MADONNA V GUY

DOUGLAS THOMPSON

MADONNA V GUY

THE INSIDE STORY OF THE MOST SENSATIONAL DIVORCE IN SHOWBIZ

JOHN BLAKE

Published by John Blake Publishing Ltd,
3 Bramber Court, 2 Bramber Road,
London W14 9PB, England

www.johnblakepublishing.co.uk

First published in paperback in 2009

ISBN: 978-1-84454-791-3

British Library Cataloguing-in-Publication Data:

A catalogue record for this book is available from the British Library.

Design by www.envydesign.co.uk

Printed in the UK by CPI Bookmarque, Croydon, CR0 4TD

1 3 5 7 9 10 8 6 4 2

Papers used by John Blake Publishing are natural, recyclable products made from wood grown in sustainable forests. The manufacturing processes conform to the environmental regulations of the country of origin.

Every attempt has been made to contact the relevant copyright-holders, but some were unobtainable. We would be grateful if the appropriate people could contact us.

For Lesley

CONTENTS

ACKNOWLEDGEMENTS

Madonna has strived over nearly three decades to conceal her true self with her version of the Official Secrets Act. All her employees must sign her confidentiality contracts pledging not to reveal anything about her or her and her family's lifestyle. So, generally, every time you scrape away a veneer there's tinsel underneath. Over the years an essential part of each persona she's presented to the world has remained to comprise the public Madonna of the 21st century.

But thankfully, there is still information out there and I would like to express my gratitude to those who helped me find it. Everyone you find in the Hollywood community, from nightclub doormen to film-studio bosses, has a point of view about her. Madonna has also created a British clique and with it an altogether different 'in' crowd. They have been most helpful in painting a total picture, blemishes and all, of one of the most significant entertainers of all time and her relationships, platonic and otherwise, and marriages. Many thanks to those in the know about the eight years of Mr and Mrs Ritchie and the others who spoke of the marriage of Mr and Mrs Madonna.

There *are* two sides to everything.

PREFACE

MADE IN HEAVEN, SETTLED IN COURT

*'Hollywood is the only place in the world
where an amicable divorce means that each gets fifty
percent of the publicity.'*

Lauren Bacall, 1967

It began, the world's most talked-about marriage, in a celebrity carnival of a Highland fling at a historic Scottish castle known as Heaven on Earth, a fanfare of an event swept by media hysteria and a gushing gale of romantic, if rose-tinted, intentions and optimism.

At moments it appeared an exquisitely orchestrated fairytale, like *Brigadoon*, but that fantasy was punctured by the feuding teams of security men and paparazzi. It was, many remarked, like a Royal wedding.

And, in a way it was.

The Queen of Pop was taking a second husband.

Madonna, as always, wanted every detail to be perfect. She also, as always, needed to control and stage the greatest performance possible.

It was Guy Ritchie who suggested the magnificent and stately Skibo Castle, standing splendid in 8,000 acres of isolation to the west of Dornoch in Sutherland and overlooking the Dornoch Firth, for their wedding gig. It was

Madonna ('I know how to put on a show, and enjoy performing') with her vast staff and advisers, who was hands-on for the elaborate arrangements. She let Guy choose the venue and play cops and robbers with the security teams and their heat-seeking equipment aimed at spotting paparazzi in the heather. But when it came to the detail of their £2 million carousel of a wedding, she wore the trousers.

Still, the theme was romantic. Before the ceremony a lone piper echoed through Skibo Castle. Madonna's four-year-old daughter Lourdes, as flower girl, surrounded by old-fashioned flower displays, scattered rose petals: stiff arrangements as painstakingly organised as the guest list and the music.

At 6.30pm on 22 December 2000, when the wedding ceremony officially began in Skibo's Great Hall, Madonna appeared in a strapless ivory silk gown, while Guy was in a Mackintosh tartan kilt. Madonna had gone all the way with formality and tradition and was very much the stunning bride. She sparkled, like her arrangements, in a diamond tiara, a 37-carat diamond cross, pearl and diamond bracelets, and a demure antique veil. Guy Ritchie went commando in his kilt.

In a 20-minute ceremony, the day after their son Rocco, then 4 months old, was christened, and before 55 guests, Madonna and Guy were subdued as they exchanged vows and wedding bands (hers a plain platinum and diamond ring, his a gold band) in front of the castle's stained-glass bay window, before being pronounced husband and wife. A guest reported that at that moment you 'could see the intense love in her eyes for this man'. It was, this onlooker advised, 'a true bonding, on every level'. But, possibly, only up to a point.

She was then – as she remains now – one of the most famous people on Earth, with a £300 million fortune, and a staff and entourage whose futures are entwined with hers. Guy Ritchie was revelling in the success of his 1998 debut, his gangster-chic offering, *Lock, Stock and Two Smoking Barrels*, which had equipped him with an extravagant confidence. But when, like Madonna, you've been liberated and famous longer than you can remember – she first appeared on *Top of the Pops* in 1984 – it's hard to always consider the next guy, even if you're married to him. We've seen many Hollywood marriages where one career soars as another dwindles. But for macrobiotic Madonna and pub-loving 'mockney' moviemaker Guy Ritchie that scenario never totally emerged: his career may not have been as incredible as his wife's but it cruised along. Surely he could never have dreamed he would not have to deal with being Mr Madonna? But many friends said playing second fiddle did rankle with him.

It is no criticism of him to say that he could not possibly have comprehended everything marrying a global superstar of Madonna's status would entail. It's doubtful that anyone, without living that life, could. I was once told that John Lennon at the height of Beatlemania had wondered aloud about driving his Rolls-Royce across the Atlantic to New York and an aide looked into the options. At times, fame and reality can be that far apart.

But in the end, Madonna and Guy Ritchie did not have a clash of careers or even egos but, rather, cultures and personalities. A family friend told the story of Madonna's horse-riding accident on her 47th birthday. She fell off a horse, breaking four ribs, her collar bone, her scapula and a knuckle in her left hand. She called the mishap 'the most painful event in my life'. She hurt. The friend said Madonna expected her husband to stop his world and be by her side but 'Guy approached the whole thing in what Madonna called "a very British way"'.

'Instead of smothering her with sympathy, he said, "Come on, darling, you're a tough bird – you'll be back on the horse in no time."' She is reported to have reacted badly, telling Guy their marriage was a mistake and he was not her 'soul mate' after all.

Madonna, it seems, doesn't do grin and bear it.

She is a truly American success story of rags-to-riches and, as you will read, that can only be achieved through often cold-hearted determination and steely ambition. Guy Ritchie is by far more laidback. His greatest effort has been to cultivate an image as a tough, street-smart Londoner, although actually the son of a successful advertising executive and his model wife. After his parents divorced he spent much of his youth at the 17th-century home of his baronet stepfather Sir Michael Leighton. When he was 25 he set his sights on becoming a filmmaker and began directing music videos, something he looks back on with marked distaste.

In the first year he did 'twenty videos back to back, really crappy ones, with sort of German rave bands. I hated doing music videos more than anything else but it helped me get on. I don't want to be too negative about it because it taught me about the business, but it can be a filthy world.' He then moved to directing commercials before a 20-minute movie short he made, *The Hard Case*, aired on Channel 4 and caught the eye of Sting, whose wife Trudie Styler became the executive producer of *Lock, Stock and Two Smoking Barrels*.

On that back of that triumph, which possibly provided a

false sense of equality, the celebrity couple introduced the young director of whom great things were expected to Madonna. Cynics predicted instant doom for their union but it lasted almost eight extraordinary years. Madonna entered the marriage with Lourdes, her first child by Carlos Leon, with whom she remains on warm terms. Madonna and Guy had their son Rocco and controversially adopted David Banda, four in 2009, from Malawi in 2006.

She made music, he made movies but after *Lock, Stock...* they were increasingly critically mauled, especially his *Swept Away*, a chauvinistic remake of a 1970s Italian potboiler, his version starring Madonna as a rich, spoiled socialite tamed and humiliated by a peasant.

On 17 August 2008, Madonna hit her half-century followed on 10 September by Guy Ritchie celebrating his 40th, by which time stories that their marriage was in crisis were appearing somewhere almost daily. Guy had organised Madonna's 50th birthday party for 90 guests at the London club Volstead. Friends danced till the early hours, Lourdes serenaded her mother on the piano and illusionist David Blaine performed card tricks. When Madonna's greatest hits were played, she hit the dance floor with Lourdes and sons Rocco and David.

'She looks better now than she ever has done,' Ritchie reportedly told the partygoers, adding with relish, 'I'm so proud. I love her so much.' But how much did she love him? Or want to be with him any more? Had their marriage emasculated him? And had that, in turn, turned off the woman he called 'the Missus'? Did she want the rough and tumble unshaven geezer with smokin' barrels rather than an agreeable husband? Was it now just keeping up appearances? As the weeks turned into months every sign was that the marriage was over. At 50, Madonna, the mistress of metamorphosis, looked as though she wanted to move on, to reinvent herself yet again and once more become a solo act.

When their relationship began she had played the girlfriend with fluttering eyelids, spouting Cockney phrases and adoring all things Guy and English, pints of bitter, soccer and hosting shoots and weekend house parties at their Wiltshire country estate, Ashcombe House, which had once belonged to that most English of beings, Cecil Beaton. And with beer-loving Guy, the pop queen bought the Punchbowl pub (asked if the pub was overcharging customers, landlord Guy replied with a laugh, 'I hope so!') in London's Mayfair.

Now, with years passed, she seemed drawn back to America, to New York, and worldwide stories appeared strongly linking her with America's highest-paid baseball star Alex Rodriguez of the New York Yankees. His wife Cynthia filed for divorce in July 2008, saying he was a 'serial adulterer' who had 'emotionally abandoned' her. She alleged Madonna and her husband were involved in a 'spiritual affair' and had discovered a letter in which Rodriguez wrote to Madonna, 'You are my soul mate.'

Some said Rodriguez, known as 'A-Rod' and 34 years old in 2009, was more supportive of Madonna's belief in the discipline of Kabbalah, mystical Judaism. Guy Ritchie, they said, viewed it with some disdain and was 'more British about it – sceptical about the more mystical messages'.

But with Kabbalah, as with everything she involves herself in, Madonna is enthusiastic: 'A lot of people join the group and don't know why. I was raised a Catholic and never encouraged to ask questions, or understand the deeper meanings or mystical implications of the New Testament of the history of Jesus, or the fact that he was Jewish, or anything. So I rejected that, because who wants to go through life being told you do things because you do things? When I started going to classes and studying Kabbalah I did it out of curiosity. I was told it was the mystical interpretation of the Old Testament. It is a philosophy, a way of understanding.'

She spoke in early 2008 and you could be forgiven for sensing she was talking about the breakdown of her marriage as she explained her understanding of Kabbalah: 'We are all responsible for our actions, our behaviour, our words, and we must take responsibility for everything we say and do. When you get your head wrapped around that, you can no longer think of life as a series of random events – you participate in life in a way you didn't previously. I am the architect of my destiny. I am in charge. I bring that to me, or I push that away. You can no longer blame other people for things that happen to you.

'There is an order in the universe, even though it looks like chaos. We separate the world into categories, this is good and this is bad. But life is a set-up to trick us. It's a series of illusions we invest in. And ultimately these illusions don't serve our understanding, because physicality is always going to let you down, physicality doesn't last.'

Arguably, like her second marriage.

As a woman with her fortune and her children, her life ahead, did she simply believe she would be better off alone? With Madonna's track record of doing what is best for Madonna it is quite possible. Nevertheless the couple's friends insisted they worked at mending their marriage, for themselves and for their children. There was a story that part of their marital rehabilitation included using empowering words like 'macho' and 'goddess' to one another. Guy Ritchie certainly seemed in denial as he appeared casually dressed in a grey sweater and slacks and with a few days' stubble at the Royal York Hotel in Toronto. It was the morning after walking the red carpet at the North American premiere of his rather more applauded gangster picture *RockNRolla* at the city's annual film festival. It marked something of a comeback for Guy Ritchie after his disastrous *Revolver*. The over-the-top tale of a Russian mobster, a crooked land deal and millions of pounds up for grabs with all of London's criminal underworld colluding and conspiring with one another in an effort to get rich quick, *RockNRolla* was a return to the style of *Lock, Stock and Two Smoking Barrels* and the Brad Pitt-headlined *Snatch* in 2000.

A week before the American showing, Madonna, who Ritchie said 'loves the movie', had joined him arm-in-arm for the photographers for its world premiere in London on 1 September. Was his marriage in trouble? At first, he didn't seem to know and then offered, 'Our close friends realise the absurdity of it although it's almost impossible to appreciate the absurdity of such sensationalism.' He then turned nostalgic about life with Madonna, crediting her for helping him to see London in a new light and renewing his appreciation for life in the city: 'Marrying an American has allowed me to look at London in the way a tourist does and see things I had never seen before. When we married I wanted us to move to America but she was seeing things I hadn't seen in London. I would complain about things but she always sees the good stuff and now I'm living vicariously through an American's eyes and enjoying being a tourist in London.'

With Madonna on her Sticky and Sweet world tour and her husband about to film his Sherlock Holmes movie with Robert Downey Jr and Jude Law, it didn't appear they'd have much time to go sightseeing in London together. Although amiable and friendly, Ritchie made it plain he would rather talk about his movie than about his marriage but did say, 'We've got to try and find times to somehow meet up.' Not, understandably, the best of circumstances for a marriage in freefall.

In a 2008 magazine interview the superbly talented actor Mark Strong, who starred in both *Revolver* and *RockNRolla*, said of Guy Ritchie, 'He's in an impossible situation. The fact that he's stayed sane and is such a lovely bloke is a miracle. I read this bullshit written about him and her and it bears no relationship to reality. He is thoughtful, kind and funny, yet the way he's portrayed is unbelievable.' But understandable. In 2008 he was even getting it from his brother-in-law Christopher Ciccone. In *Life With My Sister Madonna*, written with Wendy Leigh, he was accused of being a homophobe. He was open in his response to the book: 'What do I make of that book? I don't make anything of the book. The poor chap wrote it out of desperation. I don't think it'd be intelligent to comment on that. I can't give too much equity [sic] in what the chap's gonna write in that book. But you'd be hard pushed to be a homophobe and marry Madonna.'

Ritchie spent many months on the defensive. Madonna couldn't control the frenzied speculation that went on and on around the globe. Was she playing for public-relations purposes until the end of her Sticky and Sweet concerts were complete? Were Guy and Madonna divided about moving to New York? Had he, with a revived confidence due to the success of *RockNRolla*, established that he could hold his own with Madonna?

What was certain according to friends of both of them was that they had allowed their marriage to limp along for the sake of their children. Yet, that summer Madonna began her 51 shows across Europe and America promoting her 11th album *Hard Candy*. It was her first tour since 2006's record-grossing *True Confessions* – her anti-piracy creed: 'there's one thing you can't download and that's a live performance'. It was said they began to communicate only through their personal assistants. What seems the inevitable happened: after only a few weeks of publicly going arm-in-arm it was Madonna's longtime spokeswoman Liz Rosenberg who confirmed on 15 October 2008 that it was all over:

'Madonna and Guy Ritchie have agreed to divorce after seven and a half years of marriage. They have both requested that the media maintain respect for their family at this difficult time.' Some chance.

If the previous speculation had been sensational it was now lavishly over-the-top. Especially about who would get what percentages and real estate from their combined multi-million pound fortune. Madonna did not help matters. A few hours following the divorce statement, she was on stage in Boston, still on what the most successful tour by any artist in 2008 (£193 million), and telling the audience, 'This song is for the emotionally retarded. Maybe you know some people who fall into that category. I know I do.' She then performed 'Miles Away', which she'd explained was inspired by her often long-distance life with Guy Ritchie.

She appointed Fiona Shackleton to represent her in the divorce negotiations, who had worked for Prince Charles when his marriage to Diana ended. She also, highly successfully, represented Sir Paul McCartney in his marital battle with Heather Mills, being soaked in water if highly paid for her victory. But there were no courtroom dramatics with Madonna and Guy. Negotiations went on behind closed doors and on 21 November 2008, the couple's 'quickie' divorce was completed at the High Court's Family Division in central London. Ciccone ML v Ritchie GS was one of 17 cases dealt with that morning.

In a sworn statement signed in Beverly Hills on 4 November, Madonna petitioned on the grounds of her husband's 'continuing unreasonable behaviour'. Asked if they had lived together since the date of the petition, she'd answered, 'No.' The marriage, made in a Scottish castle, in Heaven, was settled in a small courtroom. It took 54 seconds. Madonna's life has been a circus – but she's always been the ringmaster. There has been no Svengali guiding her. In an age of manufactured music, of boy and girl bands, of *X Factor* television and singing soap-opera stars, she is unique. If you think about it, she didn't even need to change her name. And the circus is always meant to be fun. And a little bit naughty. So it was no surprise that the day her marriage ended she was cavorting on stage in Philadelphia in a basque and fishnets. She was laughing and seemed to be enjoying single life, being the solo architect of her own destiny. She'd been there before as she battled to be the world's greatest entertainer, as famous as God.

CHAPTER ONE

FAMILY TIES

'I long to have children.'

MADONNA, 1988

Madonna Louise Veronica Ciccone has drops of French and Dutch blood, gallons of Italian and is all American. Nevertheless, the world appreciated her true roots when, in 1987 at a football stadium in Florence, she told more than 65,000 fans, '*Lo sono fiera di essere italiana.*' ('I'm proud to be an Italian.') The passion and the glory? It's in her genes.

Gaetano Ciccone was 19. His new bride, Michaelina, was a year younger. They were living with his family in the easy-going community of Pacentro at the foot of Mount Amaro in central Italy. It was 1919, the First World War was over and the world was changing. In Pacentro, it changed for the worse. The people were farmers. They were also poor. But it was a pleasant place to live. Families left their doors unlocked. There was no crime. There was also no work or prospect of it in Milan to the north or in Rome to the west.

A short, wiry and determined man, Gaetano Ciccone had to make a decision for himself, his bride and the babies they talked about having. He wanted lots of sons. She wanted daughters. They both wanted a good life. They had to emigrate or starve. For Gaetano Ciccone, who is recalled in Pacentro as a feisty, driven character, there was no choice.

America, the New World, was a magnet for the poor of Europe. It offered so much. Those who had gone and returned did so in style. Between 1920 and 1930 there were 455,315 Italian immigrants to the United States and that was despite the Immigration Act of 1924, which assigned Italians an annual quota of only 3,845 immigrants. In 1920, Gaetano and Michaelina Ciccone were two of them. They arrived in America with Prohibition and a couple of battered suitcases. They could speak no English.

They had made the trek from Pacentro to Sulmona and then the 186 miles from there to Naples by road. It was a dusty and hungry trip, but they were young and strong. Emotionally, it was more torturous. They were leaving the stability of their home and families and investing their hopes, their very lives, in an alien culture and country. It was a gamble, a chance to profit by risk.

The voyage from Naples on the *SS Regina d'Italia* of the Lloyd Sabaudo line had taken 11 weeks. They were in steerage, which meant sleeping on deck in chafing, salt-water-damp blankets. On 29 April 1920, the *Regina d'Italia* entered Upper New York Bay and sailed on past the Statue of Liberty and the final three quarters of a mile towards Ellis Island. Gaetano and Michaelina Ciccone were up close to the rails along with all the other passengers. Their eyes dazzled as they stared out at their new unknown land and future.

The *Regina d'Italia* anchored at quarantine. Inspectors and immigration officials boarded to survey the latest delivery from crowded Europe. The passengers were many, the formalities swift. Along with the others, the Ciccones were put on barges and ferried to Ellis Island. All those who have walked down the gangplank and up the quay to the New World recall the noise of the ground-floor baggage room. It was in every way a Babel. And above the smell of the masses, there was the welcome aroma of thick soups, stews and freshly-baked bread. Medical and legal examinations took place in the Great Hall upstairs. The Ciccones waited on wooden benches for their turn, a manifest tag with two numbers attached to their worn coats. They were each asked 30 questions in 2 minutes. In English.

'What is your name?'

'Where were you born?'

An interpreter stood by as the Ciccones were quizzed, parrot fashion.

'Are you an anarchist?'

'Do you have a criminal record?'

'Do you have any skills?'

Gaetano Ciccone had no skills. He had strengths. He was able bodied. He wanted 'honest work' to support his family. This was still a time of the *padrone* at Ellis Island. These were labour bosses who spoke Italian and English, who understood the ways of the Old World and the needs of the New World. They had contacts with industrial concerns throughout New York, New Jersey, Pennsylvania and Southern New England.

By then, mutual-benefit societies had replaced the extended families of the Italian villages like Pacentro, which today is home to only 1,496 people. In 1920, 'Sons of Italy' had 125,000 members in 887 lodges across America. They helped with sickness, despair and death; it was a system to provide inexpensive group insurance.

When, on 1 May 1920, the Ciccones officially stepped on

to American soil, the law that was to lead to turbulent times, to the 'Roarin' Twenties', had been passed. The 18th Amendment and the Prohibition Enforcement (Volstead) Act of 26 January 1920 launched entire groups of Italian-Americans as crime entrepreneurs. At the same time, the rise of Mussolini and fascism in Italy forced many Mafia leaders to make a similar, if more comfortable, trip as the Ciccones. English was bastardised – *viscid* (whiskey) was what the *ghengas* (gangs) were selling on the *strittos* (streets).

The immigrants loved the music halls, which were free (the profits came from liquor sales) and the opera. Cleofante Campanini was the first conductor and director of the Metropolitan Opera House. Giulio Gatti Casazza was general manager from 1908 to 1934. The Italian cultural overhaul of the New World was well in progress. So was the popular one – Frank Sinatra, Dean Martin and Tony Bennett would go on to become musical legends.

And Gaetano Ciccone looked around in bewilderment. But he heard the words 'hard work' and 'best pay'. And he understood them. He and his wife went to Pittsburgh, an inland port and one of the world's greatest steel-manufacturing centres, and headquarters to some of America's largest corporations. There were ferries to transport the newcomers one mile to Manhattan or only 300 yards to the piers of New Jersey where most immigrants settled. But, again, Gaetano Ciccone decided on the longer journey and the greater risk in hope of greater profit.

The days started early and finished late. The Ciccones worked hard. They moved into a rented one-bedroom house near the steel mill in a very poor, but proud 'Little Italy' ghetto. They did not even need to learn English – everyone spoke Italian. And Gaetano got his dearest wish – sons. Six of them. And he raised them Old World style. As the father, he was the interpreter of all their needs and interests. His authority was total and he maintained it by strict discipline.

It was the same for all the families. Children were given responsibility at an early age. Daughters did not work; they prepared for marriage at home and were expected to marry the spouses chosen by their parents.

But things were changing in the New World. In 1919, a study in New York showed that 91 per cent of girls of more than 14 years old were working for wages and, in turn, of course, an independence unknown in the Old Country.

But in Pittsburgh, Gaetano Ciccone ruled the house along traditional lines. The aim was to keep the family unit together. Five of his sons went into the steel mills. Silvio 'Tony' Ciccone was the youngest and most doted upon. The 'baby' of the family, he went to college and got a degree in engineering. But there were no openings for optics and defence engineers in a steel town. Short and wiry, and similar to his father in many ways, he left the stability of home and moved to where the work was.

Silvio Ciccone wanted to better himself. He was of the New World but he was also his father's son. Discipline, honesty and hard work were the creed. Integrity was the byword; teach by example. The Catholic Church provided a helpful rulebook as a guide. He had never wanted for anything but, as the youngest of a poor immigrant family, he had had a hand-me-down upbringing. It is easy to understand the deep need to provide and provide well. And that meant having the confidence not to follow the herd. Clever and inventive, he put in the hours at several car companies in the Detroit area, in the city which would ironically become famous for the Motown 'Motor Town' sound and, later, for his daughter and anything but assembly-line products.

When he was called up for the armed services, he was skilled enough to join the United States Air Force – you had to join the Air Force; they then put you in the Army or the Navy. He was a straight shooter and well liked. Another airman, Michael Fortine, came from Michigan and they travelled from a Georgia posting together. Fortine introduced Silvio Ciccone to his youngest sister, a stunning-looking woman called Madonna. They fell hopelessly in love at first sight. A French Canadian, Madonna Fortine was born in Bay City, a chill of a place on Lake Huron's Saginaw Bay. And that is where Silvio Ciccone went to visit his future bride's family.

By then, he had left the Chrysler Corporation and was working for General Dynamics. There was a post-war boom – the motor industry sold 9.3 million cars in 1955 and suburban housing tracts were changing the lifestyle aspirations of the working and middle classes. It was the days of the American Dream of 'Happy Families' – the stereotype was TV's *Father Knows Best* with Robert Young – and colour television and a garage with two cars. Marriage seemed a perfectly wonderful idea.

The full-scale white wedding took place in a church in Rochester, which was then a new and developing community, not the urban sprawl it is today. Then, as now, much of the outlying communities were lumped together as 'Detroit'.

In 1957, with Eisenhower in the White House, their first son Anthony was born. A year later, Martin arrived. The following summer, another child was due. The family wanted to escape the overbearing heat that comes up and off the Great Lakes in July and August, so Silvio Ciccone took the family to stay with his in-laws in Bay City.

The legend-to-be was born on 16 August 1958, a hot, sunny day on which the only clouds in the sky were man-made ones from the factories and chemical dumps. It was a remarkably easy birth. The Ciccone's first daughter seemed anxious to get on with her life.

The world was changing. Castro had taken control in Cuba. John F Kennedy was on his way to the White House. Without Evita, Juan Perón had been overthrown in Argentina. Antonioni's then avant-garde *L'Avventura* was being filmed. Jack Kerouac had published *On the Road*. Americans were being told they did not have to conform and that same message was circling the rest of the world.

And another non-conformist had joined it.

The day Madonna Louise Veronica Ciccone was born, Elvis Presley was topping the American pop charts with 'A Big Hunk O' Love' having knocked Paul Anka and 'Lonely Boy' from the number-one spot. It was an important week for Elvis who was serving with the United States Army in Germany – he was introduced to 14-year-old Priscilla Beaulieu, the daughter of an army captain, who would become his wife and part of the Elvis legend.

This was the news the Ciccones heard on the radio and read in the *Rochester Eccentric*, the local newspaper, while baby Madonna rolled around in nappies. How could they have imagined that, in not so many years, their bald baby daughter's name would be as well known around the world as The King's?

Madonna was obviously named after her mother – but it was not an obvious thing to do. It marked her as something special from the start. It was rare for an Italian-Catholic

7

mother to pass on her name, especially such an exotic one with all of its religious implications.

The annual birth pattern continued. Her sister Paula was born in 1960, then Christopher and Melanie. Six kids. One salary. Tough but, for Silvio Ciccone, possible. In 2001, 'Tony' Ciccone was running his own 15-acre vineyard and winery in Sutton's Bay, Michigan, following what he calls his 1994 retirement from the rat race. With hindsight, he said, 'I was a simple man. I just wanted to provide for my family. That was always my motivation.'

Madonna also remembers, 'I think my earliest memories go back to about four or five years old and they're memories of my beautiful mother. They're really great memories. When I was four and younger, I remember not being able to sleep at night. I would walk to my parents' bedroom and push the door open. They were both asleep in bed and I think I must have done this a lot, gone in there, because they both sort of sat up in bed and said, "Oh no, not again," and I said, "Can I get into bed with you?"

'I always went to sleep right away when I slept with them. I felt really really lonely and forlorn, even though my brothers and sisters were in my room with me. I wanted to sleep with my parents.

'I remember, because my mother had a really beautiful red nightgown, silky red. My father was against me getting into bed with them and I remember getting into bed and rubbing against her nightgown and going to sleep – just like that.

'To me, that was Heaven, to sleep between my parents.'

What happened next was to tear the young life apart and mould her future. More than 30 years later she is still dealing with it, and, over the years, has regularly consulted a female psychiatrist in Beverly Hills, California.

Her mother died of breast cancer at the age of 30. A couple of years later, her father remarried. She felt abandoned by one and betrayed by the other. A lost little girl. It is in her work, in her videos and songs. She will live with it for ever. One friend, Lori Jahns, explained that even when they were out on wild dates, her 'best friend' Madonna – she called her 'Mud' and they wrote affectionate letters to each other for several years – would often grow quiet and say, 'I miss my mother.'

Years later, Madonna kept a photograph of her mother in a silver frame on an antique bedside table in the bedroom of her art-filled home in the heart of the Hollywood Hills. It moved with her, as did some of the art, over the years to other homes in Los Angeles, Manhattan and London. The art is worth millions but the snapshot of a 16-year-old, dark-haired girl in a long white dress is priceless. Another favourite is of herself, aged seven, wearing her mother's wedding gown and veil.

The death goes on hurting. Painfully, it is always in her words: 'When I see my girlfriends with their mothers even now I can't even imagine – it's unfathomable what that sort of nurturing would have done for me. I really miss it. My role models who nurtured me when I was growing up were all men. It's true. Life is just too short and I should have too many goddamn things to do, so I'd better hurry up. That has a lot to do with my mother's death – I've felt that way since I was a child. I think the biggest reason I was able to express myself and not be intimidated was by not having a mother. Women are traditionally raised to be subservient, passive, accepting. The man is supposed to be the pioneer. He makes the money, he makes the rules. I know that some of my lack of inhibition comes from my mother's death. For example, mothers teach you manners. And I absolutely did not learn any of those rules and regulations.'

She watched her mother waste away from breast cancer. It took a year, an agonising one of futile treatments, painkillers and then the morphine-induced hazy, hanging-on days until the end. Of all subjects – and she has proven she is not afraid of any, from the spiritual to the profane to the previously taboo – this is the one in which she finds most eloquence for her emotions:

'I remember her being a very forgiving, angelic person. I have a memory of my mother in the kitchen scrubbing the floor. She did all the housekeeping and she was always picking up after us. We were really messy, awful kids. I remember having these mixed feelings. I have a lot of feelings of love and warmth for her, but sometimes think I tortured her. I think little kids do that to people who are really good to them. They can't believe they are not getting yelled at or something, so they taunt you. I really taunted my mother.

'I remember, I also knew she was sick for a long time with breast cancer so she was very weak but she would continue to go on and do things she had to do. I knew she was very fragile and getting more fragile.

'I knew that because she would stop during the day and just sit down on the couch. I wanted her to get up and play with me and do the things she did before. I know she tried to keep her feelings inside and not let us know. She never complained. I remember she was really sick and was sitting on the couch. I went up to her and I remember climbing on her back and saying, "Play with me, play with me," and she wouldn't. She couldn't and she started crying and I got really angry with her, pounding her back and saying, "Why are you doing this?" Then I realised she was crying.

'I remember feeling stronger than she was. I was so little and I put my arms around her and I could feel her body underneath me sobbing and I felt like she was the child. I stopped tormenting her after that.

'She spent about a year in the hospital and I saw my father going through changes. He was devastated. It was awful to see your father cry. But he was very strong about it. He would take us to the hospital to see her and I remember my mother was always cracking up and making jokes. She was really funny so it wasn't awful going to visit her there.

'Then my mother died. I remember that right before she died she asked for a hamburger. She wanted to eat a hamburger because she couldn't eat anything for so long and I thought that it was very funny. I didn't actually watch her die.

'Then everything changed.'

And so, she says, had she.

'That was the turning point. The die was cast. I think that made me grow up fast. I knew I could be either sad or take control and say it's going to get better.'

After his wife's death, Silvio Ciccone was forced to separate his family. It was crushing – the patriarch was meant to keep his family together. But how could he work and care for his children? The solution, some months later, came from hiring housekeepers. This brought the children back together. First one housekeeper, then another and another. The children's behaviour was wild – a throwback to their easy-going mother.

'I think my parents pissed a lot of people off,' Madonna remembers, 'because they had so many kids and they never screamed at us. My older brothers were rumbustious and they would start fires in the basement or throw rocks at windows, and my mother and father would never yell at them. They would just hug us and wrap their arms around us and talk to us quietly.'

It was a cosy time before death intruded. Madonna recalls her father's 'integrity' — she did not agree with all his Old World values or, come to that, some of the New World ones — and his living by example.

'A lot of parents tell their kids not to smoke cigarettes and they smoke cigarettes. Or they give you some idea of sexual modesty — but my father lived that way. He believed that making love to someone is a very sacred thing and it shouldn't happen until after you are married. He stuck by those beliefs and that represented a very strong person to me. He was my role model. I was my father's favourite. I knew how to wrap him around my finger. I knew there was no other way to go besides saying, "No, I'm not going to do it." I employed those techniques.

'I was a very good student. I got all "A"s. My father rewarded us for good grades. He gave us quarters and fifty cents for every "A" we got. I was really competitive and my brothers and sisters hated me for it. I made the most money from every report card. I'd pit myself against all of them. It wasn't because I was going to learn; it was because I wanted to be the best. Of course, all my brothers and sisters wanted to beat me up.'

She could handle that. But the piano was an altogether different challenge. Her father made all his children learn a musical instrument and take a daily lesson. Madonna played the piano. She hated it. She convinced her father with those young wiles to allow her to take dance lessons, tap and jazz and baton twirling. She says the classes were hang-outs for hyperactive girls with no other productive means of expressing their energy.

12

And she had to cope with equally rowdy brothers who would hang her up on the clothes line by her knickers. She says she always talked her way into trouble, and her sister Paula, a tomboy, and the boys would gang up on her. She ratted on them to her father. He was her 'daddy dearest'. But he also brought the news that wrecked her world and still permeates their comfortable, new-century relationship in difficult moments. Tony Ciccone declared in 2001, 'We talk all the time, things between us are better than they have ever been,' but at the time the tension among those trying to get on with living was often intolerable.

'My father told me that my mother was dead but you keep waiting for her to come back. We never all sat down and talked about it. I guess we should have.'

The tragedy turned Madonna into a pre-teen anxiety case, totally over-dependent on her father. She would be physically sick when he left the house for longer than it took to put out the garbage. She was frightened he, too, would leave. She thought she had cancer. She would creep into her father's bed every night.

'I kept telling him that if he ever died, I was going to be buried in the casket with him. He would say, "Don't talk like that — that's really disgusting"'

What she found utterly disgusting was his decision to marry again.

'I hated my father for a long, long time.'

And after her father's decision to remarry, Madonna took some peculiar revenge. Even she does not know where her mind was then, but she decided she would never again visit her mother's grave. For now, she wanted to be Cinderella. She eventually reconsidered this warped decision — but only many, many years later.

CHAPTER TWO

PAPA DON'T PREACH

'Doesn't every little girl want to sleep with her father?
Isn't that normal?'

MADONNA, 1994

Madonna and her brother and sisters never took to their housekeepers. Who could replace their mother? Madonna felt that she, too, would die young. There was loneliness, a longing for ... something; later, she would call it 'an emptiness ... if I hadn't had that, I would never have been so driven'.

There was also fear. There was a staircase in her house with spaces between the steps. She thought the devil lived in the basement and she would always dash up the stairs so he would not grab her by the ankles. Illogical, yes, but despite being scared, she still scooted up those stairs.

She was not so quick to react to the demands of the housekeepers who seemed to spin through the house as though they were on a roundabout. Women small and tall, big and trim, young, middle-aged ... but all strangers. It was hard to accept discipline from strangers; wash the dishes, tidy the room, make the bed and on and on in a domestic litany.

But there was one, Angelica Roberts, who resembled the

late, tragic movie star Natalie Wood. The kids liked her. Their father, however, married another housekeeper, the strikingly handsome Joan Gustafson, who in 2001 helped him run his Ciccone Vineyard and Winery. Madonna had to compete with another woman for her father's attention. And then there were more babies – her half-sister Jennifer in 1968 and, on the annual cycle, Mario the following year. And there was a great deal of psychological pain.

Many years later, her father acknowledged that Madonna's hurt was 'understandable' but then he adds, 'I was not an easy father but I believe I was a good one. I did the best I could. People have never really understood our family. Madonna has said her piece over the years but I have never spoken, for, in truth, what is the point? But we have always been closer than people could ever imagine. If Madonna is happy, I am happy. She is her own woman and that is a wonderful thing.'

Much of Madonna's childhood was spent in a two-storey colonial-style house just off Old Perch Road in Rochester, in a little huddle of homes called Oklahoma. Madonna was the oldest girl. She took care of business – changing the babies' nappies. It was a difficult time but also character building, and either good or bad depending on one's viewpoint. Her father insisted on church before school every day. After school, the uniform came off and there were jobs around the house. There was homework, dinner and no television except for the Saturday-morning cartoons. Any other programmes were sinful.

Madonna recalled in 2000, 'Television was poison; to be brought up and not have a sense of responsibility, to be plopped in front of a television and not be talked to or read to, was to my father – and I understand it now – a huge mistake.' The family never went out to the cinema or out to dinner. Magazines were a luxury. It was like the gradual winding of a spring, as though in readiness for the drive and energy she would need to achieve so much fame and fortune in less than a decade. It was also the birth of the Madonna style – or lack of it.

Her father insisted they called his new wife 'Mother' or 'Mom'. But to Madonna she was her 'step-mother' and she could do no right. Madonna was not allowed tampons because her step-mother said they were the equivalent of sexual intercourse. To stop arguments, all the girls were bought similar dresses.

Madonna hated to look like her sisters, detesting the uniform required by her Catholic schools. She put bows in her hair and would wear razzle-dazzle socks. Her private joke was her brightly coloured knickers, which she wore instead of the regulation dark-blue variety. It did not stay a secret for long – the children would tease each other by lifting up their skirts, and most girls were mortified. Madonna retaliated with an unexpected flash of pink or black-and-white polka dots. If no one lifted up her skirt, teachers would recall her regularly taking matters into her own hands during school breaks and hanging upside down on the playground monkey bars revealing her rainbow of underwear.

She desperately wanted to be the oddball. Her brother Martin, now a gleaming, curly-haired, good-looking disc jockey with a Detroit radio station, recalls, 'She wasn't rich, she wasn't famous then, but she was the same girl, always being different to others.'

She was closest to her brother Christopher who is now an interior designer in Los Angeles. He commented, 'In an Italian home, socialising always centred around the kitchen, so Madonna and I both know the value of a good pot to make a big batch of pasta.' They remember Madonna always seeking attention, climbing on to tables and dancing at family get-togethers.

By the age of ten – fifth grade in the American school system – Madonna had turned into a precocious little flirt. She was socialising outside the family circle and was by now adept at getting herself noticed. She had long dark hair, a winning smile and sweet look. It was a glossy veneer and the start of the incredible play acting that would finally result in the self-sustaining phenomenon of Madonna, the Act.

The family attended St Andrew's Church in Rochester and Madonna went to the Holy Family Regional School, which is a rather foreboding-looking building on the outskirts of town. Today things are not so strict, but headmistress Mrs Sylvia Trepanier laughed when she said, 'I'm not sure we would want to acknowledge Madonna as a former pupil.'

And that was as much a reference to the past as the present. Ten-year-old Madonna was a terror. Ask Tommy, the child with bad teeth whom she chased around the playground. Madonna really went after her young man. She tore off her blazer and white blouse and went topless after him. One of the nuns grabbed her and furiously explained that little girls did not take off their clothes and chase boys.

Until that moment, she had been obsessed with becoming a nun. She thought they were special, very beautiful.

'I saw them as really pure, disciplined, sort of above-average people. They never wore any make-up and they had these really serene faces. Nuns are sexy.'

Of course, they did not chase boys. Her career goals were nun or movie star. Looking back, she says just nine months of convent school put her completely off the first idea. But not off Tommy – 'I wanted him.' The day after the playground chase, she received her first kiss. From Tommy, in the convent. Today, she still recalls the moment as 'incredible'. Madonna's first kiss in a convent. Well, what else?

It was the start of the rebellion ... and her sexual revolution.

'Probably about the same time as I began to rebel against the church, I went through puberty. That was when I really started to think about sex, about its presence, not about what I was going to do about it.'

Carol Belanger, a friend who was in the Brownies with her, recalls the convent days, the interest in sex – and what the nuns had beneath their habits. 'Madonna and I went peeking through the windows of the convent to see the nuns without their habits. We found out that they had hair.'

Belanger, who is married and still lives in the Rochester area, often attended church with Madonna. Once they went naked – under their coats. As they sat through the service, they exchanged knowing glances and suppressed giggles.

Schoolfriends remember Madonna as the girl who was willing to take all the risks. If there were apples to steal, she would lead the group. When they went on shoplifting sprees, she would regularly get away with the most loot. She wore trousers to church, which her father hated.

'As soon as you tell me I can't do something, I feed off that judgement. It started when I was a little girl. The boys could wear trousers to church but the girls couldn't. I used to say, "But why? Is God going to love me less if I don't wear a dress?" It just irked me – the rules. So I would put trousers on underneath my dress just to fuck with my father. And after church I would tell him I had trousers on and I'd say, "See, lightning did not strike me." '

She's been rebelling ever since. Her first great public dare was at St Andrew's annual talent show. She was in the seventh grade, but a fast-developing 12-year-old. The parishioners gathered early in the church hall. Fathers had come home early from the car factories, showered and put on collars and ties. Mothers were wearing their Sunday dresses. And most of the kids were in their Sunday best, reciting poetry or tap dancing or singing or playing the piano.

Madonna came on stage nude. Well, she looked naked. It was her turn as Goldie Hawn from the 1960s *Laugh In* show when Hawn used to gyrate her lithe, youthful body, adorned with a skimpy bikini and painted graffiti. Silvio Ciccone's little girl wore green fluorescent paint and what could be mistaken for a 'monokini'. The music started, blasting 'Baba O'Reilly' by The Who. Under an ultra-violet light, which highlights fluorescent colours and 'kills' other images, Madonna wiggled and undulated and leaped about on stage with a strobe flashing. The only things not moving were the parents' eyeballs. They were frozen in shock. The kids, especially the boys, were turned on by Madonna's first public performance. She had spent weeks planning her act, the costumes, the antics. Her father took 30 seconds to grab her as she left the stage. She was 'grounded' for two weeks. She can smile about it now: 'He was mortified. He just dismembered me.'

As she entered her teens, Madonna became wilder rather than tamer. And also curious. About her body, about boys. About everything.

There were also the other kids at school.

'You want to identify with somebody as you are growing away from being a child. You're starting to think differently and you want to be independent, but before you reach that independence you want to attach yourself to someone. In school there were hippies – the more free group, the guys with long hair who took a lot of jewellery and shop [trade] classes and smoked a lot of pot during lunch hour. I didn't identify with them because I thought they were extremely lazy. Then there was a jock group and they were drunk on beer every day. I was a cheerleader for a little while, but I couldn't get into it. It wasn't that I didn't like athletics – I couldn't get into the sensibilities of cheerleaders and athletes. They were only interested in sports, drink and girls. I had this idea that everyone went to junior high and high school with blinders on their eyes and it really pissed me off. I was sure everyone was missing something and I wandered around aimlessly. My best friends were the guys who were really studious, like physics majors.'

But it wasn't easy being anybody's friend. The boys wrongly thought she was easy. The girls thought she was too. An attractive blonde called Katrina made her suspicions known after her boyfriend started flirting with Madonna. She slapped Madonna's face. On the street. In front of many of the school. Madonna was devastated. But not enough to slow down. She was listening to Diana Ross and the Supremes and young Stevie Wonder. Frankie Lymon's songs made her weak at the knees. And she would let everyone know what she thought.

'Sometimes, I literally put my hand over her mouth to shut her up,' says Carol Belanger. 'A group of bikers dropped firecrackers on us. Madonna yelled at them and told them to knock it off. One of the biker girls came down and started hitting her in the mouth. We finally got away, but she had a black eye and a bruised cheek.'

At home, Silvio Ciccone still ran a strict ship. Madonna

had to go to a friend's house to see television shows like *Dark Shadows* (the cult black-and-white vampire series which, in the 1990s, was revived on US television with British actor, Ben Cross, as the lead vampire) and drool over David Cassidy in *The Partridge Family. The Monkees* was another favourite show.

She had fights with her father, mostly about religion. She would find ways to say she was going to a different Mass from him and then take off with her friends. But she always thought ahead and worked out the 'sermon' she had heard, to stop being caught out by her father if he quizzed her.

The Rochester school system had a more solid reputation than Madonna did in the school playground. Silvio Ciccone decided to take his oldest daughter out of Catholic school and she joined Rochester West Junior High.

Madonna wanted to be 'European'. She stopped shaving her legs and her armpits. She wore gypsy-style clothes, and she became friends with Lori Jahns, who is now an attractive married woman, living an hour's drive from Rochester in a smart suburban area near Hummer Lake. 'Mud' Ciccone and Lori Jahns spent a great deal of time together. Lori, a quick, smart blonde, sipped her Miller Lite beer and fondly recalled her days with Madonna.

'We were real close in eighth grade. She had other friends, but it was *us*. We sent letters back and forth and we'd call each other all the time ... spend the night together if we could. I guess back then you always had a best friend. We had friendship rings and all that kind of jazz. She'd had a tough time at the Catholic school. Too strict. I guess the nuns were real bitches. They were just too strict and nasty and she would tell jokes about stuff she and the other kids would try and get away with.

'That's why she was going nuts when she got to public school. For someone who had had to wear a uniform to school, to just go to your closet and say, "I wanna wear this!" was wonderful. Or to go to a friend's house and go, "Oh, I have twice the wardrobe now." Hot pants were big back then and those God-awful bell-bottom jeans, those hip-huggers. She loved to borrow clothes and stuff. If it's your best friend, it's fine. The clothes she had weren't that great. I guess it wasn't as big a deal to her family as it was to some others.

'My mom didn't like her very much. She thought she'd lead me astray. She thought there was something different about her. She would never say why. Maybe it was because of her independence or because she was very headstrong.

'Her family was different from my family. My family always seemed to be close and dinner time was when you sat down and chatted. And it didn't seem that close at her house.

'We were into boys, boys and more boys. Girls mature quicker than guys and she wrote to me about two boys saying she wished they'd grow because they were so adorable. They were short and really cute but she was like, "Hmm, this doesn't look right."

'We did a lot of boy talk and girl stuff. We'd sit around and sing. She would sing. Carole King was real big then and we'd sing her songs. And there were just all kinds of guys who would get together and practise music in someone's garage or basement. That was a big thing so they could play at high-school dances. She knew a guy down the street and we went there dancing. They said, "Let's just goof around, why don't you guys sing back-up?" I don't even know what song it was – "Proud Mary" or something like that. I didn't sing. I danced. And she got up and sang back-up. She wasn't frightened at all.

'She was fearful at times. She didn't get along well with her step-mother.'

Lori recalled it as a hard time for Madonna's family.

'Her father was doing two jobs. There was a new woman in their home getting her dad's attention. She was her mother's baby because she was the first girl. It was seldom that she would talk about it, and when she did, she was very emotional about it. She mentioned her mom's suffering and when she did talk about it she would always say, "I wish my mom was here." It was always sad. I couldn't pinpoint anything that started conversations like that. She must think about her mom all the time. I'm sure she does even now.'

And what about being a loner?

'She said it gave her commitment, she wanted to do something. She'd say, "Fine, I'm gonna do this. I can do this." I think that has a lot to do with her today. It was like her dancing. We did a talent show in the eighth grade and she wanted me to do this dance number with her. She choreographed it herself and everything and I still remember the song and the lyrics: "Let our body feel the music and feel the beat and just kind of groove to the music..." I mean, she would just dance like you could not believe. She was loose. She could really do it.

'Madonna didn't care what anybody thought. She would just be her own self. "I wanna do what I wanna do" was her motto. And that's what she eventually did.

'Her father was one stickler for homework. You did your homework before you did anything else. She was very intelligent. I would have to study, study, study to get my "B"s and "A"s. I had to work a lot harder than she did to get the same results.

'She shared a bedroom with her sister Paula and Melissa

then. A lot of times I'd ask her to come over to my house and she couldn't because she had to watch the little kids because her step-mom was doing something. Her father wasn't around a lot. He worked a lot of hours. It was a hard time for her. It was a development time. And she was a lot more developed than some of us. But she wasn't easy or a "sleaze" as we'd call it back then. I've read things that say she's had her boobs done and this and that. She never did. She always had a gorgeous figure.

'Was she bisexual? It raises a little controversy and gets people talking. But back at school, it was just boys as far as I know. But kids experiment.'

The friends began going to catechism together.

'I wasn't a Catholic. My mother asked, "Why do you want to go to catechism?"

"It's interesting, Ma. You learn about different things."

'I learned about boys and so did Madonna. That's when you're finding out your sexuality and everything else. We'd do a lot of heavy petting. In a sense, there was peer pressure to be cool. But at the same time, we wanted to be our own individuals. And that's hard at that age when you're trying to find out what and who you are.

'Rochester was a very small, beautiful town then. You wouldn't know it any more. It's over-developed, the roads can't handle the traffic. When we all first lived there, there was the golf course and the cow pasture and we could ride our bikes and go to Baskin-Robbins for ice cream. Or we would skip catechism and go to the movies – kissing with the boys in the front row, of course. Necking with the guys from catechism. It was then that Madonna invented her "floozy" look. The girls knew their parents didn't like it and that made it even more fun.'

Indeed, Madonna recalled, 'We got dressed to the nines. We got bras and stuffed them so our breasts were overlarge and wore really tight sweaters – we were sweater-girl floozies. We wore tons of lipstick and really badly applied make-up and huge beauty marks and did our hair like Tammy Wynette. We posed. We took turns lounging on the bed with our hands behind our head. We took pictures of each other and developed them and these were our ten-cent-floozy pictures.'

Madonna the floozy moved to Rochester–Adams High School and her friend Lori Johns to Rochester High. They were rival cheerleaders. But Madonna mastered solo-flirtation, and started going steady with big-smiling Nick Twomey, who eventually became a Michigan pastor. And she developed her long-lasting fascination with Marilyn Monroe, turning herself into a Monroe wannabe.

CHAPTER THREE

LIFE AFTER SEX

'Men feel safe with a guy who dresses like a female but might feel intimidated by a woman wearing a pinstriped suit with her tits hanging out, grabbing her crotch.'
MADONNA, 1999

The Reverend Nick Twomey is a neatly dressed, dark-haired man with horn-rimmed glasses, a picture of propriety. He is pastor at the Faith Reformed Church in Traverse City, Michigan. He used to 'go steady' with Madonna and they were friends until they both graduated from Rochester-Adams High School in 1976. She was a cheerleader. He played on the football, basketball and baseball teams.

'We did some serious flirting. We sort of hung out together,' recalled the pastor. 'You do that more, I suppose, than going steady in seventh, eighth and ninth grades.'

Neither of them belonged in the popular, mainstream crowd at school. He became a Christian. She took on her 'European look'. They were different.

'Even when we were no longer super close, we had mutual respect for one another because neither of us cared what the other kids thought. My life zigged, her life zagged.

'We've heard all about her rebel life, but I'm not so sure

she was *such* a rebel. Neither of us had halos on our heads, but I don't know that either one of us was any worse than the other.

'I've thought about Madonna and I remember how she was. She was often confused. I wonder if she is happy. I suspect that underneath all the fame and fortune is a person in need of love, forgiveness and hope.'

The teenage Madonna was constantly misunderstood. The boys would call her a 'nympho' and girls would put her down as a 'slut'. She was still a virgin. She was never one to wait to be asked for a date. If she liked a boy, she asked him out. She got a reputation, and necked and heavy-petted with the best of them. She also took precautions; to necking parties – known as 'make-out' nights – she wore a turtle-necked blue bodysuit. No matter how hot it got, there were several zippers between her virginity and lusty, teenage boys. But teenagers – or, more appropriately, walking hormone factories – are on a constant sexual voyage of discovery. She could not go on for ever being the girl who went to church every Sunday morning in a starched, white dress and who knelt with her brothers and sisters, father and step-mother in the third row from the front.

She lost her virginity in the back of a Cadillac. Later, she would regret describing it – in a joke that backfired – as a career move. But she did not go 'all the way' until she had been dating Russell Long, who was two years older and drove that infamous Cadillac, for several months.

'I don't know if it was anything to do with me,' says Russell. 'I think it was more to do with adventure, of the experience of the unknown. She really wanted to find out what it was like.'

Sex was now very much on her mind. She and Carol

Belanger would joke about it – they even stripped Ken and Barbie and put them face to face under the covers of Barbie's bed. Madonna spent hours reading *Glamour* and *Seventeen* magazines. They gave her the sweater idea, which was a way of brightening up her school uniform by wearing hot pink, purple and orange sweaters. She was never frightened of others laughing at her or jeering. Most of us do not like to be stared at for being different, the odd one out. Madonna's strength in the playground – and now – is that she does not care what others think. She says she knew she was different from the age of five.

So, having her first sexual experience was not because of peer pressure; it was simply because she wanted to see what it was like. She was 15. There is some amusement for her when she conjures up that moment of intimacy a lifetime and two children later: 'The idea that the first guy I ever slept with is married and has kids really breaks me up. I wonder if he still loves me – he probably does.'

But there were sexual adventures before that. In her 1991 documentary *Truth or Dare* (the UK title was *In Bed with Madonna*), she confronted the woman she says 'finger-fucked' her when they both lived in Michigan. The woman in question could not recall the particular incident. Madonna asserts, 'All children experiment with each other sexually when they're little. These are things that people just want to sweep under the rug and treat like dark, dirty secrets, when they shouldn't be.'

And Madonna says that from her earliest sexual longings, she was attracted to *all* sides of sexuality. As with everything else in her life, she wanted to know *all* about it.

Reflectively, in the late 1990s, she offered this view: 'The most interesting people to me are people who aren't just one way. I'm attracted to it because I have been described as being very male-like or very predatory or having a lot of male traits. But that's because I'm financially independent and I have spoken about my sexual fantasies in the sort of frank and blunt way that has been reserved for men. And the more people have criticised me for behaving in an unladly-like fashion, the more it's provoked me to behave in an unlady-like fashion.'

Behaving 'properly' was part and parcel of those growing-up years, during which Madonna felt great pressure to 'fit in', to be part of a group. You had to be a member of the church, a participant in neighbourhood and school activities. That pressure made her angry. The escape was to dance to Motown records at her friends' homes. They would stack portable turntables with 45s – The Supremes, Martha and the Vandellas, The Shirelles, The Ronettes – and dance and sing. 'Oooooohhh, baby love' and 'be-bop-de-bop'. She made up routines. The other kids would give her standing ovations and she liked the applause.

Another pastime was to go to what today we would call an 'art-house' cinema, one that showed foreign and old movies. She saw flickering black-and-whites with Carole Lombard, Judy Holliday, Bardot ... and Marilyn Monroe. 'She was my first movie idol. When I first saw her, I wanted my hair blonde and to wear pointy bras.'

Madonna saw herself in those screen sirens. Her humour, her need to be the boss, to be in control and at the same time to be cared for. She was then the paradox she is today. She had knowledge. She also had innocence. And years later, in December 1986, she would pose Monroe-style in the pages of *Life* magazine. And she did it again, even more spectacularly, on the cover and pages of Italian *Vogue* and worldwide editions of *Vanity Fair* in March 1991. And on 25 March that year, she also played Monroe with co-star Michael Jackson, at the Shrine Auditorium in downtown LA – at the Oscars.

She had appeared on stage by backstage magic – an elevator lift from the orchestra pit – to gasps from the celebrity-studded audience. Her mock strip routine was a wow, especially when she turned her rear end to the crowd and simply wiggled. Even her high-profile 'date', Michael Jackson, in his gold-tipped cowboy boots, played second fiddle to Madonna, who appeared on stage more like Marilyn Monroe than Monroe. The 63rd Annual Academy Awards celebrated 100 years of film. The traffic started jamming up around the Shrine Auditorium around 4.00pm. The Shrine holds 6,200 people, which is twice as many as the Dorothy Chandler Pavillion, long-time home of the Oscars; more people but less class.

There were the lines of limousines, the formally dressed men and the carefully coiffured and gowned women. But they were serving hot dogs and snacks, and wine in paper cups on what is supposedly Hollywood's champagne and caviar night. This was tacky in Tinseltown. By 6.00pm, the atmosphere at the Shrine was decidedly down at heel. The excitement level measured a zero on the Richter scale. Then came a seismic roar from the thronging crowds. Madonna had arrived. With Michael Jackson.

The tinsel was back in town. Madonna waltzed her way into the Awards as though she owned them. Her dazzling gown was like another of her snake skins. You expected her to slither out of it at any second. It shimmered. She shimmied. The pearls on her white gown played laser games with popping flash-bulbs. This was paparazzi heaven. Once inside, Madonna and Jackson, also in white and bejewelled, took the two front-row aisle seats, centre stage. Throughout the auditorium people craned their necks to get a better look. Dustin Hoffman stood up to see what was going on. *Dick Tracy* co-star, Al Pacino, waved. Everyone wanted Madonna's attention. Later, during a commercial break and away from the television cameras, master of ceremonies, Billy Crystal, peered down from the stage at Madonna and enquired, 'Who do you have to fax to get on the show?'

Ironically, it was the evening that Kevin Costner, who Madonna regarded as a 'white bread' entertainer, and his *Dances With Wolves* rode off with seven Oscars. The good guys won. But so did the Bad Girl.

No one had ever worked the Oscars – and the ceremony's one billion television viewers worldwide – with the brassy bravado of platinum-blonde Madonna. She bumped and ground, wearing $20 million worth of a girl's best friend. The diamonds twinkled despite the competition of her pearl-encrusted, lethally low-cut dress. The veterans ogled and said she had brought the glamour back to Hollywood and the annual cavalcade of self-acclaim, with a bang ... and the roll of a hip and thrust of a buttock. If she had performed like that in the street, she would have been arrested rather than grandly and most approvingly applauded.

She sang the Oscar-nominated 'Sooner or Later (I Always Get My Man)' from the film *Dick Tracy*. The song was written by the legendary Stephen Sondheim who was besotted with her. She ignited and then fanned the flames of the torch-song, which won an Academy Award. Sizzling Madonna won the evening.

The entertainment world's commercial chameleon had just performed to her biggest audience ever. And it was a captive audience. Satellites in the sky had beamed her backside to the world's television audience. She had shook it at them. A super-confident superstar.

Probably only from the front-row seats at the Shrine, where you could see close-up and 'live', could you also see the shakes. Watching from there, you could see that she was as nervous as anyone might be performing on such an evening. Madonna nervous? Oh, yes. For despite her backside-to-the-world image, this is still an insecure multi-millionairess. She still does not have all that she wants. Every bump and grind on Oscar night had been rehearsed again and again by this perfectionist performer. She had 'become' Marilyn for the camera. She posed and pouted like her idol and a few weeks later appeared at a Beverly Hills benefit concert in a short black dress – a mirror of Monroe. This was not a teenage thing.

Psychologists have warned her about this obsession. But she believes Monroe, whose mother was committed to an asylum soon after Marilyn was born, rose above her difficult start in life. She is irritated when warned off the Monroe imitation track: 'Marilyn Monroe was a victim and I'm not. I know what I'm doing and what I want. If I make mistakes or fall into traps, they're mine, not Marilyn Monroe's.'

Madonna has a collection of Monroe memorabilia. In the videos for 'Material Girl' and 'Papa Don't Preach', she struts Monroe-style, recalling her idol's hit films *Gentlemen Prefer Blondes* and *There's No Business Like Showbusiness*. She shrugs off stories that she consulted psychics who told her she was Monroe reincarnated, as well as the story published in America saying that she has bought a crypt so she could be buried near Marilyn Monroe at Westwood Memorial Park in Los Angeles. She hasn't ... yet. But Monroe is a subject which she has pursued since her mid-teens, a continuing, haunting presence.

She was always the person, the performer, to call on for a different take. At junior high school, classmate Jonathan Gilbert decided to make a short 8mm film. For his cameras, he wanted a naked tummy on which to simulate frying an egg. Madonna obliged.

By 16, dance, as well as Marilyn, had become a passion. Whenever touring dance companies visited the Detroit area, she would fight for tickets. She took every dance class she could. It was then that her teenage anger subsided. She had orientated herself.

'I was a little girl from Michigan and I had a dream and I worked really hard and my dream came true.'

She wanted to dance seriously. And Christopher Flynn taught serious dance.

Flynn, a lean man with thinning hair and glasses, was 45 when Madonna met him. He was a homosexual and a Catholic. She adored him. Her family was not in the least worldly and Michigan is not America's most arts-orientated state. It is a hard-working, blue-collar place, and no more so than Detroit and its suburbs. Flynn understood Madonna. She looked to him as a mentor, a father figure and even as an imaginary lover and brother. Lover, brother and father – a trinity the 17-year-old felt she did not have close to her.

Flynn did not disguise his sexual preference. Instead, he took Madonna to gay discos in downtown Detroit. The crowd was swallowing 'poppers' (capsules of amyl nitrate) and talking literature and poetry. They could not be more different from all the school playground jocks whose lives revolved around sports, drinking and girls. This was glamour. This was sophistication. What it was, of course, was new and different. He took her to museums and art exhibitions in Detroit. And they would go dancing, which Flynn was later to recall.

'She was hot. We would dance our asses off. People would clear the floor. But she's that way about life. She was always trying to be better, always positive, always filled with urgency, always wanting the most of it and she had this tremendous thirst for everything. She was [that word again] insatiable.'

And that even extended to 'knock-knock, who's-there?' jokes. Flynn remembered a two-hour drive in which she made them up one after the other, and he marvelled, 'They were good.'

Madonna graduated from Rochester High and won a dance scholarship to the University of Michigan, an achievement that did not thrill her father. He wanted his daughter to stay in single-sex accommodation at Michigan's Ann Arbor campus. She vented some of her frustrations by letter writing, and sent one to Odina Sweet, her friend in Montreal, Canada, saying, 'My two room-mates are enough to kill anybody – one's a Jesus freak and the other's in the Air Force. My father said I had to live in an all-girls dorm – they call this one the Virgin Vault. That's a pretty good description.'

In another letter, she told Odina Sweet, 'There are a few gay discos and somewhat kinky people that keep me going. I guess I'm turning into a degenerate, isn't that wonderful? The dancing is great and there are some African rain dances that are very sexual and primitive. That's why I like it! The jazz class is taken by a crazy French woman. It's the hardest class because she works very fast with little explanation plus you can't understand a fucking word she says, so you can only watch.'

The Virgin Vault. Afro rhythms and bongo players. The exasperating but totally talented jazz dance teacher Sylvie Lambert. Madonna loved it all.

By then she wore her hair in a short, spiky punk look. There was discipline including a tough *plié* exercise – low knee bends with the stomach held tightly in while maintaining a perfect posture. Madonna broke the class up one day during the exercise with a loud belch. On a hot day she wanted to take off her leotard and just wear a bra, no knickers. She hammed it up in ballet class. She ripped pieces out of her leotard and wore safety pins, and scratched runs into her tights.

Flynn had told her she had a face like a Roman statue. She was extremely well built for her age with breasts that had the neighbourhood boys goggle-eyed – something she did not encourage. But Flynn told her she was beautiful. No one had said that before. Even Russell, in his moments of passion, had praised her body rather than her total look. She understood Flynn to mean that she was beautiful not only in appearance but inside. It was then that her mind took her one step further, to theory, and later to the fantasies she would capitalise on in her career. Anything was possible.

Madonna has no doubts about Flynn's influence. 'I'd say that, after my father, the most powerful, important relationship of my life was with Christopher Flynn. I didn't understand the concept of "gay" at that time. I was probably twelve or thirteen years old. All I knew was that my ballet teacher was different from everybody else. He was so alive. He had a certain theatricality about him. He made you proud of yourself, just the way he came up to me and put my face in his hands and said, "You are beautiful." No one had woken up that part of me yet. I was too busy being repressed by my Catholic father.

'By the time I was fifteen or sixteen, he took me to my first gay club to go dancing. I'd never been to a club. I'd only been to high-school dances, and no guys would ever ask me to dance, because they thought I was insane, so I'd just go out and dance by myself.'

Flynn's gay world made her feel 'normal'.

'In school and in my neighbourhood and everything, I felt like such an outsider, a misfit, a weirdo. And suddenly, when I went to the gay club, I didn't feel that way any more. I just felt at home. I had a whole new sense of myself.

'Until that point, I kept seeing myself through macho, heterosexual eyes. Because I was a really aggressive woman, guys thought of me as a really strange girl. I know I frightened them. I didn't add up for them. They didn't want to ask me out. I felt inadequate around them, and I felt not beautiful, and I felt like I could never fit in with the prom queens and the cheerleaders and the perfect girls who all went out with the football players. Ballet is such a female thing. I was surrounded by male ballet dancers and, to me, that's gender confusion. I mean, a bunch of guys walking around in tights putting their toes in the air, and they're incredibly effeminate. I started spending a lot of time with dancers, and almost every male dancer that I knew was gay. Then I went through another feeling of inadequacy because I was constantly falling in love with gay men.

'I wanted to be a boy when I was growing up because I was in love with the male dancers I knew and they were all gay. And I thought that if I was a boy, they'd love me. So I got into role playing. When I was at school, I cut my hair short and I was anorexic – I had no boobs. I would dress like a boy and go to gay clubs and my goal was to trick men into thinking I was a boy.' And, she says, the Gwyneth Paltrow *Shakespeare In Love* ploy worked. 'It did actually, a few times.'

You can understand Flynn's attraction for this 'misfit'. Madonna explained further.

'I was really down on myself. When Christopher introduced me to this life, I suddenly thought, that's not the only way I have to be. I felt that my behaviour was accepted around him. My father didn't know. At the time, he would have freaked out.

'People didn't talk about gay life in the Catholic Church. They barely talked about sex. So I didn't see it as something I was supposed to be wary of or afraid of. All I knew was, I was attracted to Christopher and his lifestyle. I fell in love with him and the way he treated me. Of course, I was so miserable that I wasn't a man.'

She had the 'balls' to move on. It was Flynn who encouraged Madonna to stretch herself, to move away, to try New York. Flynn died of AIDS at the Hernandex House hospice in Los Angeles on 27 October 1990. Madonna was distraught. A California newspaper contacted Flynn a few weeks before he died. He told them that he and Madonna had kept in touch.

'We still remained friends after Madonna found her own way in life and achieved her dream. We had a special relationship. She was a very worldly sort of woman even when she was little more than a child.'

Flynn had told her to try New York. She told her father. He was against it.

'My father was not behind me. I was angry that he was not supportive. I wanted to leave his house, get out, be my own person.'

Other family members and friends were just as opposed to the idea of New York. But Flynn had told her she was beautiful, she could do it. She felt she was simply marking time at the University of Michigan Dance Department, just tuning her technique. She dropped out and took a Northwest Airlines jet – her first plane ride – to New York. Her ticket cost her $88.

CHAPTER FOUR

BIG APPLE, BIG AMBITION

'She wanted it more than anyone.'

MUSIC MANAGER CAMILLE BARBONE ON MADONNA'S

DESIRE FOR FAME, 2001

Michigan to Manhattan? It is a lot further than the miles involved. Madonna was nearly 19. And budding. There was no hiding her figure, and she did not try to. And she did not have any thoughts about the perils of the big city. She was totally self-absorbed and hardly noticed the passengers on the jet. She was the one heading for New York City and the big time. If there were any regrets about her leaving her home town, they belonged to Steve Bray.

Some months earlier at the smoke-filled Blue Frogge nightclub, a favourite of the University of Michigan's preppy crowd, she had picked him out. She had been dancing up a storm and fighting off attention from a crowd of students when Bray caught her eye. He was black. He was a waiter. He was also funny. And, more importantly, he was cool. Bray was also a gifted musician, a drummer with a local band that worked the Detroit lounge circuit. Bray – like so many in the years to come – was captivated by Madonna's energy and what he would later call her 'aura of

41

ambition'. And it was that insensitive ambition which allowed her to leave Steve Bray, a man who would later have an enormous impact on her life and career, at home, barely realising his feelings for her.

It was mid-summer when Madonna landed at La Guardia Airport, hot and sticky. She was carrying the dark-blue winter coat that she could not fit into her suitcase, which held her ballet shoes, tights, underwear, a couple of outfit changes, two pairs of street shoes and a picture of her mother. She gathered her belongings together and, weighed down by her case, staggered down the escalator and through the sliding glass doors to the yellow cab rank outside. She told the cab driver to take her to the middle of everything.

She was lucky, something which was to influence Madonna's life again and again. The driver took her to Times Square and only wanted $12 of the $37 she had for the trip. She walked east on 42nd Street and then south on Lexington Avenue. There was one of those open-air summer markets going on Lexington. By now she was wearing her coat rather than carrying it. A man started following her. It looked as though all her father's predictions about coming to a sticky end in New York were coming true faster than even he could have foreseen. But this man was no rapist or mugger – rather, a Good Samaritan. He quizzed her about why she was wearing a coat in the heat. She explained she was just off the plane and had nowhere to stay.

She stayed at his apartment for her first two weeks in New York, with breakfast provided. He showed her the city and then she was off to one cockroach-infested slum after another. She would try to eat one apple a day, but mainly lived on popcorn. It was cheap. It filled her up. She also dined out of street rubbish bins. She would look for the McDonald's bags because there were usually a few french fries in them. She was also adept at 'borrowing' $5 from every other man she met. She was sexually ambivalent to these men – come hither but go no further.

'She was definitely not trampy, not free with her sexual favours,' said Camille Barbone who was Madonna's first manager and mentor. 'She never lost her sense of pride. She always carried herself with a great deal of dignity.'

Madonna spent a long time living in a rooming house on 30th Street between 8th and 9th Avenue. Steve Bray and other friends recall the stench; vagrants peed or did worse in doorways. When she traded up a place, Bray, a gregarious, round-faced and friendly character, says the smell was better, although when he visited, 'I always thought I was going to be killed by junkies.'

New York, New York. Madonna gritted her teeth. She was a cloakroom girl at the celebrity Russian Tea Room (the venue for Michael Douglas and Catherine Zeta Jones' pre-wedding reception) on West 57th. She was lonely. But there was nowhere else to go. She went to work for Dunkin' Donuts, which had a less jet-set crowd than the Tea Room. She left after a disagreement with an overbearing customer. She could not drive (she got a California licence in 1985 after a back-to-back series of lessons) but she would dress up and just wander around the city with people gaping at her outlandish outfits. She would ride the subway, enjoying all the attention. The Lower East Side of New York was her territory.

She got a job serving at a Burger King fast-food outlet just down from Central Park. The pay was $1.50 an hour. Over at art school, they paid $10 an hour for nude modelling. She suddenly felt 'financially and emotionally' rampantly artistic. Her body was in great shape, if a little underweight, from her popcorn diet. Her muscle definition and skeleton were on display for the student artists. She was their favourite model – she was easy on the eye and easy to draw. She started modelling privately in people's homes. And that included photographs. Her attitude was that Michelangelo was not a pornographer and neither were the artists and photographers she posed for. There were many, many modelling sessions from 1979 to 1980, but the truth of it was that they were more to put food on the table and pay the rent than for the artistic endeavour. Later, of course, like Marilyn Monroe before her, the nude pictures would surface after she became a worldwide phenomenon.

Today, it is relatively hot stuff. Back then, it was cold work.

'It was cold in my studio,' remembers photographer Martin Schreiber. 'I had two heaters on Madonna but she was laughing.'

Schreiber founded the Photographing the Nude course at New York's New School. From 10 February up to Valentine's Day in 1979, his students snapped away at a new model who their teacher called 'a beautiful, intelligent, unconventional lady'. He says now, 'She was skinnier. There was something special about her, that's for sure. I think she's quite beautiful now, but she had a different kind of beauty then. I don't think she really knew what she wanted then, but she had some ideas.'

She was experimenting. She would do whatever it took to get to where she wanted to go. Schreiber said of those photographic sessions, 'There was no hesitation on her part. "Here I am – it's no big deal." That was her attitude. With lots of nudes I don't photograph faces, but with her I wanted to include the face. The nudes I've done are lovely. There's something wonderful in a beautiful form that happens to be somebody's body. One of my roles is to make people look at nudes differently. I'm trying to make people feel less uptight about their bodies because we're living in a puritanical age.'

He said that his students had to pay cash to Madonna for modelling; she couldn't take cheques because she did not have a bank account. Lee Friedlander, who was awarded a Medal of Paris in 1981 and has three Guggenheim fellowships, says of model Madonna, 'I was curious to try my hand at the nude. She seemed a very confident and streetwise girl. She told me that she was putting a band together, but half the kids that age are doing that. She was a good professional model.'

The Friedlander and Schreiber photographs reveal Madonna still in her 'European mood'. Her armpits are unshaven. Her hair is dark and curly. In some pictures she is pouting, in others she looks pensive. In one she stares warily at the camera, as well she might have. By the time she was a pop sensation, her naked body was stapled all over the pages of *Playboy* and *Penthouse* magazines. The black-and-white nudes of the $10-an-hour (occasionally discounted to $7-an-hour) model sold for more than $100,000 to *Playboy*. But Schreiber and Friedlander revealed that their picture sessions with Madonna, which were published in *Playboy* in 1985, were a 'job lot'. They paid her only $25.

She did a little better from photographer, Bill Stone, who sold his pictures – he will not say for how much – to *Penthouse* magazine.

'I was going to write her a cheque, but she wanted cash. I fished in my pockets for all the money I had and it was $50. She said, "I can't take that much money." As she was leaving, she said, "I can't take all of your money – take some back." And she handed me a few dollars.'

Others were also cashing in on Madonna's modelling days. Madonna had attracted many people during her months in New York. One was Stephen Lewicki who persuaded the 19-year-old to appear in *A Certain Sacrifice*, a soft-porn exercise, which could be judged both exploitative and boring. You'd have thought that, if Madonna had made a porno movie, the viewer at least would be anything but bored.

In the film, she is involved in a rape scene in a coffee shop, an orgiastic dance session and a ritual sacrifice. *High Society* magazine paid out $100,000 for out-take nude shots of Madonna from the film. She had been paid $100 to appear in the movie. (Madonna later sued Lewicki to stop him using her name when he released the film – Madonna nude suddenly made this sex-slave confection a marketing possibility in 1985.)

Madonna brazened out the nude pictures. But they did get to her.

'At first, the *Playboy* pictures were hurtful to me and I wasn't sure how I felt about them. Now I look back at them and feel silly that I ever got upset, but I did want to keep some things private. It's like when you're a little girl at school and some nun comes and lifts up your dress in front of everybody and you get really embarrassed; it's not a real terrible thing in the end, but you're not ready for it. It seems so awful and you seem so exposed. It's other people's problem if they turn them into something smutty. That was never my intention.'

Back in 1980, her dream of stardom was still that. It was time for Little Orphan Annie to meet Mae West. Another example, as Miss West would surely have said, of goodness having nothing to do with it. It was the perfect time for flash/trash. Her desperation showed in her choice of outfits – she was hanging out in New York bars wearing little more than her underwear. She craved attention. There are the tales of her scholarship with the famed Alvin Ailey American Dance Theatre, but they are just stories. She was asked to work with the Theatre's third company, which is much like being in the reserves.

What she quickly found out was that she was not the only ambitious girl in New York. It was like being in the movie *Fame* – everyone could sing and dance and wanted a break. Madonna, spiking her hair, tearing her leotards and being different, lasted for 13 weeks at the Dance Theatre before she went to train with Pearl Lang who was a protégé of dance legend Martha Graham.

Madonna's father came to visit. Her apartment at 232 East 4th Street was cockroach city. Silvio Ciccone pleaded. His daughter told him fame and fortune were just around the corner. But not quite the next corner. There were still many hurdles. Madonna and Pearl Lang did not agree about training methods and they split up. And it was time for a change of personality as well.

She was still taking dance classes. She was also partying and, while doing so, she met Dan Gilroy. Gilroy was here, there and also renting an abandoned synagogue in Corona, Queens. He and his brother Ed were both musicians, and lived and rehearsed there. They were also Madonna's passport out of the cockroach gulch. She moved in with them.

'She never really liked modelling,' says Gilroy, adding, 'She would come home and complain about it sometimes or she would talk about how some photographer had tried to come on to her. She posed for me too. I did paintings and sketches but she didn't like staying in position so I'd let her read and relax when I was painting. She made better money modelling than any other job she could get. Madonna was beautiful and alive and wanted to be a star. She'd wake up every morning, a quick cup of coffee and get right on the phone calling her contacts, getting her career moving. She'd call anywhere and everyone. She worked hard. She learned to play drums with us. She'd practise five hours a day. She was a dancer and she had a sense of the beat. We got to be very close. We were living in the basement of the synagogue and using its large meeting room as a rehearsal and recording studio. My brother Ed and a beautiful blonde girl named Angie Smit were also in the band. We were pretty good but the gigs just weren't there. We might get one or two paying jobs a month and if you got $80 a night, that was a lot. And we were dividing the money four ways.

'She modelled once or twice a week. Sometimes she enjoyed the sessions if the photographer or artist was very good and professional. Once she gave me some beautiful nude photos that she was very proud of. She even wrote a little Chinese poem on a card attached to the pictures. It talked about how some people want women to have bound feet but others want women whose feet are free. I think that maybe it was her way of saying she was free and liberated.

'Madonna would go to the corner markets and bargain with the stall holders for the best vegetables and fruit she could get for the money. One time, we were on hands and knees looking for loose change to buy a few potatoes.

'We had fun too. We'd go dancing, but only on week nights when it wasn't too crowded and we could really move around the floor. Our only luxuries were bicycles. Madonna was young. She was influenced by the people around her. When we played our gigs, Angie dressed really sexy with see-through clothes and she moved sensuously on stage. And Madonna began to do these things too. She was dark haired then, but she saw Angie's long blonde hair got the attention when she was on stage. Maybe that contributed to her finally going blonde.'

Gilroy and Madonna and the band they called the Breakfast Club stayed together for a little more than a year. If things had gone differently in Europe, it might have been more a matter of days. Madonna has always taken every opportunity. Back then she had little thought about anything but advancement.

Patrick Hernandez was a disco pin-up, all movement and not too much substance, and enjoyed some success with a disco ditty titled 'Born To Be Alive'. Madonna was offered a job dancing and singing back-up for him in Paris. She squeaked her delight to anyone who would listen. Michigan to Manhattan, and now April in Paris. *D'accord, cherie.*

CHAPTER FIVE

BOY TOY

*'Even when I was a little girl, I knew I wanted
the whole world to know who I was, to love me and be
affected by me.'*
MADONNA, 1985

The Eiffel Tower. The Champs-Elysées. The city where a young girl's thoughts turn to … misery and loneliness. In Paris, Madonna had an apartment, a maid and a voice coach. Producers Jean Claude Pellerin and Jean Van Lieu, the two Jeans, said they would make her the new Edith Piaf. Like so many before her, Madonna was to hear the immortal words, 'We want to make you a star.' It was a *Pygmalion* fantasy for the Frenchmen who had brought Hernandez's act to France. Now they would work on Madonna. But she was no fair lady. She wanted to work, to sing and dance, and not be touted around town as an upwardly mobile urchin. She had picked up enough French to get the drift of the pitch from the two Jeans.

Madonna reacted quite typically. She rebelled. If they wanted her to be at a certain restaurant, she would be out and about with a Vietnamese boyfriend who had an enormous asset – a motorcycle for scooting through the Paris traffic. When she went on tour with Hernandez to

Tunisia, she was more enthusiastic about the nightclubs than his act. During her stay, she went swimming, in a one-piece body stocking. She stood out on the beach.

Back in Paris, she would order a string of desserts in very proper restaurants just to embarrass her hosts. This was not the France of Bardot and the films she saw in Rochester. She was all but dismissed and no one talked to her in Rochester. She was annoyed and upset to the extent demanded by her personality – mad as hell. She was an ornament, and not the star ornament or the star of this particular road show. And she did not like it. The two Jeans gave her money to keep her quiet. They introduced her to French boys, whom she liked with their trim hips and interest in fashion. The more effeminate the men she met, the more intrigued she was. She feels the same today.

'I see them as my *alter egos*. I feel very drawn to them. I think like a guy but I'm feminine. I relate to feminine men. I just wanted *somebody* to ask me out. Actually it would be great to be both sexes.'

Jean Claude Pellerin's wife, Michélle, recalls Madonna's impact on the men of the French capital: 'She stayed with me and my husband here in Paris. She was very beautiful and she dated a lot of French boys. She thought they were very old-fashioned and she was very free. Very free and very liberal. She wanted a lot of boys. She liked the attention. But she *really* only wanted to be one thing – to be a star. And when she left Paris, she promised me she would come back as a star.'

Of course, she kept her promise. She returned a star, but in her individual way, as always. She distracted the catwalk models at 1991's spring fashion show by wandering around in short skirts that often revealed she was wearing no underwear.

Madonna had spent five indulgent months in Paris.

However, her French mentors had flopped at their attempt to pull off a Professor Higgins double-act. It was that young man back in Queens, New York, in the rented synagogue, who was to provide the initial spark for the Madonna magic.

Dan Gilroy had kept up a steady stream of letters to Madonna – 'We miss you. You must return to America.' She did, driven back by frustration and a disabling attack of pneumonia. She called the synagogue from Kennedy Airport. She was back on stage with the Breakfast Club.

Madonna, the Gilroy brothers and Angie Smit made beautiful music together. It was a free-wheeling time and Madonna felt the happiest she had ever been in her life. She felt loved. She felt wanted and needed. She was writing songs now, and not just playing the drums, but any instrument that Dan or Ed Gilroy would help her with. Madonna had the business brain. She was also the 'balls' of the group as the others recall it. She went about trying to set up appearances, record deals.

'I think I was just naturally more charming to those horny old businessmen than Dan and Ed Gilroy.'

From her earliest days with Daddy, she had known how to twist men round to her point of view.

And there was always fear. A morbid fear of death ever since her mother died. Madonna had lived longer than her mother. What about Marilyn? She had died at 36. She thinks about that now. But there was no fear when she jetted in from Michigan, suburban-street-smart but still naïve in the ways of Manhattan; she was a ripe, well-built cherry, parachuting blind into Times Square, the Big Apple's rotten core of pornography, drugs and prostitution and any combination of all of them. There was no fear in going to Paris and literally living off the kindness of strangers.

But deep inside herself, there was an irrational fear — of failure, of being alone, of dying. Most of us share some of these fears, but most also tend to push through them and get on with living. She fed off her fear. It was the catalyst, the blue touch-paper for her unique and exceptional career, which was about to explode like a fireworks display. But there were some flying sparks to deal with first and she was not in the least fearful of them.

The Gilroys had been trying to make it for five years. They knew their music. Madonna's motto was, 'What do you know? Teach it to me.' She was pushing and pushing hard, and later it would sound harsh when she talked about those particular early days.

'I took advantage of the situation. I wanted to know everything they knew because I could make it work for my benefit.'

Gilroy found himself something of a Dr Frankenstein. He had created a problem — Madonna wanted to sing in the band; the band already had a singer. He was torn between his loyalty to his brother Ed and to Madonna, who also wanted to sing her own songs. She had turned into a monster for Dan Gilroy.

'She was fun, you know. But I knew that, with that kind of drive and devotion to getting ahead, something had to happen. I don't know if she was more talented than the rest of the group. More driven, and an incredible attention-getter. It was fun. It was a good year.'

The romance, the learning and her role with the Breakfast Club was over. She left the synagogue. Queens was dead. Long live the big city.

Back in Manhattan, she called on the contacts she had established. She rapped her knuckles on record company doors. There were boyfriends – one for Sunday, Monday, Tuesday, and so on and – if she didn't get confused – it would all work out on Saturday night. One man invited to a party asked if he could bring a date and was told, 'Sure, bring a date. We can *all* do something.'

But Camille Barbone still says all the boyfriends did not mean a roundabout of sex. It was contacts.

'Her first encounter with me was a flirt. I was getting into an elevator in a building in New York and she was in it. "Did you do it yet?" she asked. I was completely confused and said, "No, not yet." What "it" was a mystery, but the question got me and Madonna working together.

'Madonna knew I was a music manager and organised a gig where I could hear her perform but I was ill and could not attend. The next day, she came into the office slamming things.

'"It's my life," she shouted at me. "I set this gig up just for you."

'I really enjoyed that and I thought then that she would be a superstar. Not because she was slamming things and acting up but because she wanted it more than anyone. Everybody has a dream but not everybody has the balls to go after it. I think I've worked with other artists who have far more talent than Madonna but never have I worked with an artist who has had as much drive. The musical side of the songs was kind of simplistic but she wrote great lyrics and it was my job to pair her with great musicians.

'But the first thing I had to do was to pay Madonna's rent and try and make sure she had food. She'd show up at my studio and be weak from hunger. She would never complain about personal stuff like that; only if she didn't have a piece of equipment she needed, or a costume. She was very careful and showed her vulnerability. I gave her security and support because I thought she needed a friend and someone who would take care of her without extracting a great repayment from her.

'The sexuality of Madonna is so played up but it's almost an asexuality because it's universal. It's across the board. It's a powerful tool and she wields it beautifully. And in the early days, she relied on it very heavily. But I don't think there is anything dodgy about the fact that men – and probably women too – are more than willing to sponsor beautiful and attractive women. Would Madonna go on a date with someone because she was hungry? Yes, she would. Would she sleep with him? Probably, if she liked him, she would. Probably, if she didn't like him, she'd be smart enough to manipulate it so she didn't have to sleep with him and still get dinner.

'She called herself a Boy Toy, but in no way was she in any way like a career prostitute. She didn't have to be. Madonna is a sexual creature who has men eating out of her hand. She knows about timing. A simple word like "Hi" delivered by Madonna and men are reduced to stuttering and stammering. She had men lending her money and musicians rehearsing and giving their time without pay – and she wasn't sleeping with any of them.'

She was sleeping in New York's garment centre in a 12-storey structure called the Music Building, simply because it had been converted into a series of rehearsal rooms. Madonna was still scrounging food on the streets – and accommodation in the building. When the last group left the place, she snuggled down for the night. In the morning, before the first group arrived, she would use the basic toilet facilities.

Madonna took pride in making do. People could not

understand how she lived – the popcorn, the daily apple, the bought meal, the borrowed five bucks. She was feeding on fear and she was ravenous.

Around the New York clubs, she was known as a bit of a 'prick teaser'. A pragmatic one. After she got things – shall we say 'stimulated'? – she got her way, but those stimulated did not necessarily get theirs. But for most men it did not matter. It was a turn-on, a thrill. She was funny. Rude. Terrific to look at. Sexy. Fun to be with. She was an all-round entertainer. A dangerous and different one. Because you never knew what you were going to get. It is the same today. She frightens. She fascinates.

Back in New York, she was more interested in being fascinating. Again fate blessed her. Steve Bray, the tall, pony-tailed waiter from the Blue Frogge in Detroit, called. She needed a drummer. He was in New York in six days. He brought some musical know-how and 'cool' to the motley band Madonna had gathered around her.

Bray moved in with her in the Music Building. Once there, he sensed Madonna was not held in the greatest awe by the crowd who used the rehearsal halls.

'I think there was a lot of resentment of someone who had obviously got that special something. There are so many musicians out there, but there are only a few who really have that charisma. That community frowned on her. She had trouble making friends.'

It was like a commune, and Madonna was not a commune person. She was a Madonna person. A solo act. She wanted to call the group 'Madonna'. The self-effacing Bray told her that was an upsetting idea. So they called themselves the Millionaires (bottom dollar as it turned out) and then Modern Dance (no one stepped out to them) and Emmy (a nickname Dan Gilroy had given Madonna, but that still did not bring good luck). She made a demo tape, which Camille Barbone, who was managing other rock bands around the city at the time, agreed was good enough for a business arrangement to be made. A deal was done. Madonna, for the first time in her life, was on a salary. She knew how to spend. 'Outtaaahere!' was the cry. The Music Building was history. She moved to New York's Upper West Side. Steve Bray moved uptown too.

Camille Barbone found herself counselling Madonna. 'There was a great transition that took place from the moment Madonna met me to the end of our relationship. My premise with her was that she was the key, she was the core, the power, she had to begin to own that. I gave her the idea of strength and support so that she was capable of that. I got her on the Manhattan social and business circuit. One of the first meetings we had was with the William Morris talent agency and it was at a Japanese restaurant. We were all sitting there talking and Madonna let out the most gigantic belch in the world and everybody looked at her and she just smiled and laughed. Other times I'd be in a meeting in my office and she'd come in and start shaving her armpits in the mirror. It was shock value. She'd make me laugh and make me shake my head and sometimes she'd make me really angry. Madonna pushed me to my financial, patience and loyalty limits. She'd give me thirty reasons why she had to have something – a guitar, a weekend at the beach with her boyfriend – and I found it difficult to say no. I suppose I was a little bit in love with her too. It's hard to talk about her and not sound in love with her. I guess I did love Madonna. She is a very attractive woman with amazing sex appeal.

'I take credit for jump-starting her performing image. We

started doing performances in Long Island and it was only a matter of time before people started to dress like her. I remembered Brian Epstein, when he was first pushing the Beatles, paying people to scream and I grabbed a few kids and gave them twenty dollars and told them to go out and buy a few accessories that she was wearing and show up at the shows. The Madonna wannabes were born through that.'

But Madonna wanted more and the magic word was *now*. Her new band was called 'Madonna'. Camille Barbone had been promised old-fashioned rock 'n' roll. Madonna wanted funk, funk and funkier. There were shouting matches. 'People said I was trying to turn Madonna into Olivia Newton-John but I disagree with that. Madonna's mould would have been whatever she wanted it to be. I showcased her in a boa, a coat and tails and black leather, and I don't think you've ever seen Olivia Newton-John in that. It was much more Chrissie Hynde than anything. But that was where she was musically at that stage of the game.'

Madonna would leave Camille Barbone in her wake. In 2001, the woman who had 'adopted' Madonna recalled the end of their musical affair.

'One day I was asked to attend a meeting with her lawyer and the message was blunt: I was fired. I had spent everything I had on her; it bankrupted me. I later sued for breach of contract and settled for an amount that covered my loss of earnings. Not that many years ago, she contacted me and said, "You're a bitch and I'm a bitch but we work well together – let's find a job for you." I wanted more than she was willing to give and we have not talked since. I don't think I've ever felt bitter. I've felt sad about it and obviously being in the music business and having lost an opportunity like Madonna is quite searing, to say the least.'

Madonna went with rock 'n' roll but she was, as always, influenced by those closest to her. They wanted to be cool. Even cooler. All day she would write the songs that they wanted with Steve Bray and at the clubs they would play the music the management – both their own and the clubs' – wanted.

They would play the Roxy, or the Danceteria, which was where Mark Kamins changed Madonna's life. 'I think Madonna has slowed down, in a good way. She was once the wildest person I knew. There was really nothing she wouldn't do if she thought it would be fun.'

Well connected, in many senses, Kamins was a disc jockey who mattered. And his Saturday-night crowd liked to impress him. For Kamins, his popularity meant less lonely nights at home. At Danceteria, he was a star and he had his groupies. He came on to Madonna. And she flirted right back. She got what she wanted. Kamins listened to the demonstration recording made by Madonna and Steve Bray, which included a song called 'Everybody'. Kamins adored it. It became one of the specials at Danceteria. The kids danced to it – they had to. Kamins recalls, 'Everybody going to nightclubs has other ambitions, but she was special.'

So special that Kamins helped finance a re-recording of that demonstration tape. And negotiated – solo – a deal for her with Sire Records. It was a *big* rung on the ladder.

Steve Bray and Kamins were beside themselves; Bray would produce Madonna's first album, and Kamins would produce Madonna's first single. Wrong. Both of them. Madonna was scared. She felt that she had been handed a golden egg – and she wanted it hatched by experts.

CHAPTER SIX

HOT ROCKS

'She is her own woman.'

SILVIO 'TONY' CICCONE, 2000

The challenge of channelling Madonna's enormous but often erratic energy into her first album went to Reggie Lucas, who had previously produced for Stephanie Mills and Roberta Flack. It happened in a roundabout way after Madonna had put herself in a position of being an investment worth hundreds of thousands of dollars. And it followed much Madonna-manipulation behind the scenes.

Both Mark Kamins and Steve Bray had their hopes, but Madonna had her own dreams and also her own way of pursuing them at the Danceteria, the four floors of the Chelsea disco that offered funky music and hospitality to the crowd who favoured skin-tight leather and purple hair – anything exotic, but always different. Mark Kamins had contacted Michael Rosenblatt, a music-industry talent scout who worked for Sire Records, the 'New Wave' arm of the giant Warner Brothers Communication Group.

Rosenblatt caught what amounted to performances by Madonna at the Danceteria. These were the days of the belly-button look. Madonna wore cascades of jewellery (she got it free from Maripol, a French designer who was on the scene) and every piece of cloth had a suggestive rip or tear. Some of the Danceteria crowd say that, at times, Madonna looked as though she had been through a spin dryer attached to her 'Boy Toy' belt.

Not everyone got the humour. When she was living in the East Village, her hangout was the Roxy. It was full of graffiti artists and break dancers. All of them had nicknames, which they would write on the club walls. There would be 'Hi-Fi' or 'Whiz-Kid'. The game was to see how many times you could get this tag name up on the wall. The slang was you 'threw up' your name on the walls. Madonna 'threw up' her 'BOY TOY'. The crowd thought it was hilarious. Madonna saw it as a tongue-in-cheek statement, the opposite of what it meant. She was not available to anyone – but outside the Roxy no one knew that.

The controversy was beginning, and the slut label that had haunted her schooldays was back again. Madonna resents that, and the talk that she slept her way to success. Sure, she learned music from a string of guys, some of whom she had sex with. It is not that she was annoyed at the suggestion she used sex to get where she wanted – she was just furious that people thought Madonna could not get there simply on her own talent and drive. That was insulting. And it was later the sexual promiscuity of some of her partners rather than her own which convinced her to take a test for AIDS. The result was negative.

Such scary thoughts were far from the heady atmosphere of the Danceteria where Madonna's ambition and plotting were about to get her the result she so desperately wanted.

When Rosenblatt saw her at the club, he scented 'a find' – a big-dollar one at that. He remembers that when he first saw Madonna at the disco club, he thought two things – she looked wild and she looked beautiful. On stage, she danced to Kamins' re-recording of her version of 'Everybody'. The word was being passed around the right circles and a deal was about to go down.

Seymour Stein was in Lennox Hill Hospital, New York, suffering from heart problems. As the boss of Sire Records, he had to finalise any recording deal with Madonna. A stocky man with what hair he has left worn in tight, grey curls, Stein is a music mogul. He reached the top spotting talent and trends. The buzz on Madonna was so strong he agreed to meet her in his hospital room. He shaved, combed his hair and brought a new dressing gown for the meeting. The nurses told him not to get so excited, to watch the stress. When Madonna arrived, he had forgotten all about his dressing gown. He had a drip feed in his left arm and was sitting by his bed wearing his underpants.

It was a strange but, with hindsight, totally appropriate beginning for the Material Girl's career. Stein, although impressed by Madonna's tape, which he had played on one of the giant 'portable' stereos in his hospital room, was still the wily businessman. He committed – but just so much. Madonna would be paid $5,000 as an advance for a contract to make three singles.

It was Easter 1982 when she went into a recording studio to remake 'Everybody'. The record was showcased at the Danceteria – and what a showcase. She got three dancers – one of them a gay artist, Martin Burgoyne, whom she had roomed with – and they put on a sensational act. It was raunchy. It was sexy. It was sensational. It blazed out dollar signs. In neon. Seymour Stein was there to watch her. So were Steve Bray and Mark Kamins.

Fans said she sounded 'black'. She was not pictured on her record covers. It was only when she appeared in public they realised this 5ft 4in-tall Italian-American was pounding the sound out. The irony of these appearances was that she was asked to lip-synch to her record and was paid more than when she had performed live. She was being heard in gay clubs. Black clubs. Transvestite bars. Rock clubs. Every place they were making music. Her next record, 'Burning Up' – again, a 12-inch disco single – was released and with it a cheaply made video (unlike the most sophisticated and sometimes controversial videos which followed).

Madonna moped for some moments, and then bounced back. She likes smooth skin, lips and the Latin look in her men. Enter John Benitez, a.k.a. 'Jellybean' Benitez. 'She didn't bowl me over at first. Then we started holding hands and buying each other little presents.' They became a solid item – she even took him home to Rochester. Her father approved of Jellybean more than his daughter's outlandish, all-black outfit worn for the Thanksgiving dinner. Now a respected producer, Jellybean was the resident disc jockey at the Funland disco when he met Madonna. Now he makes his own music. They remain very close. Interestingly, he says their first couple of years together were cemented by mutual ambition.

'We both started to move at the same pace. We're both very career orientated, very goal orientated. We both wanted to be stars.'

And Madonna never more so than when Sire Records told her that they were prepared to bankroll an album.

She then turned her back on Bray and Kamins. It was a bitter falling out with Bray. 'It was very hard to accept,' he says. But he had no choice. He joined Dan Gilroy and the Breakfast Club, another crowd Madonna had left behind.

Kamins was in the same position. 'Sure, I was hurt. At the time, I felt stepped on. But I don't think there's a mean bone in her body. Maybe a mean knuckle, but not a mean bone.'

Maybe not mean. But tough: 'All my boyfriends turned out to be helpful to my career. That's not the reason I stayed with them. I loved them all very much. I'm not Alexis from *Dynasty*. All the men I stepped over to get to the top – all of them would have me back because they all still love me and I love them.'

Professionally, the man who really mattered at that moment was record producer Reggie Lucas. He did not last long. The album *Madonna* was released in America in July 1983. The first single from it was 'Holiday', a song which had been brought to her by Jellybean. Everyone had enormous hopes for it, but it made a minor splash. Later, there were radio plays of 'Borderline' and 'Lucky Star'. They made it into the record charts.

But it was her first video which made Madonna. And it was quickly followed by a second. This was the breakthrough. Her dance background, her sense of the outrageous and her songs all blended together for the MTV generation. She knew just how to 'come across' sexually and later explained, 'I've been in touch with that aspect of my personality since I was five.'

Madonna had given Reggie Lucas the go-ahead for the 'sound' of her début album, but she did not go for the finished product. It was not for her. Too sharp, too sleek. Impersonal. She felt she was as good a judge as these professional producers. And she told them so. Lucas remembered, 'I wanted to push her in a pop direction. She was a little more orientated toward the disco thing, but I thought she had appeal to the general market. It's funny about the thing with Kamins and Bray. The same thing that happened to them pretty much happened to me on her second record when they had Nile Rodgers.'

Lucas was dropped from the Madonna express. Madonna went after Rodgers, who had worked with David Bowie and Duran Duran for her *Like a Virgin* album.

Madonna was on the move – literally. In 1983, she had gone to London to promote 'Everybody' and appeared at the Camden Palace, where a couple of years earlier she had met the then chart-topper Boy George, and had been hugely impressed with him and with London and Britain. She thought it more classy and 'cool' than America. Madonna did not even believe Boy George had a group. All she remembered was he wore high heels and was surrounded by men dressed just like him. She was intrigued. She liked everything feminine. She was not in control of this particular androgyny and she did not hang around to watch the action.

Even a year after the release of her first album, which was dedicated to Silvio Ciccone, she was not really a 'name' outside of the New York club circuit. She could go to the Danceteria – a 'Class of 1982-type' reunion – and not be mobbed. Or 'throw-up' with the boys at the Roxy. It was no preparation for the giddy world she was joining. She was quick to realise this and sought expert help. Her antennae yet again twitched at the right time.

Rodgers introduced her to her Detroit-days' idol Diana Ross. She met Barbra Streisand. She was moving in the legend league. She wanted someone to guide her to that sort of status.

'Who's the best manager in the world?' she asked Rodgers and Jellybean Benitez. But she did not wait for their answer – she'd thought it out herself. Who was the biggest pop star at that time? Michael Jackson. So she went straight to California to meet Jackson's manager, Freddy DeMann.

DeMann is always dapper, his moustache neatly trimmed and his hair slicked back. He started out as a promotions man in the record business and moved on to become an artists' representative in 1978. His first big clients were the Jacksons, the group known worldwide as The Jackson Five. In 1979, the quietly spoken DeMann (who is prone to depression – which he says is from his mother's side of the family and known as 'The Glickman Curse') packaged Michael Jackson, youngest of the Jacksons, with music legend Quincy Jones. The result was *Off The Wall*, which appeared to be the hit album of the century until *Thriller* was released in December 1982. Jackson and DeMann split in 1983, which, for most people in the music business, would have been reason enough to locate the highest window and leap.

But DeMann had something else going – Madonna. A 14-year relationship, which ended in the summer of 1997, was about to begin when Madonna appeared in his Sunset Strip offices on a hot, smoggy day in July 1983, around the time her *Madonna* album was in the record stores. She was seriously blonde at the time. And determined.

'She had that special magic that very few stars have,' he remembers. DeMann was interested enough to fly to Manhattan to see Madonna do her stuff at Studio 54, then the hangout of choice for Bianca Jagger, the late fashion designer Halston, the Andy Warhol crowd and other up-market trendies. That crowd did not worry Madonna.

DeMann was her concern. He had told her that he did not rate Prince, so how would he rate her? And Michael Jackson, like Prince, was an exciting stage performer. Would DeMann like her? Would he manage her? Yes. And yes again. A formidable partnership was struck.

DeMann was taking care of business. Nile Rodgers who had crafted David Bowie's hit 'Let's Dance', was in the recording studio with her. Madonna liked that idea for all sorts of reasons, and she was also a huge Bowie devotee.

'David Bowie was a huge influence on me because he was the first concert I went to see. I remember watching him and thinking I didn't know what sex he was and it didn't matter. Because one minute he was wearing body stockings – the whole Ziggy Stardust thing – and next he was The Thin White Duke in white double-breasted suits and there's something so androgynous about him. And I think androgyny – whether it's David Bowie or Helmut Berger – has really influenced my work more than anything.'

And so it was with Nile Rodgers. But also in the studio was Steve Bray, the friend from the crazy days of the Blue Frogge in Detroit and the squabbling days in New York. The two were writing together again and four of their songs went on to the *Like a Virgin* album.

The fireworks were about to go off. The title track of her second LP was also the first single, and the video was filmed in Italy, against the backdrop of the pillars and marble of Venice. It was almost the end of Madonna's career, and for the guardians of moral propriety it is a pity that the lion did not eat her. The lion? Yes, the tame lion that co-starred with her. It just wasn't quite tame enough, it seems. Madonna was to perform confidently while the lion wandered over to her right side. She was not to be alarmed by it. She was provocatively leaning against a pillar – 'You make me feel…' – hip push – 'like a virgin…' – roll of the belly – when, nudge, nudge, there's Leo the lion with his head between her legs. Right there! She says now that she was convinced he was going to take a bite out of her. She looked down from under the veil, looked away and then looked down again. Leo gave her the eye and then a deafening roar. 'SEX SHOCKER: MADONNA TURNS ON KING OF THE JUNGLE' – how the newspapers would have loved that one.

Madonna was hot. The crucifixes, the bare midriff, the 'BOY TOY' innuendo and her blatant sexuality also made her controversial. The 'Merry Widow' long-line bras were not uplifting to the Moral Majority. And there were millions of angry parents having to cope with youngsters who just wanted 'to be like Madonna'.

Dr Sam Janus is an associate professor of psychiatry at New York Medical College and author of *The Death of Innocence*. He stated, 'She was oblivious to the traditional standards of morality. The sexually explicit lyrics and her vulgar songs advocate prostitution.'

Oh, well. What does Dr Danilo Ponce, a renowned professor of psychiatry at the University of Hawaii, have to say about that? 'The whole image Madonna projects is that of a tramp – of a streetwalker eager to sell her favours to the highest bidder.' Of her records, Dr Ponce commented, 'She flaunts her bare navel and dresses in lacy lingerie and black bras.'

What an advertisement. The legendary Frederick's of Hollywood, purveyors of all sorts of stimulating, sexy underwear designed to give bottoms, busts and ardour an uplift, recall the height of the *Like a Virgin* controversy. As well they should. Their sales soared. Especially the black Merry Widows. In the first 6 months of 1985, there was a 40 per cent increase, says John Chapman, the company's merchandise manager: 'We knew her popularity was doing it. We were selling to a much younger element – girls were going for the innerwear-outwear effect.'

Maidenform looked back at sales reports and found that their black push-up bra was a sell-out. Lily of France said their all-over lace body briefer did 'phenomenally' that year.

There were all sorts of 'ban Madonna' outcries. Margaret Scott, who was co-director of the United Parents Under God, with headquarters in Belmont, California, was active in that. Why? 'Our youngsters were being exploited and manipulated by Madonna. She took a public-be-damned attitude when it came to morals. Our kids were being victimised. The kids worshipped Madonna.'

They called her 'a porn queen at heart', 'a corrupting Pied Piper', 'a trashy tart', 'a slut'. The lady, they said, was a tramp. Madonna worried about that reaction for as long as it took her to unhook her bra. Her attention was on the wannabes, the fans who were buying her records and sending her to the top of the charts worldwide. In America, around 75,000 copies of *Like a Virgin* were dancing off the shelves daily. And the fans were desperate to see her live – she sold out 3 nights of concerts at Radio City Music Hall in New York in 34 minutes. The old record of 55 minutes belonged to Elvis Costello and Phil Collins.

The Boy Toy was no longer to be toyed with. She says it was all her humour, the mocking and mixing of sex and virginity, of crucifix and crotch. She says the fans tuned into her humour.

'For so long people had been telling girls, "You have to

dress nondescript. You have to look masculine if you want to be in control." And here was someone being very sexy and having fun and dressing up and doing exactly what these little girls wanted to do. And making all the decisions, and having power and success. The people who adored me were the children who understood where I was coming from.

'The people who loathed me didn't get it and my success pissed them off. There's a lot of idiots in the world. It makes for more interesting magazines. Wouldn't you rather read about a slut than a plain-Jane wallflower? I know I would. Anyway, I think it would be kind of boring if everyone just loved me a hundred per cent.'

But she would love it. A poll of half a dozen American psychiatrists showed she had an I-want-to-be-loved complex. And if you do not love her, or agree with her, or do what she wants, that is it. Be gone. That is her vulnerable spot as one husband, lovers and collaborators would discover. She has trouble with the other viewpoint, which is understandable when you are the most recognised star in the world. But it does not help in personal or business relationships.

Her two years of living with Jellybean in a New York loft were almost over. He also wanted to be a star and was producing and recording on his own. There was no room in Madonna's world for two stars in the family as she was to discover.

Madonna's goals were endless. Her records were all over the pop charts. She had six at once in the American Top 40. She was working on her body, determined to be the healthiest and fittest star. She wanted to be a movie star. She had played a cameo role as a nightclub *chanteuse*, warbling two of her own songs in Jon Peters' film *Vision Quest* (titled

Crazy for You in the UK, after Madonna's theme song), and deep inside she still wanted to be a movie star – a big, major, massive, incredible, adored legend, like Marilyn Monroe.

CHAPTER SEVEN

HOLLYWOOD HIGH

*'After you get a little success in Hollywood, the next
thing you usually get is a divorce.'*
DAN DAILEY, SINGER–DANCER, 1958

In the late summer days of 1984, Madonna spent a lot of
time in her SoHo apartment in New York, simply
thinking, trying to clear her mind. She had climbed on to
the rainbow. Now she wanted to ride it. As fast as possible.
She knew she would have to go on tour. But she also wanted
the movies. And she had heard about a picture that might
just be her. In one of the most amazing – if somewhat lucky
– marketing coups in showbusiness history, her desires
dovetailed. It was as if someone had waved a wand and
granted her every wish.

Also living in a SoHo loft was Susan Seidelman, who, in
1984, was 31, ambitious and the director of the cult film,
Smithereens, which had been the surprise hit of the 1982
Cannes Film Festival. Seidelman sat on cushions to protect
her spotless, varnished floors while she read the script of a
film entitled *Desperately Seeking Susan*. It was something of a
New Wave fairytale with Susan disrupting the everyday lives
and sexual activities of all involved. The film relies on that

well-used plot device, memory loss. It is New Jersey housewife Roberta who suffers temporary amnesia and 'becomes' Susan. Mistaken identity and farce. Rosanna Arquette, who is like Audrey Hepburn masquerading as Sophie Loren – the gamine look meets the full-figured woman – was offered and accepted the role of Roberta.

Susan was a small, $5 million-budgeted film for Orion Pictures. To make it work, Seidelman needed a kooky, crazy, but believable actress in the title role. She heard on the New York grapevine – regarded as just ten minutes slower than the Hollywood buzz – that Madonna might be interested. Already, 207 other actresses had shown their interest and had been tested. Madonna did a screen test.

Why did they pick Madonna over all the others? Midge Sanford was one of the producers. 'She had this presence you couldn't get rid of. No matter how good the other people were, we kept going back to her screen test.'

Seidelman was all for Madonna, but Orion Pictures' executives had never heard of the singer. As Seidelman said – and hard as it is to believe now – Madonna was then 'just a pretty pop singer'. Ten months later, she would have been out of reach of such a small project. Then, she was prepared to work – and to learn. Her days of being the wise guy, the comedian in the school playground, helped. So did the discipline from her dance training. Her director said, 'During the nine weeks of filming, we'd often get home at 11.00pm or midnight and we'd have to be back on the set at 6–7.00am. Half the time the driver would pick Madonna up at her health club. She'd get up at 4.30am to work out first.'

Madonna admits to 'shitting bricks' during the early scenes. But she was determined to learn. 'I think I surprised everybody by being so calm – I was gonna soak everything up.' She admits that there was something of a self-caricature about her Susan. But only so far. 'At first, it was hard to get producers to take me seriously because I was a rock star. I think they thought I would throw fits or do blow [cocaine] on the set or something. I think they were shocked when I showed up every morning like clockwork.'

As Madonna's world and fame increased, so did the interest in the film. And Rosanna Arquette was sceptical. A new song from Madonna, 'Into the Groove', was worked into the film. On a film location in the Pacific-Northwest, Arquette said, 'The script changed when they got Madonna. I told them that if *Susan* was going to be a two-hour rock video, I didn't want to be part of it. A disco-dance movie wasn't what I signed on to do.'

At the time, an American magazine had quoted her as saying, 'I don't think I'd ever want to be as famous as Madonna.' Later, she would cast doubt on that, commenting, 'I never meant that. But I think it might be a bit of a prison for her to have that kind of fame. I mean, she can't go anywhere and that's a lot to lose. I'm an actor and I want to be able to do different things. I'm not a mega star – that's a tough thing to be.'

Madonna went to work on *Desperately Seeking Susan* in November 1984 and, at the same time, *Like a Virgin* was released. By the New Year, the album and the single would be sitting at the top of the American record charts. And Madonna's life was about to change irretrievably. On the business side, there was the fantastic success of the Virgin tour, which played to nearly 400,000 fans in 27 cities with the Beastie Boys as the supporting band. On the last night of the tour, her father Silvio carried her off stage. The Material

Girl was still Daddy's Girl. She renegotiated her record contract, giving her much of the $8 million up front in a cash advance. She was not climbing the rainbow, she was riding it hard.

At a personal level, it was a bumpy ride. Jellybean Benitez had all but vanished with the New Year. 'We're still friends. I know a lot of her ex-boyfriends and I don't think she used them or me. She took advantage of opportunities given her. Other people do the same thing,' said Jellybean who, like most of her men, remains loyal. It was to get even bumpier that year. She was to meet and marry Sean Penn, be rumoured to be pregnant, have her naked body from the modelling days displayed all over *Penthouse* and *Playboy* magazines and go to court to try to stop the re-release of John Lewicki's soft-porn flick, *A Certain Sacrifice*. Her lawsuit argued that it was a poor quality film with an even poorer quality plot, never mind the orgies. Around that time, a ritzy apartment co-operative in New York's Central Park turned down her $1.8 million bid for a unit. They didn't want rock stars in the building. But Sean Penn wanted the Material Girl. Very badly. So badly that he played the romance without any of his trademark aggressive and impulsive style.

Madonna was still fixated by Marilyn Monroe. Wasn't she the original Material Girl for the 'Material Girl' video? It was decided to reprise Monroe's best sequence from *Gentlemen Prefer Blondes*. Madonna would be Monroe. But she really wanted to get the feel of it. Bill Travilla, who designed for the ladies of the television series *Dallas* and *Knots Landing*, was responsible for Monroe's shocking-pink, cut-to-the-high gown in the 1953 film. He was surprised to see Madonna wearing it – or rather, a perfect replica of it – on her video. Travilla was not credited with the design but years later takes it in good humour. 'I felt, to paraphrase Madonna, like a virgin. I'd been knocked off for the very first time.'

The video was also the first time Sean Penn got up close to Madonna. It was a draughty recording studio in February 1985. He, by no accident, turned up on the set of the video. He could hardly miss her fascination with Monroe. At this time, there was no evidence of Penn the hot-head. They talked. They held hands. Madonna said at the time, 'I didn't feel swept off my feet, but he is somebody whose work I had admired for a long time. He's wild though. He'll probably die young.

'We have so much in common. We were born one day apart [Penn was born 17 August 1960] and he and I have similar temperaments. I feel like he is my brother or something … In fact, when I squint my eyes, he almost looks like my father when he was young … He's really smart and he knows a lot. He's willing to play the outsider or nerd rather than the hero that everybody likes.'

Madonna and Sean Penn – the Outsiders. When they were first together on the West Coast, the doting Penn took Madonna on a 40-mile drive from his place in Malibu to Westwood, the university district of Los Angeles. To the rear of the campus of the University of Los Angeles at California (UCLA) is Westwood Cemetery, the home of Marilyn Monroe's grave. Madonna was shaking during the visit. The rose that is always there from baseball legend and former husband, Joe DiMaggio, who died in 2000, was on the grave. Later, Madonna said, 'He really loved her.'

And love, or a version of it, was to keep her going in the months ahead. No one – not even she or Sean Penn – knew what they were getting into. Madonna's early mentor

Camille Barbone had something of an inkling when asked about that early relationship. She responded, 'Madonna has always liked the rebel, the loner, in her men. James Dean is her idol. Sean Penn was not the first or last rebel in her life.'

Penn has been around showbusiness all his life. His father Leo, who was 77 when he died from lung cancer in 1998, was an actor-turned-television producer and director, and his mother is one-time Broadway star, Eileen Ryan. They dote on Sean and his younger brother Chris, who were brought up in the surf-washed, sun-tanned community of Santa Monica. The family later paid $3 million to move down the Pacific Coast Highway and into a Malibu hillside home.

Penn was a schoolboy when he began working in local Los Angeles theatre groups. At 19, he landed a guest role on the long-running crime show, *Barnaby Jones*. He secured more television work and then stage roles in New York. His big break was when he was cast opposite fellow Brat Pack member, Tim Hutton, in *Taps*. Then he was a doped-out surfer in *Fast Times at Ridgemount High* alongside Phoebe Cates in her pre-black suspenders and sexy television mini-series *Lace* days, and before she became Mrs Kevin Kline. It was a sign of the acting technique he was developing when he 'stayed in character' after the cameras stopped rolling. Director Amy Heckerling remembers he once 'lost' his character, but jumped right into being surfer Jeff Spicoli by stubbing out a cigarette in his palm.

Bad Boys director Richard Rosenthal is another Penn fan. The film stamped Penn's screen image. He played a teen gangster and grew his hair to his shoulders, ignored the make-up department for a real tattoo (a wolf's head) and only gave in on having his teeth filed down when his mother objected.

'He likes to get into character. He's the most talented actor of his generation,' said Rosenthal, who offers an amazing insight into Sean Penn's method. 'We went out with some Chicago cops so Sean could get a "feel" of it all. During the raid, some more cops arrived and thought we were criminals and told us to raise our hands. I complied, but for Sean it was a chance to see what it was like for a gang member to take on a cop. He turned to the cop, who was the size of an apartment, and said, "Fuck you." The cop picked up Sean and threw him into a wall. His nose was almost broken, but later he told me it was at that moment he finally became his character in the film.'

However, *Bad Boys* co-star Reni Santoni recalls, 'I thought the kid had been watching too many Brando movies.' Film executive Sherry Lansing, who produced *Racing with the Moon*, which collapsed at the box office – Penn refused to promote the film in which he co-starred with one-time lover, Elizabeth McGovern – believed then that Penn had to do something about himself. 'His career will be over if he doesn't change. He's talented but he's also self-destructive.'

But for all his supposed publicity shyness, Penn eats out at places like Sunset Strip's Spago, which is always besieged by cameramen. Once, he walked out and into friend and Brat Pack 'godfather' Harry Dean Stanton. As flashbulbs popped, Penn zipped his jacket over his head and carried on the conversation with the bemused Stanton.

Penn liked proposing to actresses. First was Bruce Springsteen's sister, Pam. He met the Boss's sister during filming *Ridgemont High*. The wedding date was set for 20 February 1983. In April a year later, he was set to marry Elizabeth McGovern. Madonna intervened. Even Penn's father Leo shakes his head when quizzed about his eldest son's sex appeal: 'He has a big nose, small mouth and close-set eyes. He's moody and likes mischief.' And Penn himself tells a story that reflects just how far he is willing to go. It involves him and fellow Brat-Packer, the son of Martin Sheen, Emilio Estevez:

'One time me and my buddy Emilio planned this thing. It was one of those times when we sat around and said, "We're really going to follow through on this. All the way. Nobody's gonna laugh."

'This guy Kelly always got off the school bus with Emilio. So one day I was around the corner with another buddy in my car. We had .22 calibre machine-guns with blanks. And Emilio had a blood squib – a big bag of fake blood. So he coaxed this guy Kelly into walking down to the ice-cream parlour with him. We drive by – and open fire. Emilio does this great stuff. He squeezes the blood bag and it bursts all over his front. He hits the ground. Kelly has a skateboard in his hand, and he's freaking out. He starts to walk away in shock. So we grab Kelly at gunpoint, put him in the back of the car, and we take off. He's so scared, he can't talk. We're wearing ski masks and we're calling him Emilio as though we've got the *wrong* guy, right? We go up into the canyon. We stop and yell at him to get out of the car, and we say, "We're not going to hurt you, but we're gonna tie you to this tree and then we're gonna take off."

'This was our greatest, ever. Out of the back of the car we take this gasoline can – it's full of water – and my buddy lights the match. The guy starts screaming. I pour the water on the guy, and my buddy flips the match at him. Then we tell him. Emilio arrives, and we have a little picnic. And the guy has never been the same since.'

No one who meets Penn ever is.

He says his mother told him long ago about dealing with executives: 'She said when you go in, don't picture them sitting behind a desk, but sitting on the toilet. It's amazing how that makes you strong.'

As long as you don't get flushed away.

Penn was enjoying strong reviews for *The Falcon and the Snowman* when he first met Madonna. In the film, he and Tim Hutton starred as the title characters, two young, convicted spies. Penn sympathised with the plight of the real Snowman (he got the name for cocaine dealing), Andrew Lee Daulton, and supported his efforts for parole. So much so that he forgot his shyness to appear on nationwide television in the United States and said he would 'do what I can as things come up. During the research for the role it was more than "you can scratch my back, I'll scratch yours". I think it became a friendship and out of this, within the bounds of what a friend can do, I will. Under different circumstances, I'd like to sit down and have a beer with him. Maybe sometime we'll do that.'

But at a party for *The Falcon and the Snowman*, he spent two hours huddled behind a pot plant. You get the feeling that it would be a little unsettling if Penn was cast as Hitler because his 'research' might involve starting a couple of wars. This deep research in changing mind and body is characteristic of De Niro, but Penn insisted in a rule-breaking, talkative moment, 'One thing I don't like to see written about me is the whole De Niro thing. I think it just doesn't matter. All that matters is what's on screen. I don't need to be thought of as a hard worker. I just want to be as good as I can.'

'A lot of people will label him shy, but it's really just that he has a good sense of himself,' said Oscar winner Tim

Hutton, adding, 'He doesn't have to carry on or be an extrovert because he's got a real clear vision.'

But it is a vision clouded by Garboesque and violent acts; he appears to believe rocks are mightier than the Penn and shows a touch of the Red Indian about still cameras – he's nervous, as though a camera click will kidnap his soul. One female photographer at a publicity function attended by Penn confided, 'He told me he had a water pistol and if I didn't leave he was going to fill it with urine and squirt me.'

When Sean Penn and I met, he looked more in need of a Bloody Mary than a shot of pee. It was 8.30am on Hollywood's Sunset Strip, which, like many other city streets, had just been hosed, making it shimmer in the morning sun. A vivid contrast to the mean streets of the night. From three floors up in an art-deco hotel opposite the Comedy Store club, Penn, who is not known for laughs, is watching the traffic start to move. He starts moving around the room. He has a powerful presence but looks more like a car hop with a hangover than a movie star. There is a lot of power in his right bicep as well as that tattoo of a wolf baring its fangs, which he got for *Bad Boys*.

In 1988, Madonna and Sean Penn had been through marital mayhem, months of chaos with the world media simmering or roasting them depending on the flavour of the month or the news of the day. Tits and ass sell – Madonna would more than likely make page one of any lively newspaper for the slightest excuse; the dead ones took another dozen years to realise she was alive – and selling millions of newspapers worldwide.

Sean Penn knew she was alive, for every conscious moment of their relationship. But that Saturday morning he was as precise as he would ever be about the two of them. He used the word 'nigger' but carefully qualified it by saying that one had to understand how he was using 'this vulgar expression'. Go on.

'I think the problems come about because I wasn't a good little nigger actor who remained quiet, made films and stayed out of the way of the press.

'Instead, I think I became labelled as the bad little nigger boy who married the white girl, a girl who was as white as they come. She belonged to them, to the public. And if anyone took her I think they thought it should be someone more acceptable like Donald Trump.

'The public is very possessive about rock stars and about her in particular. They don't want to share her love.'

Neither, of course, did he. Madonna and Sean Penn were hormones in a hurry; fantastic passion but then suspicious about their own and everyone else's motives.

But, in the beginning, everyone says it was true love. 'I'd never known Sean happier,' remembers his brother, Chris.

Charlie Sheen told me, 'Sean's always been misunderstood. And probably most about how much he adored Madonna.'

Sheen's brother, Emilio Estevez, voted the same way: 'I thought that was a lifetime partnership. I'd never have written them off.'

Their father Martin Sheen, the wise patriarch and honorary mayor of Malibu and misfits everywhere, said, 'You just wanted it all to be perfect for them for they really were a well-suited couple. They both care and they both wanted to care for each other. I've often thought you can care too much and that spoils it.'

Susan Seidelman, who was part of the Madonna crowd at

the time, said, 'She could have had anyone she wanted. If it was just for the sake of getting married, she could have married someone richer, better looking and more politically correct than Sean. I don't think she needed Sean in an opportunistic way. Movie people were already beating down her door.'

For all the right reasons. She was becoming the hottest property in town. Any town. Anywhere. These were the Madonnamania days, the beginning: 'Like a Virgin', 'Material Girl', 'Crazy for You' and 'The Gambler' from the soundtrack of *Vision Quest* were everywhere. And, suddenly, so was *Desperately Seeking Susan*. Orion Pictures, who had been reluctant to hire Madonna, now wanted to promote 'her' film. It opened in nearly 1,000 cinemas across America. And it received pretty positive feedback from the critics. *Newsweek* magazine said the title star 'has not been typecast and fills the bill with delightful sluttishness'.

Ah, a slut again. But being well paid for it. Madonna saw the humour. The reviews were mostly kind and calling her 'a new star'. The clincher was that the film made money. And Hollywood, even if it had been ignoring Madonna's music, could relate to financial success; that particular bottom line was more important to them than her tantalising, gyrating and wiggling one was to the fans.

Madonna was hot. Hollywood was hot for her. From the Polo Lounge to Morton's, they were talking deals, packages and marketing. Herbert Ross, the veteran director who had made Streisand's *Funny Girl*, wanted her to star in the story of a stripper, Blaze Starr (a project that would eventually go ahead with Paul Newman and newcomer Lolita Davidovich), and Ray Stark, who was still one of the most powerful men in Hollywood, wanted her to be involved in a project about 1920s torch-singer, Libby Holman. There was also talk of her starring for Disney in *Ruthless People* (Bette Midler got the role).

But Freddy DeMann proved why he was what Madonna herself knew she needed. He caught the moment. Madonna was talking deals all over Hollywood. She was hanging out with Penn and the Brat Pack and even by the Hard Rock Café at the Beverly Centre, which was more of a tourist than a trend trap. There were also the clubs like Helena's and its incongruous location diagonally opposite the tough Los Angeles Police Department's (LAPD) Rampart Station where Robert Kennedy's assassin, Sirhan Sirhan, was held after the 1968 killing of JFK's brother.

And she was also working out. Madonna was back living out of a suitcase. Her concert tours took her to comparatively small stadiums. DeMann knew what he had. The fans wanted to see Madonna. As close as they could get. He knew it from the Michael Jackson experience. DeMann grins as he says, 'I wanted fans to be able to see her sweat.'

They saw showers of sweat first in Seattle. At the same time, her Wazoo line of clothing – lace tops, skin-tight leggings and midriff-baring, uplifting underwear – went on sale. Maripol, her friend and jewellery designer, who now has his own New York store, remembered the days: 'All the kids wanted to look like her. They were in the shop all the time. I called them the Little Madonnas.'

And variations of them turned out in hordes for every concert. The wannabes ('We wanna be like Madonna') could not have cared less when old fogey and Rolling Stone Mick Jagger said Madonna's songs were pinpointed by 'a certain dumbness'. Silly, would-be-pensioner, they thought. Madonna had been the hottest thing on Earth for at least three weeks so Mars bars to the Rolling Stones.

It was hard for Madonna, even with all the entourage help and protection, to cope with all this fame and acclaim. Her sister Paula said in a rare interview, 'Everyone needs someone to hold on to.' For Madonna, it was Sean Penn.

They found a retreat in the Hollywood Hills. It was a white building, like a castle in one of those 1950s Hollywood epics when Errol Flynn was always the swashbuckling good guy and George Sanders or Basil Rathbone got skewered in the final moment. For them, it was romantic heaven. Was it haunted? For the practical of us, only by memories. The building had once belonged to legendary actor and boozer, John Barrymore. It was not a good omen.

CHAPTER EIGHT

APOCALYPSE NOW

*'I never shot a firearm at anything I consider
to be a human life form.'*
SEAN PENN, 2000

Madonna's rags-to-riches story was catching on everywhere. Her popularity grew by every play of her videos on MTV and she was on again and again and again. John Sykes was MTV's programming vice-president as the Madonna phenomenon began.

'Madonna is a prime example of an artist who could use MTV to launch a career. We had no negative feedback. What video did was build up the expectations of her tour.'

She was preparing for the 'Like a Virgin' tour by building a workout routine around a daily six-mile jog. Then, as today, she was almost totally vegetarian. Then, she drank Tab, chewed sugarless bubblegum and pigging out for her was cheddar-cheese flavoured popcorn. The 'BOY TOY' bad girl is always willing to be controversial but also wants to be cholesterol free. She was a long way from bourbon-swigging, drug-taking, tragic legends like the dead-before-their-time Janis Joplin, Jimi Hendrix and Jim Morrison. Madonna's stage act was risqué but her energy was pure.

In the weeks before she and Penn became exclusively attached and moved into the former Barrymore home, there was much action in both their lives. She was on display. During her tour, the 'Like a Virgin' number was designed to – and did – bring the house down. She strutted on stage in a silk wedding dress with a 24-foot long train. This particular vestal virgin bride would then crawl between the legs of her musicians. Attention? She got plenty of it. And the fans loved the sub-teen sexual humour. Madonna walked on stage with a stereo boom-box and offered saucy jokes: 'Every lady has a box. My box is special because it makes music – but it has to be turned on.' Ouch! But her timing was spot on.

Youngsters were looking for an outrageous performer, someone they could 'adopt' and could emulate. They could wear the shirts, T-shirts, bracelets and cross-shaped earrings that were on sale at every concert; the marketing men were delighted because they were selling faster than anyone could remember, faster than fan paraphernalia at Michael Jackson or Prince concerts. You could see Madonna in concert, at the neighbourhood cinema, on 24-hour television and on posters in kids' bedrooms in much of the Western world.

Sean Penn was being moody down in America's Deep South where he was filming *At Close Range*. The film was being directed by his friend and eventual best man, James Foley. They got on well and it was Penn who persuaded Orion Pictures to give Foley the director's chair. His mother, Eileen Ryan, was appearing in the film and so was his brother Chris. Christopher Walken was his co-star in the murder mystery based on a real-life father-and-son crime syndicate.

Foley was one of the first to appreciate just how strong the relationship was between Madonna and Penn. Others, mostly family members, soon found out. They were surprised. While Penn got stuck into the grind of making movies, the lady in his life was rivalling the late Diana, Princess of Wales, for newspaper and magazine space. She was supposedly dating several men, including Don Johnson, who was then starring in *Miami Vice*. Dapper Don did not make the cut, although he tried. She was a fan of Billy Idol, but for his music and naughty sense of humour, not his body. There were persistent tales of heavyweight trysts with the late John F Kennedy Jr, which offered gorgeous, irresistible stories for magazines and newspapers about Madonna following through on her Marilyn fantasy with a Kennedy. One vital ingredient to a long-term liaison was always missing – the approval of Jackie Onassis. The rumoured affair with JFK Jr – who would die in a plane crash with his young wife Carolyn Bessette (they married in 1997) – ended, but they remained friends until his death. He had met Madonna several times in the months before his marriage and during his on-off relationship with actress Daryl Hannah.

But when she was madly in love with Sean Penn, the Marilyn/Kennedy-style arrangement remained what it was – a fantasy. Madonna and Sean Penn were together every possible minute. Although exhausted, she would call him every night after her performance and they would talk for half an hour. She wound down. Penn would often be winding himself up, frustrated by his self-imposed chastity. He saw her perform in Miami and San Diego when he could get away from filming. And in Detroit, where he met her father and brothers and sisters. And found out to whom Madonna lost her virginity. Schoolfriend Carol Belanger remembers flipping through her High School Yearbook with Madonna and Penn. They stopped at a picture of Russell

Long – the Cadillac Man. Belanger says she told Penn that Madonna 'broke a lot of hearts'. Penn was to turn around and do just that to the Madonna fans before the year was out. When the Virgin tour arrived in Los Angeles, the Penn family and members of the Brat Pack were there. The long, hot summer was not far off.

James Foley says he was respectful of Madonna's relationship with Penn. Of the pre-marriage days, he says, 'I'd known Sean for a long time and he'd never been happier.' Foley got lucky too. Madonna asked him to direct her new video of 'Live to Tell', which was the closing track of *At Close Range*. He was glad to but says reflectively, 'Nobody knows what a major sweat those videos are.'

Diane Keaton is a close friend of Foley's – as are Cher and Barbra Streisand – and saw an early version of *At Close Range*. They became a constructive critical group and Foley says, 'Madonna was like Diane in that she had opinions and voiced them without hesitation. Diane and Madonna had a lot of similarities and liked and respected each other.'

Sean Penn does not like or respect the press, particularly the suede-shoes variety from the tabloids of Britain and America. Lots of people don't. It is just that he is rather more exuberant about it. In June 1985, the gossip factory was mass producing stories that Madonna was pregnant. There had been hints that she and Penn were going to marry. Well, what other possible reason could there be for marriage? Love? Forget it – she's a BOY TOY and he's a WILD BOY. Some of that thinking was correct.

A writer and photographer from a British newspaper were sent to doorstep a motel on the outskirts of Nashville, Tennessee, and get happy snaps of the 'pregnant' Madonna who was visiting Penn on the *At Close Range* location. The lads got lucky – or unlucky, depending on how you view it.

They had no idea if Madonna would be there. It was part of the old journalistic tradition of 'when in doubt, send'. They had been sent. When Penn saw them, his face went bright red with rage. He hammered and punched the writer, threw a rock at the photographer and then grabbed his camera strap. Madonna was only a few steps away. She pulled a floral baseball cap over her eyes and ran back into the hotel. A very nasty incident, which was not helped by the fact that photographer Laurence Cottrell had remained as cool as possible in the circumstances and kept his finger on the camera button. The photographs of the snarling Penn about to throw a rock went around the world.

The legend of the Poison Penns were building. And so was the talk of marriage. Now it was generally agreed they would marry – but when? And where? The couple were hot. The new Burton and Taylor. They would star in a film entitled *Pipeline*, set in the Alaskan oilfields. They would do the comedy *Blind Date* (Kim Basinger and Bruce Willis finally made that one), and every other producer in Hollywood trying to pitch a package was talking to Madonna and Penn.

On 13 August 1985, Madonna performed solo and with the Thompson Twins at Live Aid in Philadelphia. She was introduced by Bette Midler as 'a woman who pulled herself up by her bra straps and has been known to let them down occasionally'. Madonna had other thoughts as she strutted in Philadelphia. She and Penn were busy planning their marriage. Something old, something new, something borrowed, something blue? Try a more military strategy. Penn was to greet his wedding guests with, 'Welcome to the remaking of *Apocalypse Now*.' He wasn't far off.

Madonna, who had boosted her career by being able to manipulate the public, was not such an artist when it came to privacy. She and Penn tried. The invitation, designed by Penn's brother Michael, read,

Please Come To Sean and Madonna's Birthday Party on the Sixteenth of August Nineteen Eighty-Five. The Celebration Will Commence at Six O'Clock p.m. Please Be Prompt or You Will Miss Their Wedding Ceremony. The Need for Privacy and a Desire to Keep You Hanging Prevents the Los Angeles Location from Being Announced Until One Day Prior.

RSVP by August 3 to: Clyde Is Hungry Productions, 6521 Leland Way, Hollywood, CA 90028, (213) 469–6208. Please include a phone number where you can be reached.

Nuptials, Hollywood style. Don't call us – we'll call you. For all those guests hanging on for the wedding location, there was time to buy a wedding present. Madonna had gone the traditional route and registered with a store a list of gifts she would like. The Michigan girl, who had begun her career living out of rubbish bins in New York, was registered at Tiffany's and had selected two china patterns: Monet's Giverny, which then sold for $260 a place setting, and Coeur de Fleur from Tiffany's private stock, which in 1985 was $660 a setting.

It was just an indication of just how far and fast Madonna had travelled. In shopping malls across America, there were regular weekend Madonna lookalike contests. She had been photographed in Hawaii for a *Madonna 1986* calendar and Barbra Streisand filmed her video, 'Emotions', clutching a handful of photographs of Madonna.

Hollywood was still at her door and the budget this time was $15 million for *Street Smart*, in which she was to appear with both Sting and Prince's protégé, Vanity, the three to star as a one-name rock trinity, in something that sounded very similar to *West Side Story*.

She was out jogging in Central Park in New York – not that healthy an activity given the high mugging rate – when she realised she could never again go anywhere public without a bodyguard. Concentrating on her running, she at first did not realise that she had been recognised. When she did look over her shoulder, she was being pursued by about 15 fans. She did not know they were just chasing autographs and panicked. She hurdled a fence and fell. She only scraped a knee, but she had lost control for a moment and swore that would never happen again.

Yet she had little control over the imminent remake, as Penn had put it, of *Apocalypse Now* on a bluff in Malibu. Penn's 25th birthday was on 16 August and Madonna was 26 the next day. It was quite a party for them both. Penn, although facing assault charges and a civil lawsuit for his bad-boy behaviour in Tennessee, seemed to have mellowed. He and Madonna had been playing house, renting the former Barrymore home for $1,300 a month. They could see the 'HOLLYWOOD' sign from the bedroom window. She recalls when he proposed, 'I was jumping up and down on my bed performing one of my morning rituals and all of a sudden Sean gets this look in his eye and all of a sudden I knew what he was thinking. I said, "Whatever you are thinking, I'll say yes to." That was his chance, so he popped it.'

She says they celebrated by going out to a 7-Eleven convenience store and buying a bag of gob-stopper sweets known in America as 'jawbreakers'.

Not a traditional proposal or celebration, but wedding plans moved along in an orderly fashion from then on. There was her wedding shower, which was hosted by Nancy Huang, the girlfriend of Nile Rodgers. She had invited Madonna's friends to her Upper East Side apartment in Manhattan. Mariel Hemmingway and Alannah Currie from the Thompson Twins were there – and six male friends of Madonna's who dressed in drag by way of celebration. The gifts were lingerie, a push-button, sequinned phone and an assortment of jewellery. Madonna had bought herself, for $44,000, a midnight-blue Mercedes. The celebrations continued a couple of days later in Hollywood with a 'bachelorette' party at the Tropicana. It is a tacky mud-wrestling club in a run-down area. Madonna went in a disguise of dark glasses, no make-up and her hair pulled back from her face, and looked just like Madonna in dark glasses with no make-up; she cheered as big-busted lady wrestlers flailed about in the mud.

Sean Penn was also getting ready for marriage, with a stag party. Madonna had had the lady mud wrestler, but her husband-to-be was entertained by Kitten, who bounces off the measuring tape at 42–24–36. The party was in a private room above the Roxy nightclub on Hollywood's Sunset Strip. Penn's brother Chris, Tom Cruise, Robert Duvall, David Keith, Harry Dean Stanton and Cameron Crowe (who wrote *Fast Times at Ridgemont High*, and directed *Jerry Maguire* and the 2001 critical success *Almost Famous*) were among the guests. The drinks were free. Used to revelation, Kitten remembered, 'They were all pretty buzzed. Sean was feeling no pain. But he didn't fall on his face or anything. When he talked, he made sense. He's a very nice guy. He reminded me of a little boy, like he was eight years old and had got so many cookies he didn't know what to do with them.'

Kitten Natividad did her strip routine with Penn slapping his knee in delight. Harry Dean Stanton arrived late and Kitten said, 'Sean picked up my blouse and said, "See what you missed." Then he shoved his face right into me. I didn't mind. Sometimes I do, but it was Sean's night and he could have done whatever he wanted. That was about as wild as it got.'

No one really knows who leaked the location of the nuptials. But by the morning of the wedding, everyone knew it was in Malibu. By the afternoon, the location had been pinpointed. Television stations and newspapers rented helicopters and, indeed, they suddenly appeared out of the sky like that famous scene in *Apocalypse Now*. I remember driving up the Pacific Coast Highway from Santa Monica to Malibu to report the wedding for a British newspaper. It was mid-Friday afternoon and the weekend traffic heading north to Santa Barbara, Carmel and other retreats were already building up. The all-news radio was babbling the headlines and at the top of the news was The Wedding. One commentator suggested it was the oddest coupling since Marilyn Monroe was turned on by the intellect of Arthur Miller, the couple who became known as The Hourglass and the Egghead. With a blazing red sun dipping down into the Pacific, it seemed more beauty and the beast that day.

The world wanted sensation. They got media mania. And star paranoia. Who was out of order? The choppers buzzed the wedding of entertainment's most visible couple, the reigning king and queen of what seemed to be daily headlines. Crowds crushed around the estate. Madonna and Penn could have slipped off to Las Vegas and avoided such fuss. They didn't. They did it traditionally, with a Grand Prix of twists, on one of the most material pieces of real estate on Earth. Malibu is where you flaunt rather than hide it. This is where you can lie on the sand and stare at the stars and vice versa. She forgot her outlaw black lace and wore an antique-style white gown, a low-cut number designed by Marlene Stewart, who costumed Madonna for her Virgin tour. It was, recalls Ms Stewart, designed as 'a fairytale kind of thing with sort of a baroque feeling. We wanted a 1950s feeling, something Grace Kelly might have worn.'

Well, we are talking rock royalty. The Queen of Pop added one of the twists to the traditional by giving the finger to a buzzing helicopter as her mother-in-law, Eileen Ryan, dabbed wedding-day tears from her eyes. The groom also stuck his head up the bride's dress. A new tradition? Maybe a Malibu one.

To set off her Cinderella gown, Madonna wore her hair in a French twist with a black bowler draped in cream-coloured tulle on top of it. What appeared like a beauty contestant's sash was draped across the dress, a silver and pink metallic neck covered in encrusted jewels. She walked down the white-ribboned aisle set out at the $8 million estate in shoes decorated in pearls and gold embroidery. Silvio Ciccone was at her side as the helicopters buzzed around like annoying flies in the clear blue sky above the ten-minute ceremony in which the couple exchanged plain gold bands.

The groom wore a dark, double-breasted, $695, off-the-rack Gianni Versace linen suit. The bride and groom are Roman Catholics and the Malibu clifftop where they took their vows had been blessed by a priest. White ribbons had fluttered on the bluffs all day like an open invitation to the helicopters that chattered all over them. White seats and benches, in sectioned, serried ranks and enough to accommodate 200 guests, had been laid out 2 hours before the ceremony at the lavish home of film producer Kurt Unger. Unger, a neighbour of America's major talk-show host, Johnny Carson, is a close friend of Penn's parents. The massive catering tent was toothpaste-white like the bunting and ribbons covering the tennis courts. White lily pads floated in the swimming pool. But there was anger among the guests over the helicopters, which delayed the ceremony. Producer James Day who was there as a guest commented, 'Guests were hoping Sylvester Stallone would turn up and do a Rambo on the "copters".' He did not. Many others did. And they went through what seemed like presidential security.

Tom Cruise, David Keith, Andy Warhol, Christopher Walken, Martin Sheen, Diane Keaton and Carrie Fisher were all formally dressed. Cher set off her not-so-traditional outfit with a spiky, all-purpose hair-do. 'I thought this was a secret,' complained actress Rosanne Arquette as she, along with other famous faces, submitted to being frisked by security men in smart slacks and blue jackets, which hid their two-way radios. Penn had also arranged for guards with infra-red binoculars to 'frisk' the perimeters of Unger's estate. An Italian photographer wearing camouflage gear and a blackened face, for all the world looking like an SAS man, had been caught and ejected from his hunter's hide in the shrubbery just before the 6.30pm ceremony.

Judge John Merrick, who conducted the bizarre event, recalls that, despite the choppers, he thought it was 'dignified'. 'I was shouting but she was answering as loud as she could. I think she enjoyed it all.'

Best man, James Foley, smiled through two weeks' growth of beard for most of the ceremony, and Madonna's sister Paula, who was her matron of honour, helped pacify the bride and groom as the choppers continued to hover overhead. They told them to forget about the intrusion and concern themselves with their own lives – and it was with a brave face that Madonna turned to her father before taking her vows and said, 'Bye, Dad.' The music was 'Moments of Love', but as the melody was drowned out by helicopters, Penn's face got redder and redder. Sixteen years later, Penn is still hesitant to talk about whether he found a rifle and took pot shots at the big, thundering birds in the sky. He says he doesn't recall shooting at press helicopters on his wedding day to Madonna. 'I don't remember on the grounds that it could incriminate me. Let's put it this way – I never shot a firearm at anything I considered to be a human life form.'

'The ceremony was lovely. Madonna was lovely, but I couldn't hear a thing – nobody could,' recalls *Deer Hunter* Oscar winner, Christopher Walken. As the official ceremony ended, the *Chariots of Fire* theme started up. Penn lifted the veil pinned to Madonna's black bowler hat and gave her a lingering kiss. Then, hand in hand, they clambered up to the balcony and, grinning, began waving to their guests. Madonna leaned backwards towards the crowd before hurling her bouquet of white roses into the sky. It was aimed towards a group of her single girlfriends. 'Catch it, catch it,' she yelled at them. The BAD BOY and the BOY TOY were wed as Penn toasted 'the most beautiful girl in the world'.

Service was quick for the 200 guests after the ceremony. Malcolm McClaren's *Madame Butterfly* blasted from loudspeakers as waiters scattered around pouring $100 bottles of Cristal champagne. A feast was served by the chefs from Spago: a five-tier hazelnut cake with sugar flowers, lobster ravioli, rack of lamb, swordfish, and baked potatoes stuffed with sour cream and caviar. Wines included California's Acacia Pinot Noir. There were three fully stocked, 8ft-long bars.

Cher remembers a wonderful moment. When it came to cutting the cake, Madonna turned to her, saying, 'Hey, you've done this before. Do you just cut one piece or do you have to slice up the whole thing?'

Outside, the press were still gathered. One man armed with a two-way radio was trying to talk to his airborne colleague:'Mad dog to mad dog one ... do you copy?' Inside the guests were gasping at the wedding presents, which had a room of their own. There was a 1912 antique silver tea service from British producer John Daly, who was responsible for *The Falcon and the Snowman*. An antique jukebox with two dozen Motown numbers from Michael Ostin, an executive of Warner Brothers Records. And there were several sets of Tiffany china. Disc jockey Terence Toy had got the dancing going with some Big Band Swing numbers, but by 8.00pm was beginning to liven things up. He blasted out Motown's dance numbers and then Madonna's own 'Into the Groove'.

And that was exactly what the couple planned to do on their four-day honeymoon at the Highland Inn in Carmel, the seaside community quietly settled between Los Angeles and San Francisco, and known around the world because of the two-year tenure of Mayor Clint Eastwood. For $225 a night, the Highland Inn offered peace, quiet and privacy, which Penn and Madonna needed. One room-service waiter told me of the day he delivered to their suite: 'I couldn't believe my eyes. They were both sitting in the bath together – and they had their clothes on. And the bath was full of water. They were not embarrassed about it, but I was.'

The couple were in room 429 and registered as M Ochs. It was an in-joke on the play of 'Madonna Ochs'. The late Phil Ochs was a 1960s protest folk-singer who was overshadowed by Bob Dylan. He became a disillusioned, forgotten and extremely difficult character. 'Phil was an asshole long before it became fashionable,' said Penn, who liked the idea. He had driven them north in his black Mercedes. Madonna was wearing a black sweatsuit.

'She wore the same sweatsuit for three days,' recalled a maid, who revealed, 'They brought their own beer cans with them. They gave me one and we all held hands while we had a drink.'

Madonna appeared to survive on room-service strawberries and cream, and supplies of champagne, orange juice and popcorn from the hotel's food shop. One night, they went out to dinner at the Hog's Breath Inn, which was then owned by Clint Eastwood. It was a favourite eating place for Carmel locals, but also popular with tourists. By going there – and why did they? – any belief that their whereabouts could be secret was gone. By morning, the fans, the press and the paparazzi were heading for Carmel. The honeymoon was over.

Reality and the business of finding a family home took its place. They had been looking for a long time. Penn favoured something in Malibu with a good number of acres. One of his Pack remembers asking him if he planned to fence off any property he might get and was told by an unsmiling Penn, 'A fence, nothing. We're going to have gun towers.'

Madonna had not seen any gun towers in Beverly Hills

or Bel Air where she had been looking. Her search almost led to an embarrassing run-in with another material girl, Nancy Reagan. Playwright Neil Simon had put his lavish Bel Air home up for sale. Former First Lady Nancy was interested but dithering. She looked around twice. Then she brought friends over. Then she arrived at separate times with three different sets of decorators. The Simon asking price was $3.5 million. All of this was unknown to Madonna who was being shown property by a Beverly Hills real-estate agent. She fell for Simon's property instantly and offered a bid closer to the asking price. Simon was stuck. He pleaded a change of circumstances and took the house off the market.

Madonna and Penn eventually headed for a $3.5 million estate, shielded by the mountains that used to be roamed by the Chumash Indians. They created more barriers with a high, electrified wall fence. Penn wanted more security. Steel spikes were ordered and placed along the top of the walls. It was a sort of martial Fort Knox. Despite that, it was the scene of some of Madonna's happiest moments.

But for the moment, they were lovers, scouting shops in Los Angeles and New York for furniture, for bric-à-brac for their home. By October, there were already rumours that the marriage was in a desperate way. Years later, Penn says they never had a chance. And that he was drunk for most of their marriage.

CHAPTER NINE

JAILHOUSE ROCKS

*'I have my insecure moments and that puts a lot of
strain on people. You take things out on the person you
love and that causes fights, alienation, grief, shrink
sessions and a lot of ca-ca.'*

MADONNA, 1987

It was only a few weeks after the wedding on 16 August
1985 that Madonna sought psychiatric help. Her friends
also urged her to persuade Penn to seek professional help.
When Penn had turned extraordinarily violent, into a wild-
eyed madman during his attack on the two British
journalists in Nashville, she had been speechless.
'Throughout the whole thing she never said a word to
either of us,' recalls Laurence Cottrell, the photographer at
the scene, adding, 'She just stood there and watched us as he
did this thing with the rock.'

Now it seemed like another day, another brawl. Seven
weeks after the wedding, Penn was spitting and swearing at
photographers outside Wolfgang Puck's West Side celebrity
hangout Chinois in Santa Monica. Madonna was covered
up with a coat and laughing as she asked, 'Where are we? I
can't see where I'm going.' Penn did not find any of it
remotely amusing.

A Certain Sacrifice with a brunette Madonna went on sale

in video stores in October 1985, just as Madonna and Penn were driving, running or hiding from photographers in Los Angeles and Manhattan. Penn went to Nashville to face his assault charges. He was fined $100 and given a 90-day suspended sentence.

Madonna and matrimony seemed to be bringing out all the acrimony in Penn. Around the celebrity crowd hangouts in New York and Los Angeles, they were known as 'S & M'. They were also one of the best-known couples in the world. Madonna had convinced herself that acting was what she wanted more than anything. But she was still deeply in love with Penn and determined, as a good Catholic girl should be, to keep the marriage intact. She also had a great deal of respect for Penn as an actor, and as a mentor.

This was the start of another obsession for her – to win the title role in *Evita*. She had met quietly with producer Robert Stigwood and Penn was unaware how keen she was on the role. With him, she was talking about a joint project. But then Madonna wanted movie stardom on the Marilyn Monroe scale. She saw *Evita* as the vehicle to provide that.

Seymour Stein, who had launched her career, was in the know: 'I knew from the moment she walked into my room that she would be a star. She had the kind of self-assuredness that convinced me she was a very determined lady. I don't know about ruthless. When men are ambitious they're called ruthless. There's no ego problem there. She was in a hurry. She was very, very serious about what she did. She knew what she wanted. Her talent had been obscured because of the fuss about everything else. But nobody tells her what to do.'

It also seemed that way to Hollywood producer Julia Phillips, who had been involved in major box-office successes like *The Sting* and *Close Encounters of the Third Kind*. When Phillips had a meeting with Freddy DeMann at Morton's restaurant in Hollywood, she was won over by him. 'He was managing Madonna, the hottest female to come along since Barbra Streisand.' In her often embarrassingly honest, brassy, sensationally bitchy book *You'll Never Eat Lunch In This Town Again*, which chops up many Hollywood notables, she also wrote about 'taking a meeting' with Madonna and Sean Penn, whom she calls the Prince and Princess. She says her martini arrived at the same time as the couple:

'I am torn for a moment between saying hello, changing seats, and taking a long sip. I do all three without embarrassing myself. She is dyed platinum and dressed from head to toe in black leather. He is in jeans and leather jacket – what a surprise. He is a dim bulb in her supernova aura. She has the same amazing pale perfect skin that Barbra Streisand has. I have always imagined Marilyn Monroe's skin was like that too. It is impossible not to think of Marilyn Monroe when you see Madonna, even if you know that that's because she has designed herself so that you will think that way.'

Phillips asked if they wanted drinks. Madonna ordered a Perrier water. Penn looked at Phillips' martini and started to order a beer. Madonna squeezed his knee and he changed his mind. The film discussions really did not go anywhere concrete. But Phillips and DeMann continued to talk, to meet. She was pushing a female version of *Carnal Knowledge*, the 1971 film that starred Jack Nicholson as a sexual adventurer. In Phillips' working of the film, Madonna would play the sexual experimenter. Madonna was taken by the thought of the memorable Nicholson role and, in turn, gave DeMann permission to pursue the idea with Warner Brothers. But there were complications because of a similar project.

Still, every studio in town wanted Madonna in 'something' – in anything. And they were miffed when Handmade Films – in Hollywood terms an upstart company – run by former Beatle George Harrison, won her services. Handmade had produced *The Life of Brian* and *A Private Function*, and now had Madonna starring in the $15 million *Shanghai Surprise*. The hook had been her co-star, Sean Penn, who would play a down-at-heel adventurer to Madonna's missionary in 1930s China. They were getting $1 million each, as well as some surprising perks. The couple would have total script approval, which was a nerve considering Madonna's lack of film experience. And they would have a double bed with Japanese screens in their dressing room. Their involvement in publicity for the film could be 'requested', not 'demanded'. Publicity? They got more than they ever imagined.

Macao has been a magical movie location since the RKO Studio days when Robert Mitchum wooed Jane Russell and chased William Bendix. A city of intrigue, gambling and mystery, the Portuguese settled here in 1557. Relations between them and their one billion neighbours in China have always been reasonable – a reasonable people who were about to encounter a rather unreasonable young man.

Penn was becoming more and more insecure by the day. His wife was the entertainment world's hottest new talent and he was increasingly being regarded as difficult and excess baggage. Was he worth the trouble? The *Shanghai Surprise* film company set themselves up in the Oriental Hotel, a tower block of East meets West accommodation with

A younger Madonna, desperately seeking fame and fortune.

An early look.

One of Madonna's earlier, and less acclaimed, film roles was in *Shaghai Surprise*.
Here, she is pictured with the film's producer, former Beatle, George Harrison.

Madonna's live shows have always been provocative and daring. Here, she performs a raunchy version of *Like A Virgin* (left) and (right) performs *Holiday* as an encore at Wembley.

With ex-husband, Sean Penn. Their stormy relationship was constantly scrutinised in the press.

Above: Madonna performs on The Girlie Show Tour.

Below: Madonna's stage costumes (or lack of them!) always made headlines.

A sombre-looking Madonna at the MTV Music Awards. She wore black in the wake of the death of Princess Diana.

wonderful service. The couple were assigned two bodyguards trained in martial arts. Security men would seal off the swimming pool when Madonna wanted a dip. They put on disguises to go out to restaurants. It was Leonel Borrahlho's job to see through the disguises.

He was 61 and the correspondent on the island for the *Hong Kong Standard* when the Penns arrived in Macao. Mr Borrahlho, who soon after retired to live in Macao, was a member of the *Leal Senada* – the Loyal Senate – and a man of propriety and dedication. He was asked to get photographs of the famous Hollywood couple. While others doorstepped the lobby of the Oriental Hotel, the enterprising Mr Borrahlho found out which floor the Penns were staying on. He then found himself a hiding place on the 18th floor near their suite. Late one afternoon he got lucky – and unlucky – at the same time. He was in position as Madonna, Penn and their bodyguards emerged from the elevator. From behind the door of a 'dumb waiter' he and his camera popped. Penn panicked. 'Who let you in? What are you doing here? Can't you see my wife's trembling?'

Mr Borrahlho says he saw Penn's fist coming towards him but it was stopped short by one of the bodyguards. The noise, the scuffling, left everyone seeing events differently. A bodyguard tried to grab the camera that was hung around the photographer's neck. Mr Borrahlho remembers karate chops and kicks as his camera strap held and he was injured in the tug-of-war.

'I was only doing my job. I didn't expect this kind of "ugly American" behaviour,' says Mr Borrahlho. Seemingly, Penn's reputation for never meeting a photographer without delivering a punch had not reached that far East. Now it had arrived with such force that Penn was to be called uglier things over the next few days as all manner of legal wrangling went on. Leonel Borrahlho used his platform at the *Hong Kong Standard* and his political clout in Macao to make things as difficult as possible for the film-makers, and particularly Penn. Madonna was angry and frustrated by the Penn-inflicted circumstances. She had liked the script for the film, which was based on Tony Kendrick's novel, *Faraday's Flowers*, and saw it as a chance to create something like *The African Queen*, with her and Penn as the new Bogart and Hepburn. She enjoyed the feel of the era and the dressing up as Gloria in the period clothes. She turned herself into a Jean Harlow-style platinum blonde as Gloria, a woman who runs away from the Depression in America to seek fulfilment in the Orient. Madonna wanted to be fulfilled as an actress. She wanted to prove she could act. Gloria, she felt, was a woman so different from her that she would have to give an Oscar-worthy performance to pull the role off. Gloria, unlike her, she thought, was not in touch with her emotions. But both she and her character had to contend with Penn.

As did George Harrison and his Handmade Films. Chris Nixon was the publicity man on the film. It was a thankless task. But Nixon knew his job and how to turn the nasty fracas and publicity around; give the reporters and photographers something to write about and point their cameras at. Penn thought the suggestion preposterous. The Prince and Princess were not posing. Or talking. Nixon who, in hindsight, was proved correct, suggested that the film needed all the help it could get. He was sacked. His comment? 'Penn is a very aggressive, arrogant little shit.'

But Madonna was standing by her man, while at the same time reading everything she could about *Evita*, which was about the only distraction she enjoyed. She was in the

Oriental Hotel sauna when a girl reporter cornered her and asked if she was enjoying herself in the Orient. 'What? Being harassed? No. We didn't think we'd have any problems here.' She was also asked about the Borrahlho incident. 'That guy acted like a real jerk.' But, despite the bravado, Madonna was worried. This was not how it was supposed to be. It certainly was not looking like *The African Queen*.

George Harrison flew to Hong Kong to referee an increasingly difficult situation. Madonna saw it as a test. There were big black rats under her trailer. The two-legged kind were on the streets and Chinese gangsters began making extortion demands. Extra security men were brought in because of a death threat made against Madonna, according to a source who worked on the film. Madonna was depressed. This was only her second film. The go-for-it-I-can-do-it young girl who had conquered New York was feeling totally insecure and inadequate in a foreign land.

Penn, as Mr Wade, a drifter on the loose in the Orient, seemed to be staying in character around the clock. Director Jim Gorrard, then 50, had earned his spurs on television mini-series and had been strongly recommended to Penn by Martin Sheen. But Madonna had seen her young husband challenge Gorrard's decisions and that ruled him out as a shoulder to cry on. And she couldn't rely on Harrison either, the quiet Beatle, whom Madonna regarded as a rather sweet character. There was no father figure for her anywhere in the Orient.

Under all this emotional stress, she clung on to Penn. It was them against the world and she had never before now, and would never again, get on so well with her husband. 'I think Sean and I set ourselves up for a challenge being married and working together. A lot of people were saying that's a sure way to end a relationship, you'll be divorcing afterwards. It was my second movie and I had all the feelings of insecurity and being inadequate – I'll be a terrible actress, he won't love me any more, all that stuff. But I'd seen Sean work with other people and he is a very giving actor. He would never make you feel you weren't adding up in a scene. That is his main thing when he's making a movie – making it work for whoever is in the scene with him. Strangely enough, we never got along better. We took turns being strong and not letting it affect us. There was a time when I was so overtaken by it that I was crying and he said, "Don't worry, baby, we'll make it work – we'll make it work despite all the problems." Then, in a couple of weeks, he'd be miserable and he couldn't stand it and I'd be holding him and saying, "We'll get through this, you're really good in it and that's all that matters." '

With hindsight, Madonna's remarks at the time – just before the movie's release – could be, at best, charitable, rose tinted. Whatever happened, she retained her self-belief.

For her, Harrison was an old-timer, someone from the past. She had displayed such youthful arrogance before. Just before leaving New York to begin filming *Shanghai Surprise* she and Penn had been invited by Yoko Ono to a private dinner party in honour of Bob Dylan. Wandering through Ono's Dakota Building apartment, she went into the kitchen where Dylan and David Bowie were talking. When she returned to the living area, where there was a crowd chatting over drinks and nibbles, she could not stop herself blurting out, 'Thank God there's somebody here to talk to – there are only old folks in the kitchen.' She was about to discover how hot the 'kitchen' can get as she flew off to England to continue filming.

At Heathrow Airport, the press waited for her arrival. Penn was to join her later at Shepperton Studios in Middlesex and on location at a former sanatorium near Virginia Water in Surrey. The madness began long before Madonna got anywhere near the lunatic asylum. Libby Krall, 5ft 10in tall and a 'minder' to Tina Turner, Tatum O'Neal, Goldie Hawn and Liza Minelli, and the first female security officer at the Xenon nightclub in London's Piccadilly, had been asked to take on Madonna's protection on the basis that she could guard her even in the toilet.

'I said thanks, but no thanks,' said Libby understandably. 'I just didn't want the hassle.'

But there were enough enthusiastic male bodyguards around Heathrow. They had been told to get Madonna out of the airport quickly. No pictures. No press. And the cloak-and-dagger appraoch was, of course, the only way to ensure a rumpus. Madonna's Mercedes sent one photographer flying. MAIMED BY MADONNA, shouted a headline.

The war of the press against the Poison Penns began and enjoyed a good run at the beginning of March 1986 because it was all quiet on the other Western fronts. Bodyguards with dogs patrolled the perimeter of the sanatorium. And no one seemed to know where the film was going. Because of the problems in Macao and Hong Kong, several action sequences had not been filmed. Madonna and Penn thought they were making a love story. The producers were looking for a *Raiders of the Lost Ark*. Both were to be terribly disappointed.

Madonna told Harrison that she felt she was working through the Third World War. He called a press conference at the Kensington Roof Gardens. For him, the scenes were a reminder of being mobbed in his Beatle days: 'In the 1960s, all people could do was knock the Beatles, so I've been through it myself.' But Harrison admits he was astonished at the pandemonium Madonna's press conference started. He feared for their safety. Police were called to escort Madonna away. There had been one notable quote from her: 'I have nothing to apologise for.' At that time, she had not seen *Shanghai Surprise*. And not many people ever did.

Penn hated the film and told his friends never to see it. 'I got myself into a situation with a bunch of cowards. We made a cowardly movie together. I was pissed off and preoccupied with other things that it's the one time I took a movie entirely for the pay cheque. And also there were people who wanted me to do it. Madonna wanted me to do it. Yeah. I just said, "I don't give a fuck." I just stayed drunk the whole fucking time.'

Madonna regarded it as a miserable experience but bounced back as she always does. She had no regrets. She had learned from it. And mostly what she had learned was to take and keep control – of the work in progress, and of the press. What had begun as a game of titillating and teasing the media was now a serious part of the business. It knocked out her plan to co-star in *Blind Date*. She had been told she would have approval of her leading man. Bruce Willis, who was hot from *Moonlighting*, had already been cast. That took control away from Madonna – she was out of the project. She threw herself into making her third album, *True Blue*. She dedicated it to Penn, whom she called 'the coolest guy in the universe'.

The inside word was that Madonna was on the way out. She had had her run as a slut rock queen, as the Boy Toy, or the Pied Piper of porn as some would have it. Then the critics began hearing *True Blue*. Almost all the reviews talked of the control and character in her singing. She co-produced the album with Steve Bray and friend and record producer Patrick Leonard, and with them wrote the songs. She also made a few lyrical changes to a song written by songwriter Brian Elliot called 'Papa Don't Preach'.

The first single from *True Blue* was 'Live to Tell' from Penn's and James Foley's film *At Close Range*, a film for which, ironically, Penn received rave reviews. 'Live to Tell' would be a worldwide number-one hit and make much more impact than the movie. It was then that Madonna easily declined the invitation of Don Johnson, then the hottest thing on TV, to sing on his new album and, instead, 'Papa Don't Preach' was released to record chart success and an almighty controversy.

Robert Hilburn, then pop-music critic of the *Los Angeles Times* and one of the most highly regarded in America, had watched the Madonna backlash build up in the music world. He says *True Blue* proved that those betting against Madonna's longevity were going to lose.

'All along she had shown hints of ambition and sharp showbusiness instincts that suggested she was a survivor. Some people will never take Madonna seriously, just as many never took Marilyn Monroe seriously. Novelty images – especially that of the sex symbol – are hard to erase. But talent far outshines novelty. Like David Bowie, she visualises music.'

And 'Papa Don't Preach' could have been created for MTV. The song tells the story of an unwed girl who decides to keep her baby but wants her father's approval for doing so. 'Papa don't preach, I'm in trouble deep, Papa don't preach, I've been losing sleep, but I made up my mind, I'm keeping my baby. I'm gonna keep my baby, mmm...'

Madonna delivered the song in a passionate, immediate

near-sob. It started trouble. Alfred Moran of America's *Planned Parenthood* wrote, 'The message is that getting pregnant is cool and having a baby is the right thing and good thing and don't listen to your parents, school, anybody who tells you otherwise – don't preach to me, Daddy. The reality is, what Madonna was suggesting to teenagers was a path to permanent poverty. Everybody I've talked to believes she has had more impact on young teenagers than any other single entertainer since the Beatles.'

The pro-lifers backed Madonna. First Parents Resources Center founder Tipper Gore (who almost, *almost* became America's First Lady in 2001) endorsed the song as it told of a woman deciding against an abortion. Feminist lawyer, Gloria Allred, and the National Organisation of Women demanded that Madonna speak out supporting their pro-abortion view. Madonna tried to steer away from such an emotive issue. She thought the song was about a celebration of life. Her video, with the fine actor Danny Aiello as her father, featured Madonna as a shivering waif waiting for her father's answer. Waiting for Daddy's approval. Aiello called her a 'true superstar' and recalled being so impressed by her that he told her, 'Madonna, I look into your eyes and I can see your heart.' He says she told him, 'I'm not that soft.'

The song could have been written for her. It wasn't. Brian Elliot was responsible for this landmark in Madonna's career. Elliot was then a bearded, jolly, 40-year-old, with a studio office close to North Hollywood High School.

'My studio window was the biggest mirror in North Hollywood – girls stopped to look at their reflection, fix their hair, talk things over. Their gossip was unbelievable. I developed an empathy for the things they got themselves into. The girl in the song is a composite. It's a reflection of things overheard. I wrote it for another singer, but someone at Warner Brothers heard it and thought it would be perfect for Madonna. If someone else had sung it, then it would have had an entirely different resonance. But Madonna is larger than life. I didn't think of the social consequences. I knew it was freighted with all kinds of reality. But basically I wanted to write a good piece of drama, something that would fit into *West Side Story*. Picture that song sung by someone waif-like and it becomes something entirely different. It's more of a plea for compassion from the father, not a "Hey, I'm going to keep my baby whether you like it or not." I thought it was very strange casting, matching the song with Madonna, but it worked.'

Ironically, in the months leading up to the 'Papa Don't Preach' debate, the gossip mill was insisting that Madonna was pregnant. But then there was the incident that started the real decline of Madonna's marriage. It happened in Helena's nightclub where Penn, like Jack Nicholson and Anjelica Huston, had become a 'regular'. So was musician and songwriter David Wolinski, who was sitting with a group of record executives a little after midnight. 'Hawk' Wolinski, who had worked with Madonna and played drums for Chaka Khan, was chatting away. Celebrity couple Farrah Fawcett and Ryan O'Neal were at the bar. So was Drew Barrymore, then still known for *ET*, and Harry Dean Stanton, Robert Duvall and singer Glen Fry. They all saw Wolinski go down after a sucker punch.

Penn and Madonna were leaving the club when Wolinski, who was sitting with a party of mutual friends, saw her.

The never-before-seen official police report on the case gives the most dramatic account of the inexplicable madness of the moment. And the worrying violence. File

86–0217877 from the Rampart Police Station dated 12 April 1986, and timed 00.30 hours, reads,

Victim stated at the above date and time victim was seated at a table when the singer and friend Madonna walked by. Victim stated to Madonna, 'Good night'. The suspect, Madonna's husband, stated, 'Why did you try and kiss my wife?' Suspect then appeared to go mad and with his right fist struck victim on the left side of the face. The victim fell off chair and was on the ground. Suspect picked up a chair and started hitting victim with the chair and kicking victim while on the ground. Suspect then picked up a podium and was about to throw it on victim, however, was stopped by unknown citizens. Suspect then departed the location along with wife Madonna.

The next line reads, 'Injuries: Victim has bruises and swelling on left side of face. Victim further has large bruises on legs and lower body. Victim will seek meeting with his own doctor.' A follow-up report reads,

Investigating officer spoke to the victim who stated that he was attending a private party at a club known as Helena's. The suspect's wife came to the victim's table and spoke to several members of his party as well as the victim. The victim was then approached from the rear by the suspect who accused the victim of bothering his wife and struck the victim several times with his closed fist. The victim fell to the floor and in a semi-conscious condition. He was then kicked several times by the suspect. The suspect walked over to the entry section of the club and picked up a small podium. He then ran towards the victim and attempted to strike him in the head. The suspect was stopped by several patrons. He was then forcibly removed from the premises. Contacted Michael Ostin who was present during the fight. Mr Ostin stated that he saw the suspect kick and hit the victim. Mr Ostin further indicated that the victim did not fight back as he appeared dazed from the first blow.

The report reveals more than details about the incident. It shows the attitude of those around Madonna and Penn. The Michael Ostin in the police report was none other than the executive of Warner Brothers Records' creative department and the very man who had lined up Madonna with Brian Elliot's 'Papa Don't Preach'. But rather than protect Penn by saying little, he told the investigating officers that not only did Wolinski not start the brawl, but that he was also knocked out of any proper contest by Penn's first blow.

That night, Madonna had seen a colleague and friend hurt by Penn for no reason and another colleague indicate the blame without any hesitation. She talked to her psychiatrist about it all the next day. In the meantime, other witnesses said Wolinski did not start the fight. The matter-of-fact police notebook report of the incident gives the immediacy of the incident. It does not reflect the cold fury all those at Helena's that night saw in Penn.

Madonna always knew just how far it could have gone that night and suffered nightmares because of it. Some of her closest friends found Penn spoiled and immature. And they were scared by his temper tantrums – one of which she had just seen in full, bloody close-up.

'She seemed to be having a great time at Helena's. She was really bubbly and smiling a lot,' says one of the Warner Brothers' party. Madonna still records for the company so they are guarded, but he added, 'When Penn pulled that ambush punch, her mood changed just like that.' Ryan O'Neal rushed over from the bar and tried to help Wolinski. 'The marriage had been undergoing stress all the time,' said an actor friend of Madonna's who called the Wolinski incident 'the first real traumatic episode for her'. He explained, 'Wolinski was someone she knew and it really shook her up.'

Despite being disturbed and shaken, Madonna contacted Wolinski and, after apologising for the attack, asked him not to press charges. Wolinski said that an apology from Penn would be more in order. There was talk of an out-of-court settlement but, in the event, the Los Angeles City Attorney went ahead and Penn was prosecuted. Behind the scenes in the City Attorney's Office, the mood was that Penn, be he Mr Madonna or not, needed to be brought into line. Later, he would be fined $1,700 and put on a year's probation, which was not exactly the Alcatraz treatment that the prosecutors had been pressing for. However, Madonna was relieved. Penn had not been showing great restraint before his court hearing. They had bought an $850,000 Manhattan apartment on Central Park West earlier that year, which was to be the location for more run-ins with photographers. For Penn, the brawl never seemed to be over.

Madonna detests failure and that made her work even harder at her marriage. The thought of all the carrion 'told-you-so's' around the world picking over her divorce made her cringe. But it did not stop her from taking precautions. The Central Park West apartment was in her name only. As were the various companies she was setting up to develop projects, particularly films, for her. She still had not lost sight of *Evita*, but James Foley brought her a film initially called *Slammer*, which was never to have the impact that title implied. It became *Who's That Girl?* – a dizzy-dame movie with Madonna as a wrongly jailed ex-convict who is released to find revenge and fun. Her Nikki Finn takes Griffin Dunne's straight-arrow lawyer, Loudon Trott, along for the ride. It is quite a long one and Madonna's voice grated. The critics snarled. Madonna had seen it as her Judy Holliday turn. Or a *homage* to Cary Grant and Katharine Hepburn's *Bringing Up Baby* – during filming, a wild cat, a cougar, got loose on the streets of Manhattan – but it did not match such lofty aspirations.

'Madonna has been made up and costumed to look like an aspiring bag lady with the skin of a pneumonia victim,' offered one of the more polite American critics. Her fans stayed away from the film. But they bought the album and the title-track single, which became an international hit. Don't cry for Madonna quite yet, appeared to be the message. She fobbed off the critics. She had learned from the film. Nikki has cleared her name and that was important. Madonna said she was always having to do that with the public.

Penn was not helping. He had gone out to dinner at the West Beach Café in Venice with a blonde girl and had been spotted by photographers who patrol such celebrity hangouts. Why don't stars like I-want-to-be-left-alone Penn eat dinner at home?

That night, cameraman Cesare Bonazza wished he had. He claims that after he took some pictures of Penn and the unknown girl, the actor chased after him in his truck.

'He jumped from the truck and yelled, "Come out of the car, you motherfucker!" He reached under his T-shirt and pulled out a gun. He got in a shooting position with both hands grabbing the gun and pointed at me. He said, "Give me the fucking camera, give me the fucking camera." He was crazy, a lunatic.'

Bonazza says he did not take a picture of Penn threatening him with the gun because he feared that the threat could turn fatal. 'I couldn't believe the guy ... one of these days, he's going to get killed. I was just lucky to escape him in the traffic.'

Another day, another brawl. This time a more far-reaching incident involving Penn. He was working for reformed Hollywood bad boy Dennis Hopper on the film *Colors*, costarring Robert Duvall. The actors played veteran/young lion cops in the film about Los Angeles street gangs. For an article on the gangs, whose territory spreads across many of the sporting venues used for the 1984 Olympics, I had spent several frightening weeks on their 'turf'. *Colors* was to be a grand and accurate picture of the horror and squalor and violence in gang life. But to make it on location, using gang members for most of the extras?

Madonna made three very secret visits to Penn during location filming. Hopper told me, 'All the gang members knew Sean – they'd all seen *Bad Boys*. They'd say, "Hey, man, we know you're playing a cop but we don't know, you know." They thought he was one of them. One of the Mexican gangs – the White Fence Gang – asked him to sign a homeboy [gang member] symbol for them. He said, "I don't want to sign that." They couldn't understand and asked him why. He said, "Because my homeboys are the Los Angeles Police Department." He was aggressive about that too.'

The film's producer was the soft-spoken Robert Solo, who had cast Penn in *Bad Boys*. Sitting in a Hollywood hotel, he said, 'I have always liked Sean Penn and I have always had a great admiration for him. You know, when they were making the film they were in jeopardy a lot. I think most of the crew were carrying weapons. People were nearly getting killed while we were filming. One of the gang members we were using on the film was called Destroyer and Dennis asked him why. Destroyer told him, "Sometimes I gotta do my business." Sean and Dennis didn't have any protection but their images. The gang-bangers [gang members] liked them. "Hey, Sean Penn. Hey, Sean Penn." The image sticks. It's hard to remove.'

Penn himself talked to me about Madonna's visits and said that even in that most violent arena he was not concerned for her or his own safety.

'We all have a certain sense of ability to be and not to be bullshitted. I think I can pretty well tell when someone is being who they are around me and when they're not. So, if I was going to say something good about these guys, it's that they stay pretty much as close to who they are no matter who they are talking to as about anybody I've ever met. That is that everything they say is a lie.'

In *Colors*, his cop character was called 'Pac Man' because he eats up the streets. What was his definition of masculinity? 'My definition for what?' he mugged. 'I can only say for the character.' Go on. 'In a world full of cunts, I'm the guy who can make sure the manhood stays around. That's what.'

It was during the filming of *Colors* that Penn not only landed himself in trouble, but in jail. It was in April 1987, a clear spring day out by the Pacific at Venice Beach. Jeffrie Klein, a scrap-metal dealer from Orange County, an hour's drive but decades in mentality from Hollywood, was one of a couple of hundred non-union extras getting $35 a day to fill out background scenes along Ocean Front Walk. One scene called for Hopper to film Duvall and Penn strolling along. As they approached Klein, he took a camera from his jacket pocket and took some souvenir snaps. The camera lens was the red flag for Penn and he dashed towards Klein, swearing and shouting, 'What are you doing taking pictures?'

Six-foot tall and weighing 210lb, Klein explained he was an extra and that other people were also snapping pictures. 'Sean Penn then spat in my face and said, "What are you going to do now?" ' Klein spat back. Penn started a series of punches to Klein's face. Three times the crowd of extras separated the two of them and three times Penn broke free and went back on the attack. Meagan Montgomery, another extra there that day, recalls, 'I saw Penn try to leap over security guards and try to hit Klein on the head with his fist.'

It had only been two weeks since Penn was fined and put on probation for the Wolinski incident. This was a blatant breach of probation, although Penn's lawyer Howard Weitzman, who was later part of OJ Simpson's defence team, argued that his client had not breached his probation.

It was an awful mess and Madonna was distraught. She had a husband who thought he was a heavyweight contender. He was also a champion boozer. A few weeks later he was stopped for running a red traffic light; a blood test showed an alcohol content of slightly over California's legal limit. The charge was reckless driving, another probation violation. For weeks, Penn was to play cat and mouse with the press and the California authorities. And to sour the mix even more, Madonna said publicly that they were having marital problems. It looked like her marriage was going to turn out like her most recent films – rather a miserable learning experience.

Even before Penn went to court to be sentenced for the probation violations, she had determined that the marriage was over. But publicly, she was standing by him.

CHAPTER TEN

FORTRESS MALIBU

'I like to be in control of my life.'

MADONNA, 1987

While Penn prepared for his court appearance and juggled his commitment to film his father Leo's *Judgement in Berlin* on location in Germany, his wife was taking total control of her career. She had had 11 consecutive top-5 singles – only the Beatles and Elvis had matched that – and she wanted to build on the achievement with her *Who's That Girl?* world tour and the release of the film. In long strategy meetings, which would start at breakfast and often not finish until around midnight, she and her advisers were working on a new sweep of Madonnamania. She had trained for it. Two hours a day – every day.

Within Fortress Malibu, there had been some additions; a dance studio and a personal home gym with a trampoline and swimming pool as well as weights and other equipment. She would take a bike out and spin up and down the Pacific Coast Highway or go for runs at Pepperdine University. She was 20lb lighter, trim and muscled, and her bust was even tighter. To go with a new svelte body, she had new hair – the

Marilyn look. Although she was one of the best-selling recording artists in the world and the 7th-highest earning – $26 million in 1987 – she was still desperate to escape her continuing image as a media curiosity, a bimbo who got lucky. The same drive that got her through the early days propelled her forward now.

Penn, meanwhile, had got himself in a jam and he would have to cope. For her, it must have seemed at the time that someone at Warner Brothers Studios, who were releasing the film of *Who's That Girl?*, was psychic, for it would have been just too much had it retained the original title of *Slammer*. Penn was sentenced to 60 days for his probation violations. There were all kinds of rows and outcries when the California courts agreed to allow him to serve the time over two sessions so he could complete *Judgement in Berlin*. Now, he was seen at a Beverly Hills restaurant and then strolling down Fifth Avenue in New York with Madonna. They went to Marigold's restaurant for lunch, window-shopped along Madison Avenue and visited a well-known lingerie shop. Penn should have been in Germany.

Arrest warrants were then issued and cancelled. The City Fathers of Los Angeles demanded to know what was going on. It was all farcical. Finally, Penn did serve 32 days of his sentence in the spit of a town called Bridgeport (population 500) in California's Mono County near the Mammoth Lake ski resort. Penn paid $80 a day to go to jail there rather than do his time in the Los Angeles County Jail. The difference in conditions would have had a more likely market value of $8,000 a day. The food was hot but not haute, the blankets grey but not Ralph Lauren grey. In California, such sentences for bad boys and girls in showbusiness are laughingly called 'celebrity division programmes', much like corporate offenders serving their time in open prisons known as Club Feds. Nevertheless, for an edgy, nerve-driven energy freak like Penn, any sort of confinement must have been hard to take. Madonna was in Japan on her Who's That Girl? tour when Penn was sentenced.

Madonnamania? More than they ever expected. Thousands of fans stood outside the stadium in Osaka. Ticket touts wanted $700 a seat in Tokyo. Storms shut down the first show, but the fans did not go home. They stood outside her hotel in the rain and chanted her name. On stage, she did not disappoint. She was all energy in her clinging, skimpy black corset and fishnet stockings; then she changed to giant sunglasses and a feather boa over black pants. Her thorough preparation showed when she used Japanese phrases to encourage the audience to sing and dance with her. Later, two geishas made her up in traditional style. In return, she taught them how to wink and blow a kiss. She jogged for 90 minutes every day and also did a great deal of sightseeing, going unnoticed under a dowdy brown wig. The Far East was more fun this time, and she could finally bury the ghost of *Shanghai Surprise*. But every day Sean Penn was on the phone.

Madonna was enjoying herself alone. The tour was such an instant success, one she had worked for; it proved to her that her ethic of hard work and preparation did pay off. She thought of Penn as a dedicated and 'honest' actor. But hadn't she really married her image of him? The reality of the flying fists and boozing was a wedge between them. It had sent her from their home; she had spent nights in hotels only a half-hour drive from Malibu. Or she would take off to New York and the apartment. But now it was not so easy to hang out with the gang from the past. The days of anonymity were long gone. She made her first chat-show appearance with America's king of that format, the remarkable Johnny Carson, to promote her upcoming tour of the United States. She put on a brave face and played the flirt, telling Carson, 'I'm just a Midwestern girl in a bustier,' and then added, 'I figured if I was going to present myself as a virgin to anyone it should be you.' Carson shot back, 'I suppose there has to be a first in my life.' It got the intended laughs. Yet it was a sad time for Madonna. Professionally, she was getting it right. More than two million people on three continents would see her and adore her and lust after her. Privately, though, she had no answers in the weeks running up to her second wedding anniversary.

Martin Burgoyne, who had attended her wedding and with whom she had shared an apartment and her life in the New York days – he danced in her first video – had died of AIDS. He was a bartender at the Russian Tea Rooms when she was the hat-check girl. When Burgoyne had been diagnosed, his old friend had insisted on paying his hospital bills. She supported Burgoyne all through the illness. 'I still cry when I think of him,' she says.

There were dark clouds all around. She decided to take control. The United States leg of her tour was to start in Miami. It took a 747 jet and a DC-7 to get the equipment from Tokyo to Florida and required 23 trucks to transport the specially built steel stage. It took a crew of about 50 technicians to set up. Coati Mundi of Kid Creole and the Coconuts was close to her. 'She's very conscious of how something looks. She likes to be in control of things. She pays a thousand and one per cent attention to everything.'

Out on Turnberry Island, a hedonist island on the Florida waterways where one-time presidential hopeful Gary Hart was to climb aboard the *Monkey Business* with Donna Rice and lose his White House chance, the Who's That Girl? tour group set up luxury camp. Madonna brought an extra guest – her husband. Penn played the suitor, plying Madonna with white roses and orchids. Even when photographers tried to move in, Penn gently moved Madonna and himself out of range. He even said, 'Thank you,' to a cameraman who asked to take his picture. Slugaholics do not reform overnight; the riot act had been read.

Nevertheless, Penn resented the close contact between Madonna and her crew on the tour. They had their private jokes. One regular Madonna worker revealed, 'We gave his wife a lot of attention and care, and he resented that. Sean thought Madonna should be treated like everyone else's wife and she resented that. It always ended with everyone feeling awkward when he was around.'

Penn had to leave Miami, finish his film and go to jail. The bombardment of flowers continued, as well as the phone calls as Madonna performed her way across North America. One crew member says that while they were having a tactics meeting, Penn got through to the switchboard of her hotel in Washington. Madonna kept him on hold for 45 minutes. That is control. And confidence. Penn, who had said he did not care who wore the pants in his house as long as he took them off, could have pondered that while he was filming in Europe.

It was not long before geography changed, if not the attitude. Penn in jail in the California countryside of Mono County – strip-searched, deloused and wearing a blue prison uniform bearing the Mono County Jail stamp – was allowed 15-minute phone calls. Between the ones from his wife, he wrote a one-act play, *The Kindness of Women*, which he later directed on stage in Los Angeles. It is the story of a man involved in a stormy marriage involving sexual flings and heavy drinking. The dialogue ('You jerk', 'You bitch') sounded close to home. Penn admitted to me that it was.

Madonnamania was sweeping Europe. In Britain, fans swooned and louts demanded, 'Show us your tits.' Bodyguards and photographers jogged along after her. Not with her. She was in control this time. There would be no more *Shanghai Surprise* surprises. In France, she got involved in the politics of Premier Jacques Chirac who, for popularity reasons, suddenly became very interested in rock 'n' roll. 'Everybody likes you very, very much,' he told her. 'I like you too,' said Madonna. Chirac hugged her and the fun began. 'Who's that girl at the side of the gentleman?' was the picture caption in the Paris tabloid *Libération*. An editorial about rock singers and politics asked, 'Who's that girl?' and replied, 'That girl is Jacques Chirac.' The debate roared on with other papers joining in.

What astonished the people of Paris even more was Madonna's eating habits. She was actually on two baked potatoes a day and popcorn, but for a 'banquet' dinner she served up clear turtle soup, avocado mousse and a choice of white wine or Perrier. A choice? She told her dinner guests, 'You didn't think I was going to sit here and watch you eat fancy food that I can't eat?' She was not so unforthcoming in the Old Country.

'*Siete gia caldi?*' [Are you hot?] '*Allora, andiamo!*' [Then let's go!] got her cheers of approval in Florence as That Girl blasted through Italy. In Turin, Madonna met members of the family of her second cousin Amelia Vitucci, who gave her a painting of the original family home in Pacentro. Madonna was delighted. She did a little two-step skip and turned to 11-year-old Giuseppe Vitucci and asked, 'Do you want to dance with me?' The crowd did, but the young boy was not sure and showed embarrassment as he told her, 'I don't know.' His mother Amelia later said it was 'one of the wonderful moments', and added, 'Her family left Pacentro very poor. There was not work and it's magnificent that she came back to us like that, as a great lady, a great success. Her family must be very proud.'

Bambina de Guilio was then Madonna's closest relative in Italy. She was 82 in 1987, but has since died. She was not well enough to make the journey from Pacentro in Turin with the seven town councillors who did. They gave Madonna a parchment proclamation as an honorary citizen of their town. When photographers crowded around her and her distant relatives, there was no problem. Madonna turned to everyone and said, '*Formaggio*.' [Cheese.] While Madonna was playing to standing-room-only crowds – in Turin a dozen people were injured in the crush to ogle her – an enterprising Italian journalist went for a drink with some of the folks in Pacentro. He quoted one customer as saying over sips of grappa, 'That girl sings and dances and shows her thighs. She is a *malafemina* [loose woman]. No Madonna she. The devil is more like it.' A prisoner who shared a cell with Penn says that Madonna talked every day on the phone with him. There were calls from France and Italy. But when she got to Malibu, there was silence. She was busy. There were several 'heated' phone chats before Madonna made it to Mono County Jail. Other inmates had got him going with stories about her being out on the town with Cher and Scottish singer Sheena Easton. On her first visit, they argued. Twenty minutes later, she stormed out. When Penn was released, Madonna made a lot of optimistic noises. They went to a marriage counsellor. She started house hunting, telling the Beverly Hills realtors of Hyland, Young and Alvarez that she wanted a place of her own. Elaine Young, once the wife of the late actor Gig Young, revealed, 'There was not a question it was a place for a bachelor girl.'

Then she stopped house hunting. Madonna was convinced she was pregnant. She and Penn had been celibate during her tour and his jail time. She was sure that all that self-denial had resulted in something 'cosmic' and positive when they did get together. But shy of publicity about this, she made her prediction on the basis of a home-pregnancy test kit. It was incorrect, as her gynaecologist on Rexford Avenue in Beverly Hills quickly discovered. No baby – well then, no marriage.

Penn was on the road alone, as a surprised journalist found out. In Los Angeles, the film critic for the Santa Monica *Evening Outlook* was driving out to the Pacific Coast from a movie screening. He saw a rather bedraggled, sad-looking chap thumbing a lift. He stopped and asked, 'Where are you going?'

'Malibu,' said Sean Penn, who was hitching his way around town, fearful of another spell in jail if he dared to drive a car without insurance. Penn was hitting the bars of Malibu and Venice Beach. He was seen with friends and girls. The paparazzi loved this. Madonna spent Thanksgiving in New York with some of her family and without Penn.

After being out of touch for four days, her husband turned up late in New York looking for his celebratory turkey dinner with all the trimmings. The story was that she served him with divorce papers instead. In reality, after discovering she was not pregnant, she decided to go ahead with the divorce. When Penn turned up that Thanksgiving, she announced her decision but did not start talking to lawyers until the following week. She went public with it too, saying the divorce was not the result of one incident but 'a series of cumulative pressures'. Liz Rosenberg, the Warner Brothers publicity person who has supported Madonna for many years, then explained, 'There were so many moments in their marriage when it was shaky that Madonna was finally forced to face the reality of the situation ... that they weren't happy together.'

The best career move since losing her virginity, laughed the wags. Loyal Rosenberg rebutted, 'She wanted the marriage to work, all the jokes about the marriage motivated her to work hard to making the marriage go. I don't think she considered him in terms of her career.'

An unhappy Penn slopped off to Los Angeles. Madonna stayed with her sister Paula out in Brooklyn. Penn went to Helena's. British singer Billy Idol was at the bar with photographer Vinne Zuffante (Penn had hit him the previous year) and, as the drinks went down, so Penn's ire went up. Finally, he demanded that Helena – a long, dark-haired Greek woman protective of her celebrity clientéle – throw Zuffante out even though he was without a camera. Penn went off to the bathroom but saw the queue and decided against waiting. He went outside and peed against the wall of the building. Normally he would have reacted differently and drowned his sorrows in yet more drink and violence. He did not. It was certainly a different way for Penn to behave. And Penn would sit in the Hollywood Hotel saying of the lawsuit, 'The divorce was more for the magazines than reality. Making any family work is an endless job that's hard enough when the family isn't public.'

But for the couple who had married their images it had

been, as Penn was to discover, rather like peeing into the wind, despite the efforts of James Foley.

It was James Foley, the director who had worked with and admired both Penn and Madonna in their separate ways, who had brought about the reconciliation. While the lawsuit was still being pursued, they began talking on the telephone. Their conversations got longer. Foley encouraged them. Then Penn promised Madonna something he had always written off as simply for wimps. He would see a marriage counsellor, whenever she wanted him to. The boozing would stop, the punching days were over – this was a promise-her-anything reconciliation. Over Christmas, they renewed their marriage vows. It was their last happy Christmas together. And it was going to be a rocky New Year for the woman who had become one of the best-known entertainers in the world. And, although she could never have realised it, she was just starting to soar to even greater, dizzying heights. Then, she was just a popular Princess. She would have to wait a little longer for her Coronation.

CHAPTER ELEVEN

STORMY WEATHER

'I can't conceive of living happily ever after or happiness
for a long period of time with one person. I change so
much and my needs change also.'

MADONNA, 1984

The rains came early to southern California in 1988. The storm clouds swept in from the Pacific one after the other as Madonna tried to settle back into marriage and concentrate again on her career. Her annual pre-tax earnings were around $25 million.

Madonna's discipline is more than a dancer's or a businesswoman's. It is the discipline of a driven workaholic. Her appearance is a business asset – she works out for three hours every day. There are hours to be creative, to write songs, work out routines, read film scripts and plan tours. There are hours for business on her fax machine and multi-line phone systems. But were there enough hours in the day for her marriage? A good Catholic girl should always find time for marriage.

She and Penn were certainly trying. But whether they were star-crossed or not, they could not stay away from publicity. And it was not anything to do with them. First, truck driver Steven Stillbower drove his pick-up through the front gate of their Malibu estate. He wanted to 'see' Madonna. Penn made a citizen's arrest.

More worrying was an incident when the couple arrived home with her brother Mario at 12.30am one night. They had been grocery shopping at the all-night supermarket on the Pacific Coast Highway and found five people wandering around their property. Penn drove back to close the gates and at the same time called the police on his car phone. Mario drove another car down to the gates to back up Penn. Malibu Deputy Sheriff Bill Wehner recalls the evening.

'Sean, with the help of Mario, approached these guys and attempted to stop them. One of them tried to punch Sean, and Sean, looking to defend himself, found a bottle of tofu salad dressing he had just bought and hit the guy with it.'

When the police reporters discovered the incident, the salad-dressing-Sean-Penn-brawl got the actor some of the most positive publicity he had ever had. But it was still publicity and more evidence that whatever happened in their lives would go on in the public spotlight.

Even Madonna's morbid fear of death was to become painfully public. She never expected to live longer than her mother, whom she had watched suffer and die so painfully. When Madonna discovered a lump in her left breast, she panicked. Initially, she did the right thing and went for an examination. There were uneasy minutes in the reception room of Dr Jerold Steiner, a cancer specialist who treated the late Sammy Davis Jr and the late actress-comedienne Gilda Radner.

Steiner, a soft-spoken man with a salt-and-pepper beard, spent 20 minutes explaining the problems and treatments available for breast cancer before examining Madonna. After he'd done so, he asked Madonna to return in another two weeks for another examination and test at the Cedars-Sinai building in Los Angeles. For the first time in her life, Madonna ran away from the confrontation. She had seen her mother waste away and the haunting memories and possibilities for her were too agonising to deal with.

Finally, nearly a dozen weeks later – months which, in other circumstances, could have proved fatal – she braved it out and, after taking a mammogram, Steiner carried out a biopsy, which proved negative.

There was some joy from Madonna's fears. The cancer scare brought her and Penn closer together. They would entertain at home in Malibu. One of the guests was Scandinavian journalist Sindre Kartvedt. A serious film journalist, he was someone they could easily accept in their home. But Kartvedt says he was never really comfortable during the visits.

'They both seemed to be playing out their roles. Sean was the husband. Madonna was the housewife. And neither role fitted them. They both had opinions. They both wanted to give their point of view. In that relationship, it was clear they could never be equals. They both felt as though they were more important than each other. She always seemed to be play-acting. I think she enjoyed the role of home-maker but that's all it was – a role. All the insecurities, the need to be in control, to be the boss, fit that sort of psychological profile.'

Indeed, what would Freud have interpreted from the Madonna–Penn union? They would go off and make love for hours at a time, happy in their own pleasure and in themselves, but it was an explosive match.

'I was raised to believe that when you marry someone, you marry him for life. You never give up,' said Madonna.

She also said something that pointed to Penn's attitude over her success. 'Sean used to make fun of me. You know, those cut-off jeans I wear? Sean would bring someone back to the house and I'd be wearing those with my hair all *yeuch* – I mean, I'd be looking like a hag. And he'd bring a friend in and drag me over and say, "Look at her, she's one of the richest women in America." There's a difference between being born into money and making money. I'm from a poor background and basically I'm still a working-class girl. I've been known to wash a dish or two, make a bed or two.'

Penn was to go off to Thailand to co-star with Michael J Fox in *Casualties of War*, a Vietnam drama to be directed by Brian De Palma. Penn said he would miss his wife but sighed, 'But we've been through worse things than that, I guess.' Had they?

Credibility was what they both desperately wanted. Madonna was a big star and a big earner, but still wanted to prove she could act, and decided the place to prove it was Broadway, where they have been known to butcher veteran stage stars before breakfast. She had been a long-time fan of playwright (and film screenwriter and director) David Mamet. She had enjoyed his *Glengarry Glen Ross*, which had won Mamet the Pulitzer Prize, but it was when she saw his film *House of Games* that she decided he was a 'genius' and 'I knew I had to work with this man.' She went out and auditioned with more than 300 other would-be Broadway stars for the 3-character drama *Speed-the-Plow*. Ron Silver and Mamet regular Joe Mantegna had already been cast as a couple of Hollywood sharks hustling a film deal. The female role is of a secretary 'temp' who becomes a pawn in a power game.

'I'd wake up every morning with butterflies in my

stomach,' said Madonna of her time in *Speed-the-Plow*. The tickets were $35 a time – twice what Madonna fans would then pay to see her in concert – for an orchestra seat at the Royal Theatre in New York. In the preview week, the theatre was packed. Madonna on Broadway brought out autograph hunters, hustlers, memorabilia dealers and even theatre-goers.

It was 15 minutes before Madonna appeared on stage carrying a coffee tray. A year earlier she had been parading on stage in her underwear. But here, she was in dark hair, skirt, glasses and sensible shoes. Mantegna's character wants to take the 'temp' Karen to bed. Silver bets him $500 that he can't.

The New York papers had fun. NO, SHE CAN'T ACT shouted the *Daily News*. In Britain, the *Guardian* – the most non-Madonna of papers – was more enthusiastic: 'She's plays what looks like Mamet's version of the early Marilyn who also had an ambition to star on Broadway.'

Madonna only had her big chance because first choice Elizabeth Perkins, who had created a tremendous buzz co-starring with Tom Hanks in *Big*, suddenly dropped out. Director Gregory Mosher had helped Madonna in her only other stage work previously, as a gangster's moll in a 1986 workshop production of David Rabe's *Goose and Tomtom*. When Madonna heard Perkins was no longer going ahead, she called Mosher and asked for an audition.

'Madonna didn't Bogart her way into the role,' remembers Joe Mantegna, who played a gaudy hoodlum in *Godfather III*, adding, 'A lot of high-powered actresses also auditioned.'

There were six weeks of rehearsals and the Madonna discipline of preparation and rehearsal kicked in. Ron Silver, who starred with Oscar-winner Jeremy Irons in *Reversal of*

Fortune, recalled, 'She was funny and feisty and the first one to know her lines – a professional. I liked her *chutspah*.'

Vanessa Redgrave, who flew from London to see the show, sent on congratulations. Mosher said, 'Madonna could have made a spectacle of herself, thrown her weight around or even tried to capitalise on her sexy image, but she didn't. She was a real actress – just right. She wasn't the Material Girl or her version of Marilyn Monroe.'

At the opening night party at the Tavern on the Green, she appeared wearing a pale blue dress with pearls. It had a subdued effect and designer Marlene Stewart – always one for the moment – said it was entirely intentional. But, as often with Madonna, it was an illusion. She was nowhere as cool as she looked. Throughout the run of the show, she had constant changes of costume. Even the dressers remarked – and two even complained – about the smell of her costumes, the stench from the perspiration. The fear of putting herself out there – and it must have been an incredible pressure – she has always dismissed as 'butterflies'. It may have been one of the most terrifying stage appearances, but Lindsay Law, who was executive producer of her next film, *Bloodhounds of Broadway*, said, 'It was one of the smartest things she'd ever done.'

Madonna worked with a string of established acting talents – Randy Quaid, Rutger Hauer, Matt Dillon and Jennifer Grey – on *Bloodhounds*, which was sort of a *Guys and Dolls* romp. Screenwriter and director Howard Brookner took four Damon Runyon short stories and set them over one night, New Year's Eve 1928. The theme was death, near-death and the threat of death; a black comedy. Madonna's story involved Quaid, as Feet Samuels, who has agreed to sell his giant feet to a crazy doctor to pay off gambling debts.

Then he learns that Madonna's Hortense Hathaway loves him and life is not so bad. He wants to keep his feet. It was a small-scale project, which retains an oddball charm. Madonna says she realised halfway through filming that something was wrong with Brookner, who was later to die from AIDS. In turn, he asked her about watching her friend Martin Burgoyne die from AIDS. The theme of *Bloodhounds* and the tragic reality – an eerie surrealism, a Fellini movie – made Madonna her most reflective about sexuality. About risks. About how far you, or rather she, could go. About homosexuality. About lesbianism.

Apart from this sexual dark side, *Bloodhounds* more happily gave her a friend in Jennifer Grey, the talented daughter of Joel (*Cabaret*) Grey, who had co-starred with Patrick Swayze in the surprisingly huge box-office success *Dirty Dancing*. Grey had broken up with actor-boyfriend Matthew Broderick, currently married to Sarah Jessica Parker of television's *Sex and the City* and, with Penn away on location in the Far East, there were many girls' nights out.

Grey took her new best friend to a birthday party for Sandra Bernhard, the off-beat actress who had slipped into the mainstream in Martin Scorsese's *King of Comedy*, co-starring with Robert De Niro. Madonna liked Bernhard's cool, caustic humour and went to see her one-woman show *Without You I'm Nothing*. Much of Bernhard's act is playing out fantasies. The evening Madonna was in the audience, Bernhard told a joke about how she and Madonna survived the Third World War; the punchline was that Penn did not, which got lots of laughs at the time because of the publicity surrounding their relationship.

It was the start of an ongoing and controversial friendship. And it was Midwest girls together. Bernhard was another escapee from Michigan, from Flint, another Motor Town sprawl. Relate? These ladies were almost related. Sandra Bernhard provided a shoulder for Madonna through the last gruelling months of her marriage. The performer, a couple of years older than Madonna and known as 'The Mouth That Roars', is tall (5ft 10in) and skinny (7st 12lb) and she remembers the moment they became best friends: 'I was talking to her on the phone and I said, "I can't imagine being you," and she said, "I can't imagine being you." I thought that was a very nice thing to say.'

By now they were quite literally bosom buddies. Wearing sequinned bras, they bumped and ground on stage, belting out Sonny and Cher's 'I Got You, Babe' at a benefit concert in New York. When the on-stage fondling got a little too much for the celebrity audience, which included Glenn Close and Meryl Streep, the high-spirited Madonna screamed, 'Don't believe those stories.' Leaning into the microphone, the other side of this dynamic duo shouted, 'Believe those stories!' Which is absolutely Sandra Bernhard's style. She does not simply light up a room – she just takes over: 'I'm a control person. It's hard for me to relinquish my power. It's like my weight – I'm counting down. I want to look like I'm needy because I am. We all are. It's just what I need, I don't want, I *need* stardom. It's part of the package. I wouldn't choose it on its own but, in order to do what I do, I've gotta get people to pay to see me. I'm coming from a million places. I create a persona – the ravenous predator.'

She is certainly unpredictable, as many American television talk-show hosts have discovered. One minute she has got the hair-sprayed host and his audience wildly laughing – and then she will drop a time-bomb like, 'Joni

Mitchell hasn't left the Malibu Colony in ten years and here she is singing about Ethiopia.'

She was born in America's car country of Michigan, but raised in the country-club country of Scottsdale, Arizona, where every other open space is a golf course. Her mother was an abstract artist. 'We didn't join the country club – my mother thought it was pretentious. It's because of that I never had a nose job and consequently became the girl I wanted to be.'

At 18, she moved to Los Angeles and got a job as a manicurist working on the fingers and toes of celebrities. 'I did Dyan Cannon one time. She never looked at me as I dug the sand from under her big toenail.' While she polished and buffed all day, at night she worked the town's famous comedy clubs. On and on and on for eight years. The big moment came with Martin Scorsese's *The King of Comedy*, where Jerry Lewis, *the* Jerry Lewis, played a television talk-show host who is kidnapped by Robert De Niro and Bernhard, as a crazy in her underwear. She had arrived. Her notices for the film were sensational. Her career decisions were not so good. She turned down *Ghostbusters*, which is still the biggest-earning comedy ever ('Not a good move,' she deadpans), but was a sadistic nurse in Nicholas Roeg's *Track 29*. She was a great fan and a loyal friend to Madonna. 'We have fun, we enjoy each other's company. What more do you want me to say about it? Yes, we're best friends. And being a friend is always being around when your friend needs you.' Bernhard says that despite their hard-edge approach, both she and Madonna are 'vulnerable'. She confesses, 'I am a serious manic depressive. I get tired of being sarcastic. People think I'm always sarcastic. I try to get off in different ways, being funny, but sarcasm is very easy for me. It's the easy way to make people laugh – or being wild, being really wild. Actually, I like that better.'

She has been called many, many things – even pretty. She does not agree. 'I don't consider myself pretty. Pretty means something helpless, something unattainable and unreachable, and I don't think I'm that way.

'I think I'm sensual, I'm more beautiful than I am pretty. Pretty is a high-school cheerleader. I learned early the advantage of being funny. I knew how to make people laugh, to manipulate them. I'm not the type that gets into something and drops my own persona. I'm more of an observer and a commentator. I've never done drugs. I hate it. I like being really lucid. I like being in control. When people try to give me drugs, it's sloppy, it's ugly and it's inexcusable behaviour. I stand for total freedom and just live my life in an honest way. I'm open to a lot of different things. I mean, a girl likes to have a good time. But I don't like to classify myself. I want people just to not know what's going on. To be a little confused and irritated and say, "Who does she think she is?" That's fine.'

The madcap lady who likes biker leathers, Bon Jovi, Prince, 1970s disco, leather bustiers, glitter bras and Madonna, would also have liked to have had a child. But adoption is not an option: 'I'd rather have my own child. Better breeding. Better quality control.' And Madonna? 'She is my best friend – not my gynaecologist.'

Bernhard did get a little irritated about some of the talk about her and Madonna's 'close' relationship and uncharacteristically reacted with, 'We're friends and that's it. The press just can't be happy when two cool girls like us are tight buddies – like no competition, no bitchiness, except that mock stuff we put on, kind of like Dean Martin and Jerry Lewis.

'By the way, did anyone ever accuse Dean and Jerry of getting it on? No. The press have to turn it into some freaky, sordid scandal when they *should* be highlighting the fact that maybe, for once, two strong women are setting a positive example for the rest of the gals — it's fine to be supportive of your girlfriends, like not all women are back-stabbing, vicious nightmares. So everyone in the press can kiss my fat butt.'

I asked Bernhard about this outburst at a Beverly Hills reception.

'Oh, that? Haemorrhoids, I suppose.'

In 1991, Madonna also got testy about their relationship. She was also most revealing: 'Sandy's a great gal. Sandy's one of my only girlfriends, really. She's one of the only girls that can take me. She's really a ballsy girl. Most girls just hide under the couch. We frighten everyone out of the room. Sandy and I have always been great friends. I think in the very beginning there was a flirtation, but I realised I could have a really good friend in Sandra, and I wanted to maintain the friendship. When I went on *The David Letterman Show*, it wasn't exactly clear how things were going to go. But Sandy started playing up that we were girlfriends, and I thought, Great, OK, let me go for it. Because, you know, I *love* to fuck with people. Just as people have preconceived notions about gay men, they certainly do about gay women. So if I could be some sort of detonator to that bomb, then I was willing to do that. It was really fun. Then, of course, it went highly out of control. Everybody picked up on it and the question was, are we sleeping together? It's not really important. The fact is that Sandra sleeps with men too, and I think maybe she's trying to find happiness in her life. Maybe she was just thinking, Can everybody just shut up so I can find somebody to have a decent relationship with? Sandra's one of the most open people I know. You should see her in public. She's not trying to hide anything. I think it's ludicrous that people are accusing her of being in the closet or ashamed of being gay.

'The fact is, she's a great friend of mine. Whether I'm gay or not is irrelevant. Whether I slept with her or not is irrelevant. I'm perfectly willing to have people think that I did. You know, I do not want to protest too much. I don't care. If it makes people feel better to think that I slept with her, then they can think about it. And if it makes them safer to think that I didn't, then that's fine too. You know, I'd almost rather they thought that I did. Just so they could know that here was this girl that everyone was buying records off, and she was eating someone's pussy. So there.'

While the world was fascinated by the Madonna-Bernhard-do-they-or-don't-they? antics, Madonna was obsessed with another story – that of *Evita*. It would drive her for the next few years. With her Siren Films Company, she was negotiating a deal with Dawn Steel, then the president of Columbia Pictures who would later tragically die from cancer. She and Siren development director, Stephanie Stephens, expected to have seven films 'in full swing' by 1989. The plan was for a musical built around Madonna, dramatic roles and a comedy. It was a brave but overly ambitious scheme.

But when Oliver Stone, hot from *Platoon* and *Wall Street*, flew into New York, he had another offer – *Evita*. Stone arrived from California to screen test Madonna for the role of Juan Perón's wife, the 'saint' who died of cancer in her

30s. Elaine Paige and others involved in the Andrew Lloyd-Webber/Tim Rice stage spectacular were not so sure. Streisand had been mentioned for the role. Meryl Streep had made a demonstration tape for Lloyd-Webber and Rice. During an interview, I asked Streep to sing a few bars of 'Don't Cry For Me Argentina' and she burst into a fit of giggles and said, 'I can't go to London. Elaine Paige would kill me.' But Streep, who was later to be devastated at not being offered *Evita*, should not have been Paige's target. Madonna was the one in line for the role. But she told Stone she would not screen test. It was an absurd gesture. Stone, who would go on to massive films, including *Born on the Fourth of July, The Doors, JFK* and *Nixon*, is himself a strong personality. It appeared to be a Mexican stand-off. However, Madonna was determined. One day, she would be Evita. As always, she was in the overachieving business.

She was also still trying to be Mrs Penn. Her husband was appearing in the play *Hurlyburly* in Los Angeles where Madonna was a regular at rehearsals and would telephone much of the time. But on opening night, she was late. And she arrived with Sandra Bernhard. Later in the evening, at a Century City club near the theatre, Penn was back to being the bad boy: 'You cunt. How could you do this to me?' he shouted at Madonna. As 1988 headed to a conclusion, so did their fiery marriage. A former employee at their Malibu home said they would argue all the time, with Penn punching out doors and walls or taking off into the grounds to shoot rabbits and birds, 'anything that moved'.

But even with all this marital madness, she was still taking care of business. She knew all about Warren Beatty's *Dick Tracy* – she had been introduced to Beatty by Penn on their first date – and called him up asking for the role of

Breathless Mahoney. Within a month, she was eating dinner at the Great Greek Restaurant in Sherman Oakes just over the hill from Beatty's Mulholland Drive estate at the high-wire corner with Marlon Brando and Jack Nicholson. Their dinner companion was former Presidential hopeful and long-time Beatty friend, Gary Hart. Madonna had got her role and her leading man.

She had also lost her other one. Her marriage was over, Until now, the extent of her life as a 'battered wife' was not known. Colleagues, friends and associates of the couple would only talk about the wild days of their relationship with the assurance of anonymity. They told stories of how Madonna would always take the car keys with her so that if Penn got out of hand he was the one looking for a ride home. And how Penn's constant rages and outrageous tantrums killed any love Madonna had for him.

Madonna had agreed to work with Hollywood's leading Lothario, Warren Beatty, and even an easy-going spouse might have difficulty with that one. Penn reacted by leaving home and moving in with his parents four miles away down the Pacific Coast. He had spent Christmas with his family and drinking with his friends. She had gone to a party with some girlfriends. These were tense, estranged days.

It was just after 4.00pm on 28 December when Penn broke into his own home. Madonna had allowed all the help time off for the holidays. Penn put Madonna through terror.

Madonna told Penn, who was slugging Stoli vodka from a bottle, that it was all over for ever. He tried to tie her to a chair in what was once their bedroom, but she got away. He grabbed her in the living room. His litany of 'bitch, slut, whore' banged about her head. Police are not sure how Madonna freed herself. One officer dismissed a suggestion that Madonna had 'seduced' her way out of trouble, explaining, 'It wasn't that sort of situation.' She called the police on her car phone. Later, at the Malibu Sheriff's office, she appeared with her face awash with tears, her lip cut. But Lieutenant McSweeney remembers that she was, despite her ordeal, very much in control and matter-of-fact about the official complaint she made against Penn. She was, he said, detailed and determined. He said, 'When she turned up at the Malibu office to report what had happened, half of her was dispassionate. The other half was distressed. Her face was streaked with tears. She seemed to be making a business-like decision, which she had made analytically. She seemed to have made up her mind, made her decision. She was in control and it's rare to find anyone who can cope like that in such circumstances. She was clearly distressed and anxious to report what happened.'

The stories surrounding Penn's treatment of Madonna have told of him slapping her about and threatening to cut off her hair. She was even held captive and the police were called. But Lieutenant McSweeney of the Malibu Sheriff's Department, offered this view: 'It was all over by the time we got there. It was a serious matter that if prosecuted would have had great implications. It was fully explained to her what charges she could bring.'

There were no problems with Penn at the house. 'As far as I can recall, he co-operated with the officers,' said Lieutenant McSweeney. The case changed in a few days. 'She seemed to have made another business decision. She seemed to have analysed the whole situation and decided which was the best way to take it.'

Madonna had decided she did not want further humiliation – an ordeal that would be drawn out in court and fanfared by an international media circus if she pressed charges against Penn. To have made them in the first place reveals not how distraught and fearful she was, but how bloody angry she was, the outrage at being so brutally controlled.

The police wanted to take things further. But Madonna resisted their pressure and had a meeting with Los Angeles County's Deputy District Attorney, Lauren Weiss. The details of her assault report were sealed.

'Madonna asked there be no criminal charges pressed. There was no other evidence on which to base a criminal charge so there wasn't one filed,' said Al Albergate, the official mouthpiece for the District Attorney's office. He did not say that behind the scenes there was pressure on Madonna to proceed. She stood by her 'business decision'. On 5 January 1989, in Los Angeles Superior Court, she filed for divorce, citing 'irreconcilable differences'.

Penn, with hindsight, would reflect on the marriage: 'Madonna was a hoot — I just didn't want her living at my house. I was drunk throughout most of my marriage to Madonna. People paid too much attention to nothing.

'You have to understand — hard as it must be in the twenty-first century — that when Madonna and I got together she was an an up-and-coming star. She was not a superstar. She was not an icon. She hadn't even gone on a tour. And that tour, just before we got married, didn't indicate the enormity of what was coming. But soon she became public property and her husband-to-be was treated likewise. I knew a lot of people who were bigger stars who had much more peaceful lives. My understanding of the direction Madonna was taking was a misunderstanding. And the degree to which she would be choosing and chosen for such an intense spotlight was not something I had seen in the cards. So that *was* a surprise. It was a *big* surprise. I started to get the idea very shortly after we were together but by then there's that heart of the thing that gets involved. You don't walk away so easily just because something gets a little difficult. And you don't know how long certain things are going to go on – it might have passed. All that fame could have just neutralised itself. There was a very big difference between Madonna and just about anybody else you can name. I don't think anybody else carries around that Beatles or Elvis Presley-size persona, saturating the world. Sure, that was a surprise. I can only say the marriage ended, I can't say why. It didn't end without both of us, to the best of our abilities, giving it a Scout's try to make it work out. It just didn't work out. I guess we got to a point where we felt comfortable enough with not being together to split. In our eyes, it was just like any other romance. Apart from all the fanfare that existed in the relationship, we didn't have a single tiny problem that hasn't been experienced by millions and millions and millions of people over and over and over again.'

Years on – Penn was 41 in 2001 – he says their marriage did not have a chance. 'No waaayyyy! Under the circumstances of what happened with her? No way. But I wasn't conscious of it going in. Ultimately, we had different value systems. I am not a better expert on her than anybody else, I don't know her better for being with her. I was drunk most of the time.'

The actor-turned-director – in 2001 his film *The Pledge*,starring Jack Nicholson, Harry Dean Stanton, Helen Mirren, Vanessa Redgrave, Mickey Rourke and his wife Robin Wright Penn, was released worldwide – said that

Madonna's 'handlers' had great ideas for her and wanted to ensure Penn was not marrying her for her money. 'I don't want to get into what she wanted specifically. I'll just say it was a bother.'

Penn, who gave up his 4-packs-a-day smoking habit on his 40th birthday (he remains a self-confessed 'big drinker'), says turning 40 was not 'an area of my girlie sensibility … There's that thing – what age do you see yourself as? Always felt more like seventy-six.'

He has two children by Robin Wright; Dylan (after Bob) Frances (she was nine in 2001), and Hopper (after Dennis) Jack (after Nicholson), who was seven in 2001. It says something – and goodness knows what – that he cannot get his kids into *Harry Potter*. He's the one who reads them their stories at the family estate, which he calls a compound near San Francisco in Marin County, California. They moved there shortly after he and Robin Wright were married in 1996. She had been carjacked at gunpoint in the driveway of their Santa Monica home – and their two children were in the back seat.

'I took every bit of money I'd earned in my life and put it all into the house and built a wall around it. I built a compound – I am a parent in a small town.'

Madonna never returned to the Malibu home she had shared with Sean Penn. Friends and staff had retrieved her belongings. She never wanted to be inside the house again. Instead, she found her $2.9 million hideaway in the Hollywood Hills. And within two weeks she and Penn – who had all manner of criminal charges hanging over his head if Madonna wanted to play hardball with him – had agreed on a division of community property. Penn got a good deal because Madonna also paid him $498,000, which was his 'share' of the Manhattan apartment. He got their South-Western and Santa Fe-style Malibu furniture, while she held on to the art-deco and art-nouveau paintings and sculptures. She left behind her gold wedding band, which had been inscribed 'M LOVES S', in her bathroom cabinet.

CHAPTER TWELVE

ALONE ON THE HILL

'I'm really interested in two things in art. One is
suffering and the other is irony and a certain bizarre
sense of humour.'
MADONNA, 2000

Madonna bought her new home from Allen Questrom, the Chief Executive of Neiman Marcus, the Texas-based upmarket and expensive department-store chain. Her neighbours included former *Charlie's Angel* Cheryl Ladd and, down the road, Dolly Parton. But Madonna was alone. She was at the top of the hill – literally. But alone.

She had become one of the most recognisable performers anywhere on Earth, and lived a ten-minute drive from Hollywood's Sunset Strip. There were a couple of tight turns that lead to a narrow street that dead-ends in a cul-de-sac and the electric gates which guarded Madonna's latest dream house. You could not see the contemporary-style building from the street. You identified yourself over the intercom and there was a buzz and the gates swung open. A uniformed guard – they rotated round the clock – sat in a car and watched visitors. There was lots of vegetation. Friends would go in by the garage, around the 1957 Thunderbird and Mercedes 560SL, and into the house through the kitchen and breakfast area. There were plenty of floor-to-ceiling windows facing the pool and the small garden area. From the front, you saw brick wall. And it was also easy to see the attraction of the mix of security and serenity. An elaborate laser security system encircled the property, and if the beam was broken, the alarms blasted immediately; there was no 'waiting time' to allow for mistakes.

This was not the home of a Boy Toy. It was elegant with an eclectic collection of furniture and art placed as much for pleasure as for the effect. Everything had its place. There was not one cluttered closet. The gowns were lined up in order. The black leather jackets all hung together as did the cut-off jeans. The black kidskin gloves were together and the black coats and, of course, black lacy corsets. So were the identical lace-up, wing-tip black boots. The black looks are reserved for the maids who do not clean too well. Madonna's assistants saw that notes were left on the chrome taps in the bathroom for the maid whenever they had not polished sufficiently.

To the left and right of the tiled entrance was a different touch – Madonna's office. Bookshelves were built in and there were her desks and files with phones and fax machines. This was where the chief operating officer of Madonna Incorporated carried out her business. When you stepped through from the office, you were immediately in the main lounge. There was the grand piano and hung on the ceiling was a gold-framed Langlois (originally painted for Versailles) with Hermes' loins dangling down. Above the white-painted fireplace was a 1932 Fernand Léger entitled *Composition*. Across the room from it was that self-portrait by Mexican legend, Frida Kahlo. (Madonna had emerged as a cross-cultural icon, so much so that when the austere *New*

York Times reviewed an exhibition of Mexican art at the New York Metropolitan Museum, they made a point in the first paragraph of saying the work of 'Kahlo, Madonna's favourite artist', was included.) A nude by Kahlo's controversial husband, Diego Rivera, hung on another wall. There was a photograph of boxer Joe Louis by Irving Penn and Man Ray's nude of Kiki de Monparnasse. A Tamara de Lempicka painting was in her bedroom, which was white-painted and spartan. There was no headboard for the bed, which seemed to have simply been pushed up against the wall. There was her mother's photograph and the one of Madonna in her mother's wedding dress.

To get there, you needed to walk through the bathroom/dressing room, which is clean and ordered with an open shower. An 18th-century Italian day bed and matching chairs sat beside her weight-lifting equipment and benches in front of the back-lit glass closets. There was something gladiatorial about the room.

There were pictures throughout the house. Some by her favourite photographer, Herb Ritts, with others by Tina Madotti and Matt Mahurin. She is fascinated by Frida Kahlo, the enigmatic artist and revolutionary, who became a cult figure in the 1980s – with a little help from Madonna, who still wants to make a film of Kahlo's life. In the foyer of her home was a Kahlo painting called *My Life*. It shows Kahlo's mother giving birth. The bed sheets hide her head. What is seen are her open legs and the grown-up Kahlo's head appearing from her mother's vagina.

'If somebody doesn't like this painting, then I know they can't be my friend,' said Madonna, who says her interest in and collecting of art 'is like a disease'.

It was her friend and brother Christopher, who is gay,

who helped her decorate the ten-room house. He said they looked at 24 other properties before making their 'find'.

'I wanted to avoid the overstuffed California look,' he said of his work, but quickly pointed out, 'I refuse to be called a decorator. The house has the feeling of a grand New York penthouse except the view is better and there is a pool. We both love Italian furniture. It's grand without being gaudy like French furniture. Madonna and I were very close although we had become distant for about five years. It was difficult for me to find a niche in her work. We have a certain sibling dependency and we spend a lot of time fighting. Yet, we are each other's best critics.'

But by now, Madonna was careful about who was doing the criticising. She had got out of her marriage and Malibu, and was now in Hollywood and, most importantly, in control. When she was starting out, Dick Clark, America's pre-eminent disc jockey (*American Bandstand*) and film/television producer of shows like the telecast of *The Golden Globe Awards*, had asked her what she wanted to do when she grew up. She shot back, 'Rule the world.'

Well, by now she was at least ruling her world. Stories of her hard-headed, no-nonsense attitude began circulating. Pat Leonard, who had worked on her tours and records, has this thought: 'Madonna had learned that after you've been burned enough times, it's better to be a tyrant than be a wimp and have people walk all over you.'

Madonna Incorporated comprised Boy-Toy for her music business, Slutco for videos and Siren for her films. 'It's a great feeling to be powerful. I've been striving for it all my life. I think that's just the quest of every human being – power.'

But in Hollywood, power has all sorts of definitions. She was going to be in *Godfather III*; she wasn't. She was going to play in David Lynch's *Wild at Heart*; she didn't. She was going to reprise the Marlene Dietrich role in *Blue Angel*; she hasn't, but the project is not forgotten. Dietrich has said she would like Madonna to play her in any biographical film. And *Evita* was always, always in her sights. She threw Oliver Stone off track when she suggested she should write some new *Evita* songs with Andrew Lloyd-Webber. She maintained she was never given enough guidance of the Stone–Robert Stigwood–Lloyd-Webber project at the early discussions stage. And when the negative word about Streep circulated, Madonna simply shrugged that it had had nothing to do with her.

Jeffrey Katzenberg, now the partner of Steven Spielberg and entertainment mogul David Geffen in DreamWorks, was then chairman of Walt Disney Studios and remains one of the shrewdest thinkers in Hollywood. This is a man interested in the bottom line. Period. He does not pander to stars. He would rather make movies with animals who do not talk back and do not bark on about how many millions they are worth. A pragmatic man. And a Madonna fan. 'She has a very secure sense of her life and her business. As far as I can tell, she's always had a vision of exactly who she is – whether as an actress or a performer, or as a lyricist or a music producer, or as a businesswoman. And she's also had a strong enough sense of it to balance it all. She's always evolving. She never stands still. Every two years she comes up with a new way of presenting herself, and new attitude, a new act, a new design. And every time, it's successful. There is a constant genesis. When something like this happens once, OK, maybe it's luck. Twice is coincidence. Three times is just remarkable talent. A kind of genius. And Madonna's on her fifth or sixth time.'

Madonna's financial adviser, Robert Nichols, was putting her money into real estate and 'ultra safe' investments on which his client/boss insisted. Stephanie Stephens and others were involved in movie deals at Columbia. There were plans for records and tours. The performer who had rewritten the entertainment rules of the 1980s was chasing towards the next decade – with one of the largest media campaigns ever orchestrated. Madonna signed a $5 million deal with Pepsi-Cola, which gave her more than double that amount of money in free publicity. Manager Freddy DeMann thought it a smart move: 'The reason why I wanted to do it was because her base audience was so much broader than what record companies generally approach. No record company can spend the kind of money Pepsi was prepared to spend.' What DeMann did not expect was the tempest in the cola bottle.

On 1 March 1989, Pepsi, from their headquarters in Somers, New York, sent out word that the next day the biggest coup in advertising history was going to happen. More than 250 million people in 40 countries were going to have the delight of hearing Madonna's title song for her unreleased *Like a Prayer*. The song, entitled 'Make a Wish', was the centrepiece of a video showing her on a trip down memory lane. As she went back to her childhood, the pleasure of Pepsi would be highlighted. It was a first in many ways, but shrewd Madonna was most aware of one thing – the video going worldwide did not just showcase the soft drink but gave her unprecedented publicity.

Todd Mackenzie was the official spokesman for the Pepsi-Cola Company and he was not lost for hyperbole. 'The ad will air around the globe, all across Europe and the Philippines, Thailand, Japan, in South America as well as

North America. Just about every TV set on planet Earth will have that commercial on it.'

Oh, yes. As Freddy DeMann said when he was asked why he was pushing Madonna so hard, 'You can't take anything for granted.' Especially not Madonna. Her records were selling more than one million copies a week, but you don't just pump out more of the same, do you? Pepsi was riding on Madonna's popularity – it cost them another $5 million to put the commercial on television – but she also had her video of 'Like a Prayer'. In it, she cavorts in a black slip, wriggles between burning crosses, kisses a black saint and shows stigmata – the imagery is provocative and irreverent. But is it blasphemous? It was a wonderful mix – Madonna, sex and religion – and stirred up the hurricane of headlines with which Pepsi got splashed. It was a video certain to outrage those who feel comfortable brandishing picket signs, and who instinctively phone in protests, which may, of course, have been the idea from the start.

In the video, Madonna enters an empty church where she is drawn to a statue of a young black man robed in white – behind bars. She lies down on a pew and is apparently overcome by a vision, while the statue comes to life. In this vision, the scenario of a recent crime is unveiled. A group of white thugs attacks and stabs a white woman, but a black man who comes to her aid is arrested. Madonna is then awakened from her vision by a raucous black choir marching through the church. She goes to the local jail, where she vouches for the jailed man's innocence before the police, standing at the sergeant's desk wearing only a bra and a slip. Madonna sings in front of a field of burning crosses. Madonna handles the murder weapon, a knife, and suddenly is supernaturally afflicted with bleeding nail wounds in her palms. Madonna does an uninhibited, giddy little dance with a gospel troupe, and at one point gets down on her knees while a choir member puts a hand on Madonna's forehead, faith-healer style. Rather than fall backwards from the healing touch, Madonna appears as if she might be about to fall out of her bra.

The video began running on MTV the day after the Pepsi commercial appeared on America's NBC TV. The picket signs went up. The phones rang – especially at Pepsico, makers of the soft drink and owners of fast-food chains like Kentucky Fried Chicken. Roman Catholic Bishop Rene Gracids of Texas and the American Family Association called the video offensive. They called for a Pepsi and Pepsico product boycott. Madonna went pop. Pepsi yanked the commercial off the air. The Pepsi commercial was the first time Madonna had agreed to tout or shrill a product. Michael Jackson, Paula Abdul and Bill Cosby could go their corporate way, but not Madonna. She feared it might compromise her artistic integrity, detract from her seriousness. But she did Pepsi. Why? She made the rules. She was not viewed drinking the stuff. The closest she got was to be seen twice holding a can of Pepsi. It was a disaster for Pepsi, but Madonna got her money and virtually unlimited publicity. And did the people she offended buy records anyway?

So, did Madonna indulge in a corporate ambush? Robert Mosconi was then the senior creative director at BBDO Worldwide Advertising. He worked closely with Madonna on the commercial and remembers, 'One day, Madonna, who liked to joke with me, came up and said, "Hey, Robert, are you going to have the burning cross reflecting in the Pepsi can?" And I said, "What burning cross?" And she smiled and said, "You'll see." '

While she was being the hard-headed businesswoman, the supposed 'tyrant', it ironically turned out that *Like a Prayer* was Madonna's most personal work. Critics called it 'honest'. It was certainly effective. In 'Keeping It Together', she sings, 'I hit the big time but I still get the blues.' In 'Till Death Do Us Part', she recalls marriage: 'The bruises they will fade away/You hit so hard with the things you say/He takes a drink she goes inside/He starts to scream, the vases fly/He wishes that she wouldn't cry/He's not in love with her any more.'

On 'Promise to Try', a little girl, 'her face frozen in time', is comforted by her mother. 'Oh Father' is the freedom from a strict father: 'Maybe someday when I look back I'll be able to say you didn't mean to be cruel/Somebody hurt you too.' And there was the up-tempo 'Express Yourself', which was to become her 17th music video. It was a single finger aimed at the good taste brigade who had originally jumped up on 'Like a Prayer'. It was called a carnal mini-movie all about making love, not money. She was dressed in black stockings, suspenders and a corset, and rolling her stomach, grabbing her crotch and she was seen chained to a bed lapping at a saucer of milk. It was, she would admit, a grand fuck-you to those who had tried to control her.

Madonna was then as much a magnet for controversy as she remains in the 21st century. Then, as now, she not only sold music but also huge amounts of the newspapers and magazines all the other media that trailed her rainbow, everyone wanting to duck into the pot of gold she creates. So you wonder at the attitude of then pop queen Debbie Gibson, who piped up saying she was concerned about how ten-year-olds would react to the latest video. Madonna herself stuck it to LaToya Jackson, saying a *Playboy* layout done by Michael's sister was a sign of 'desperation' and bitching, 'She must have had a major breast job done.' It was even more fun for Madonna when LaToya answered back, 'Madonna is not a lady, never has been and never will be.' Her breasts? 'If I'd had them done, they'd have looked a lot better than they did in *Playboy*.'

At the top of the hill, it was fun, if a little lonely. Madonna was linked to many men, but there were none. The only regular overnighter was her brother Christopher of whom she says, 'Christopher's gay, and he and I have always been the closet members of my family. It's funny. When he was really young, he was so beautiful and had girls all over him, more than any of my other brothers. I knew something was different, but it was not clear to me. He was like a girl magnet. They all seemed incredibly fond of him and close to him in a way I hadn't seen men with women. I'll tell you when I knew. After I met Christopher [Flynn], I brought my brother to my ballet class because he wanted to start studying dance. I just saw something between them. I can't even tell you exactly what. But then I thought, Oh, I get it. Oh, OK. He likes men too. It was an incredible revelation, but I didn't say anything to my brother yet. I'm not even sure he knew. He's two years younger than me. He was still a baby. I could just feel something. My father's very old fashioned, traditional, grew up in that macho Italian world. I know he's probably not comfortable with it. He doesn't treat my brother any differently than all of us, but I know that there's an unspoken thing where Christopher doesn't feel like he's accepted by my father. All of my other brothers and sisters certainly accept it. God knows what my father accepts in life, you know what I mean? My father is a very silent man. He keeps a lot inside.'

The only others staying were business people sleeping in the spare room. Madonna paid for the best help. She was by then America's biggest-earning female performer; her income was more uplifting than even the most notorious of her black bras. Since 1986 – and if she is coy about any figures it is her financial ones – she has earned around $197 million ... before tax. She was the boss, the president of a corporation that employed hundreds ('I keep Warner Brothers in work!') and going nowhere but into more profit. For the Time Warner Corporation, she had sold more than half a billion dollars' worth of records – as well as the hundreds of millions more for those involved in the concerts and videos and all manner of other spin-offs.

And she was involved in every detail. Her lawyers and accountants were there to advise her, to tell her what to do. In return, they did well. Freddy DeMann, as her personal manager, made 10 per cent of her earnings; her lawyer, Paul Schindler of Grubman, Indursky and Schindler of New York, was regarded as a top professional and got 5 per cent, as did business manager Bert Pedall. But there were contract clauses, which kept these advisers within the $1m–$2m-a-year range – each. A tour manager gets 10 per cent of the box-office and it could, in fact, have cost her money to tour given her elaborate productions and narrow profit margin.

Madonna knew for a long time that the way to make money in Hollywood was the movies. But only the right movies. David Geffen who, as well as Spielberg and Katzenberg's DreamWorks partner, is one of America's wealthiest men from his record-production companies, real estate and other investments, has been a long-time friend and adviser to Madonna. They have both been active in AIDS charities, but in more than grandstand fundraising.

Homosexuals were Madonna's first fans and she has never deserted them. Her *Bloodhounds of Broadway* director, Howard Brookner, was desperately ill in St Vincent's Hospital in New York where Madonna would make regular visits. Brookner's friend, Brad Gooch, recalls, 'She was incredibly supportive – she not only visited him, but all the other patients in the AIDS ward. It was like Judy Garland visiting another sort of Oz.'

Madonna wanted the Hollywood end of the rainbow. It was David Geffen who sent Madonna to a psychiatrist to deal with her emotions over her mother's death and her father's remarriage. He also sent her to Warren Beatty. He told her to call the legendary Hollywood bed-hopper, the man who could make her a movie star just like Marilyn. Beatty was limping away from the financial and critical flop *Ishtar*, and working on a long-time project for a big-screen workout as *Dick Tracy*.

Madonna secured her role as Breathless Mahoney. And many prattled on about how she was working for actors' scale – the minimum wage – $1,440 a week. What was not revealed was Madonna's privileged Hollywood history, especially at Jeffrey Katzenberg's frugal Disney Studios. She would, in return for her services, receive 'points', a good share of all gross box-office takings – and video and merchandising sales. A casual estimate would put that at around $7 million, more than Meryl Streep makes for three movies. And, of course, there would be the $14 million from the *Dick Tracy* soundtrack album. And the Blonde Ambition Tour – America's Home Box Office cable-television station paid $1 million for one screening – as well as the other spin-offs. Madonna has an excellent sense of sell. But how was she going to cope with get-your-pants-down-as-fast-as-possible Mr Warren Beatty?

CHAPTER THIRTEEN

BUMP AND GRIND

'Probably 75 per cent of the American population have had Warren Beatty.'

MADONNA, 1990

She called him 'Old Man'. He called her 'Buzzbomb'. Everyone else called them the Odd Couple. Beatty was a challenge to Madonna. They made love on their second 'date'. But she also saw him as a serious prospect for happiness. He had a history. He would not be intimidated. He was cool. He was also 52 when they started to work on *Dick Tracy*. Beatty, the first male sex symbol of the 1960s, had been toying with the idea of the film since 1975 and the days of Julie Christie and *Shampoo*. After an early meeting with Madonna about her playing Breathless Mahoney, the couple and five others involved in the film went for lunch at the Columbia Bar and Grill, a Tinseltown hangout at the corner of Sunset Boulevard and Gower. South on Gower is the 'technical' side of Hollywood, the sound studios and the editing rooms. It is where Beatty is happiest. Inside the Columbia, the Beatty table talked over Perrier and salads with lemon-juice dressing. It was time to go. Beatty asked if he could open an account and the young waitress asked, 'Who are you?'

Madonna said, 'See, Old Man,' and paid for lunch. It was a lesson in the demographics of youth and quickly learned.

'I'd seen Madonna as a very good possibility for the movie early on,' Beatty told me as we talked at his work studio on Gower. But he explained, 'She was not cast when we were working on the script, but it's peculiar – you write a character and then you cast a character and wonder how anyone else could have possibly played it. And you could have been turned down by fifteen people.'

You can understand Beatty's instant attraction for Madonna, and it has got nothing to do with bed. It is to do with work, with Hollywood, with his movies. Beatty can drop names as well as his pants. Madonna – the impatient, anxious-to-learn Madonna – wanted to hear everything. We were talking about him casting Madonna as Breathless and it brought on other thoughts.

'When I first met Faye Dunaway, I was very impressed with her. I thought she was going to be a very important actress, but I didn't think she was right for Bonnie. I introduced her to Arthur (Penn) who was directing, and he immediately saw her in the part. Eventually, I could. Can you imagine anyone but Michael J Pollard playing CW?

'What about Jack Warden in *Shampoo* or *Heaven Can Wait*. Listen, I'll tell you a story. We'd gone to about seven people who turned us down and finally we went to Jack. Jack said "Yes". About three weeks before we started shooting, he came to me and said he'd found a picture that he'd rather do. He said, "Of course, I'm going to keep my word to you. I said I'll be in this and I'll be in it. I just want to appeal to you as a fellow actor, but keep in mind if you say 'No', the answer is 'No', and that's fine. I'd like to ask you – can I do the other picture?'

'I said, "No."

'He said, "What do you mean, no?"

'I told him he was going to be very funny in the picture and he did it and he was. We laugh a lot about it now. It wouldn't have been *Shampoo* without him, or *Heaven*. I would have preferred not to have directed *Tracy*. I always prefer not to direct, but usually I go to a lot of people, and a lot of people turn me down. I didn't ask anybody else to direct *Reds* because I felt there could be a problem of vision.

'When I originally developed *Heaven Can Wait*, I wanted Muhammad Ali to be the boxer, but he couldn't fit it into his schedule. I cast myself, but I couldn't see myself as a boxer, but I had been a footballer as a kid, so I changed it. I only decided at the last minute to direct it. I had asked Mike [Nichols] and Arthur [Penn], but they were busy.'

He also bought in Buck Henry to co-star and to co-direct *Heaven Can Wait*.

In *Dick Tracy*, he got Michael J Pollard (as Bugs) and Estelle Parsons (as Tess Trueheart's mother) from *Bonnie and Clyde* and, when asked, he considered the question of friendship: 'When you've known someone for a long time you begin to see colours and facets in their personality that you just don't see in other people because you don't know them as well. So, when you're writing, you think of them. Michael J I've known for more than thirty years. We did a play together when we were kids. I don't know if it necessarily makes me feel more comfortable. I enjoy it a lot. I see people that I've known for ever. It's just that you fantasise about someone doing something and then they kind of do it. They see what you thought. If there's a problem, you go to someone. That's very much so. Jack [Nicholson], Dustin [Hoffman], Al [Pacino], Diane [Keaton]

– these are people whose opinions I value very, very, very highly. They have tremendously fresh insights on something. When you've been editing and seen so much the whole subject becomes goofy. You get someone to come in and sometimes they can help restore your original intentions. They get you to where you were at the beginning.'

Madonna was quick to learn about profound inside knowledge from Beatty who explained, 'When you know someone a long time, you know their points of orientation. If someone has a very strong social conscience for instance, Julie Christie comes to mind – I would know that showing a piece of work to Julie Christie would be a very strong consideration. That often happens on a set when you direct. Sometimes I think that when an actor directs, he is not really directing, he is just pretending to direct – what he is really doing is listening to the opinions and sensing the opinions of people around him whom he knows and respects as he does his audience. It's very difficult to be your own audience.'

Beatty pauses for a long time and then adds, 'In fact, it's impossible. I think I try to make the type of movie I want to make and I think that I credit the audience with being at least as sophisticated as I am. Frankly, I worry more about the people who are more sophisticated. Audiences are very hip and brutally honest about things. They're not really worried about your feelings.'

Beatty is tall and so are many of the stories about him, and that is easy to understand. He is a parcel of vanity and vulnerability, a sort of paranoid Peter Pan. Which is why when you meet him, the mind turns into a flickering film of beautiful images – a gallery of faces from a celebrity concubine revolving for more than 30 years. Madonna was one – but not the last – of the faces of the 1990s before Beatty settled down to marriage and kids with actress Annette Bening. If Garbo talked, well, we all know what Betty did. And by all accounts, rather well. He is also rather good on the telephone, which is his other famous appendage. We all remember Joan Collins on that one: 'Three, four, five times a day was not unusual for him, and he was able to accept phone calls at the same time.'

It is a dusty quote and when Madonna was asked on television if she was jealous of Collins, she replied, 'Have you seen her lately?'

'Is Warren satiable?' was the next question.

Eyebrow raised, she replied, 'He's satiable,' no doubt remembering their first encounter, which she found less than satisfying.

Beatty's other passion in life is making movies. He has not made many, but most have been memorable. He was the star, the producer and director of *Dick Tracy*, which cost more than $30 million. It was the teaming of a tightly-run corporation and an indulgent, and usually indulged, film-maker. The result was Beatty's first box-office success in a decade and probably his biggest ever. The film – quite literally a comic strip brought to life in primary colours – was a huge enjoyment.

Beatty has been involved on and off with the project for years. When I went to meet him he sort of slouched around the editing room looking more like a university don than a Don Juan. He is 6ft 2in with curly, slightly thinning hair which he vigorously scratched, and you could see the pitter patter of crow's feet around those bedroom eyes. At one point, he took off his Oliver People's glasses and rubbed them. He had a full cup of coffee in his hand and swirled it around. For the next two hours, he would never drink from the cup. It was his prop.

'Am I a perfectionist? The positive way of saying it is that you are a professionalist. The negative way is to say you're an obsessive. The humorous way is to say you are anal retentive.'

Jeffery Katzenberg says he had more late nights during the production of *Dick Tracy* than in his entire life because of Warren Beatty.

'I've spent more time on the phone than I ever thought possible. It used to be that my phone conversations lasted ten minutes, but now they can go on for hours. Warren requires an enormous amount of time and support and input. He is totally collaborative. I have never ever been asked so many questions by a film-maker. I don't want to make this sound self-important. Warren asked me a thousand questions a day, but I believe he also asked another thousand people those same questions.'

The *Dick Tracy* deal took a lot of doing. The ghosts of the $40 million bomb, *Ishtar*, and the critical, but not commercial, success of the $35 million *Reds* hovered around the negotiating table. Katzenberg revealed the background to what was to be Madonna's breakthrough movie.

'We created a situation for Warren in which he was enormously rewarded for remaining disciplined to his own concept of how he was going to make the movie. I've got to give him a hundred and one per cent credit. The corridors were there, but the fact is he didn't bump against the walls very often. We must have spent two years negotiating this deal with Warren. Warren is at his best at ten, eleven at night when I'm at my worst. I think Warren wanted to prove to himself that he could take the responsibility and bring the movie in for a price.'

And what Disney got was Beatty's vision of the Chester Gould comic strip, which began life in the *Detroit Mirror* in 1931. By the 1950s, *Dick Tracy* had 65 million readers in 550 newspapers nationwide. Gould created a rogue's gallery of wonderful villains and several of them came to life through the wizardry of prosthetics. There was the story that Beatty had offered then President Reagan the role of Pruneface. True? Beatty laughs. 'No – but I'd have grabbed him if I could. I would have been very happy to get him.'

He did get Madonna, whose 1990 album, *Madonna: I'm Breathless*, as well as two other spin-offs, were 'inspired' by the film. The records were part of the behemoth marketing juggernauts, which Disney hoped would roar on and on. (Merchandising from *Dick Tracy* handcuffs, key rings and fingerprint sets to vinyl dolls of Breathless and Tracy, and coffee mugs on wheels were wrongly predicted to rival 1989's Batmania.)

Beatty was the man who got up every morning and looked in the bathroom mirror and said, '*I'm* with Madonna.' They were as likely a couple as the sexy Bonnie and the sexually confused Clyde. Or the self-important McCabe and manipulative Mrs Miller. But Beatty was smitten. Madonna joined a long breakfast list that includes Joan Collins, Natalie Wood, Leslie Caron, Michelle Phillips, Isabelle Adjani, Julie Christie. Long list? Beatty smiles and says, 'I never talk about anything to do with personal relationships in my life. I never have. I don't ever intend to. If you ever see me quoted on the subject, you'll know that someone else was making it up. These are important people to me. I don't want to hurt them by discussing them in public. As for my love life, I can't control what other people say about it; it is what it is. I know that movie actors are over-rewarded in our society and that the press has to cut people like me down to size. So they come up with all sorts of wild things. They make me into an insane, eccentric man with an incredible fear of losing my youth who lives in a bomb shelter, who contemplated or who is going through plastic surgery, who has devastating relationships with women. It goes through cycles. First, they say that woman like me too much; then women don't like me at all; then they like me too much again. Somewhere along the way they say I secretly like men – but then the men don't like me! I'm old. I'm young. I'm intelligent. I'm stupid. My tide goes in and out.'

Madonna has now become what Beatty was in his heyday – an object of overwhelming fascination. What makes such icons tick? Is all the attention water off a superstar's back?

'I'd like to say you develop an immunity to it, but I'm afraid it's more like an allergy. The only defence that you have is not to co-operate. The problem is that, by not co-operating, you give freedom to the media to invent an unlimited amount of crap because they will do it. I have decided it's best probably not to be so circumspect about it. We had a very reactionary Southern Senator who went to the Supreme Court and became a brilliant, articulate Justice. His point of view on free speech was that all libel laws should be eliminated. There should be no recourse. At least the public would know that there is nothing you can do. The problem now is that you have to prove malicious intent and all kinds of nonsense that enables the public to think the things are fifty- per cent true. But if you're a person who believes in free speech, let alone a person who doesn't want to spend their whole life and fortune fighting some sort of legal battle about what is said in the media, you ignore it.'

He was not married at the time of *Dick Tracy* but knew

what he wanted in his future. Madonna was simply not the woman to provide it for him. He talked his way around that subject by returning to the character of *Dick Tracy*: 'He has primary emotions, a man who would really like to have the joys of family but is pulled by duty and doesn't know whether he can live up to the obligations of a family. He's tempted. Me? I wouldn't mind being married. I'd like to have children.'

So, of course, did Madonna. But there was little hope with Beatty who was born in Richmond, Virginia, where he and his sister, Shirley MacLaine, were brought up by their headmaster father.

'I am close to my family,' he says. 'My father died in 1988 and I talk to my mother every day or couple of days. And my sister and I communicate. We get along very well.'

He's not too forthcoming about his sister's reincarnation ideas: 'I did make a film about it [*Heaven Can Wait*]. It makes me think of the time when my father was dying. I remember him sitting on the side of the bed, his feet were kind of dangling, and he said to me, "Warren, what do you think about these ideas of Shirley's?" I said, "I just don't know what to think of them." He said, "I just don't think I want to do what I have to do to find out." '

Beatty's father had him reading by the age of four, but as a teenager he gave up the books. He was president of his class, captain of the high-school football team (something he remains proud of) but, after a year at university, moved to New York to study acting. He did not want to be 'in anybody else's shadow' – his sister, who is three years older, had by then established herself.

'I wanted to be a stage director – that was legitimate. I wanted to write for the theatre. I sort of backed into acting as a way of learning the theatre.' In late-1950s New York, he worked on stage and on some live television shows. He auditioned for director Josh Logan with another film novice, Jane Fonda. Nothing happened. Three months later, MGM gave him a five-year contract at $400 a week. At 22, he was in Hollywood. He was also quick to catch on. He did not like the look of the studio system, so he borrowed the money to pay off his contract and went back to New York.

There, he managed to win a supporting role in William Inge's play *A Loss of Roses*. The show flopped – Beatty sailed on. Director Elia Kazan saw him on stage and cast him opposite Natalie Wood in *Spendor in the Grass*. Before the film that was to make him an instant sensation even opened, he was a 'star' – in the gossip columns. His public affair with Natalie Wood broke up her marriage to Robert Wagner (they later married again) and Peter Hall would later name him in his divorce from Leslie Caron. And that is the image we have had ever since – the lover boy, the Casanova, the Lothario who cannot keep his hands off women even when they are entangled with someone else.

Lee Grant is a veteran of Hollywood and appeared in Beatty's *Shampoo*. She says, 'Warren's conquests of women are not totally successful. His percentage is about fifty–fifty. Those whom he can't conquer don't want to be part of a crowd – one of Warren's girls. But the Peter Pan quality in Warren is very attractive to some. He teaches them to fly and they have extraordinary experiences with him. They grow up and go on and he keeps flying. Like Peter Pan, he always comes back to another little girl who's ready to fly off with him to Never-Never Land.'

Madonna? Maybe she can also be in his sequel to *Shampoo*. 'I've never done a sequel. The idea has never appealed to me. But I'm sort of interested in doing a sequel to *Shampoo*. It's a real good cast.' Such a project would revive his randy Beverly Hills hairdresser, George, who cavorted with Julie Christie and Goldie Hawn and Carrie Fisher to the backdrop of the 1960 election of Richard Nixon as President. But given today's sexual climate, would the coupling-addicted George still be around today? Beatty gave his warmest smile: 'Oh, I think he would be. If you're saying he was high risk, he's not reality. Oh, I think George would still be with us.'

The satirical sexual comedy was much discussed in the 1970s. What did this mean? Or that? It became a topic and, in some quarters, an intellectual platform. Beatty explains his motives for the film by saying, 'I wanted to explore sexuality through a Don Juan. A Don Juan doesn't get that way out of a misogynist feeling or the idea that he's a latent homosexual who's seducing all these women because he really wants to seduce men, or out of impotence or the desire to degrade women. He just wants to fuck because he likes to fuck.'

Would an older George have settled down, with a younger woman, for example? Madonna saw life in that scenario. She quickly fell under the Beatty spell. He was the Hollywood charmer and he appeared to her like a mentor, a father-figure but a cool, well-connected man who could make the deals, make the movies. He was her indulgent tutor on the movie set and in bed. But, of course, there were all the women before her. And for all her confidence, it bothered her. Could she ever be as wonderful as Bardot at age 25? Or the late Natalie Wood? Then, with her trademark positive thinking, she would tell herself she was better than any of them. Beatty was protective of her and certainly not easily shocked. He could teach her.

'Warren understands the bullshit. He's been an icon for years. He's had a lot more practice at it than I have. Obviously somebody who hasn't experienced it would be more threatened by my fame than he is. You can't understand being hugely famous until it happens and then it's too late to decide if you want it or not. Warren's been a sex symbol for so long, he's just not surprised by anything.'

Not by Madonna. Beatty lobbed back, 'I don't know that there are many people who can do as many things as Madonna. People who are in a positive frame of mind, who bring as much energy and willingness to work as Madonna does. She has in this respect a real healthy humility about the cinema. I think this is a prime requisite to be able to function in cinema – or, actually, in art. I think she's courageous in the areas she explores artistically. I think that's what she wants to explore. I think her generous spirit would be the thing I think informs her work the most. As she goes on, she will gain the artistic respect that she already deserves. She has an unlimited future as an actress.'

Beatty, true to his word, would not talk about the romantic relationship. Madonna talked about their situation. 'Sometimes I'm cynical and pragmatic and think it will last as long as it lasts. Then I have moments when I'm really romantic and I think, We're *just perfect* together.'

Of course, she should have remained pragmatic and although it is difficult to imagine Madonna as the victim in a relationship, she was about to become one – for the second time. After the divorce from Penn, she had felt a sadness which – like a good Catholic girl – she still feels today. However, she felt it was like dealing with a death.

Dick Tracy – or Dead-Eyed Dick, as the character and Beatty were known on the film set – was much more fun than her previous film encounters. Madonna was also involved in the music by Stephen Sondheim, the man regarded as the genius of modern musical theatre. The challenge for Madonna was to get the songs over without sounding like Eliza Doolittle. Sondheim remembered her impatience: 'She hates to make a lot of choices. For us, she did two and sometimes she had to be persuaded to do three takes. It was her dancing that convinced me. I was really knocked out the moment she started to move – that's when you immediately know why she's a star.'

Madonna was not sure she could do justice to Sondheim's songs. Everyone else – including Sondheim – was. As buttery haired femme fatale, Breathless Mahoney, she delivered. She was concerned – having been unsettled by the lack of success of *Shanghai Surprise, Who's That Girl?* and *Bloodhounds of Broadway* – that she should pull off the role. She had also turned down *The Fabulous Baker Boys*, which won Michelle Pfeiffer an Oscar nomination for her sizzling performance opposite the talented brothers Jeff and Beau Bridges. How did she like that film? 'I hated it. It was too mushy. Such a Wonderbread cast. I think of all these people as being Californian people – blonde and boring.' She had also again refused Oliver Stone's *Evita* test.

'The movies? I'm going to keep trying. *Dick Tracy* will help me a lot. Warren says I'm great in it and I don't think he lies about stuff like that. He's really helpful reading scripts. He has an infinite knowledge about what makes a good movie, a good director. He's a sounding board for me. He's critical and that's good. Warren should have been a psychiatrist or a district attorney. When he wants to know somebody, he goes out of his way to investigate. You feel like you are under the microscope. You're not used to people spending that much time trying to get to know you. But it's admirable. Everybody ought to examine the people they're going to work for as intensely as he does. I've been drawn to so many different kinds of men, I couldn't say if I've got a type. Let's say I'm attracted to men who are in touch with their sexuality – who are aware of it and who *work* it. And I prefer men who can acknowledge their feminine side. I think I have a lot of masculinity in me. Macho guys don't really go for me – certainly not when they get to know me. They're frightened of their femininity. You imbue men with the characteristics you want them to have. Then they're not what you expect at all. But it's your own fault for not doing your homework, the investigating, the finding out. I'm more cautious now, but I'm still a hopeless romantic.'

The filming and loving days with Beatty were fun. They were in restaurants all over Los Angeles. Once on a trip to New York they were heading out to Kennedy Airport and the 6.30pm flight to California when she leaned over and whispered, 'Let's go to Paris.' The limousine driver told me Beatty did not blink, and simply picked up the car phone and made reservations. Romantically indulgent away from the film set, the actor-director was still the boss. And a perfectionist. Take after take after take.

Al Pacino won a deserved Oscar nomination for his turn as loony bad-guy Big Boy Caprice, who is after Dick Tracy. In one sensational sequence, he shows his chorus line, including Madonna, how to strut their stuff. Madonna remembers too well co-starring with one perfectionist in front of the camera and being directed by another behind it.

'As Big Boy, he was always smacking my butt and my face. I hated him. I loathed him. He'd tell me the dirtiest jokes, suck on his cigar like it was some sort of weird phallic symbol and just be a pig. So off-camera, I'd always move away from him but he'd always grab me and go, "Get over here." This is exactly what happens in the movie – he made me cry sometimes. There was a scene where Al kept smacking me in the stomach. It would sting and what made me cry was not so much the hit, but that Warren wouldn't shout, "Cut". Al just kept going and I was humiliated. And, of course, that was what they intended – they wanted me to show the right emotion as Breathless.'

Madonna plotted revenge on Pacino, who was shy with her when they were not filming. As they rehearsed the big dance scene in which she wore a fur coat, she suddenly dropped the fake fur to the floor revealing she was naked. Pacino blushed. He didn't know where to look and only got the joke when Madonna's co-prankster Beatty burst into laughter. In another scene, Madonna walks into a room, takes off her jacket and runs her hands down her sides. It took a number of takes. Perfectionist? Anal retentive?

Away from work, they were at the Catch One disco, a predominantly black gay club where a scene from the film *Beaches* was shot. Or eating at the Columbia Grill or the Great Greek and on to the funky Club Louis.

'They were at all the parties,' remembers Lonny Roland, a Club Louis regular. They were also at Adriano's just of Mulholland up in the hills or at the popular Citrus restaurant on Hollywood's ever-so-trendy Melrose Avenue. At most places, Madonna would finally find her way on to Beatty's lap.

Madonna and Sandra Bernhard remained great friends. They still had their 'gang'. As Penn was a member of the Brat Pack, the girls called themselves the 'Snatch Batch'. If she wasn't with Beatty, she was with the 'Batch'.

On *The David Letterman Show*, as a joke Bernhard confessed to having slept with both Sean and Madonna. And Madonna said the two of them hung out in a Greenwich Village lesbian bar known as the Cubby Hole.

'I've never been to the Cubby Hole. That's the joke of it. My brother Christopher lived around the corner and I've walked by it with him and I'd sort of go, "Oh, yeah, look, there's a lesbian club." Sandra and I were just "fucking" with people. But then when I realised the reaction we had gotten, I, of course, couldn't leave that alone. So Sandra and I decided to tease everybody. Then, of course, it got out of hand and I didn't want to do it any more, because it was more important for me to have a friendship. But we had our fun with that and it sort of worked itself to death.'

What about, say, her supposed relationship with Jennifer Grey? 'That came out of me and Sandra Bernhard. Then it became a question of whatever female I had a close relationship with who is an outspoken girl – which Jennifer is – then I must be sleeping with her.'

A waitress at Odeon, a restaurant in New York, remembers a night when Madonna and Jennifer and five other women came in for a late-night supper. 'Madonna ordered a house salad and everybody else ordered a house salad. She said she didn't want dressing on it – or cheese. The others – except for Jennifer Grey who was bold enough to order cheese – said they didn't want them either. When the salads came, Madonna ate hers with her fingers; all the others ate with their fingers, too. Weird. And she kept looking at me. Maybe she just liked my outfit, but she was so obvious about it. Like it was a dare. Or *something*.'

The hopes or fantasies or both of a New York waitress were far from Madonna's thoughts. She and Beatty were on the rounds. She celebrated her 31st birthday with him at actor Mickey Rourke's Rubber Club. She was also working and creating. Her Siren Films was making plans to film Frida Kahlo's life story – doing for the Mexican artist what Beatty had done for radical writer John Reid in his Oscar-winning film, *Reds*. Then there were the songs for *Madonna: I'm Breathless*. Sondheim penned his three but Madonna believed hers were 'the real shit'. They included 'Hanky Panky', which tells of the pleasures of being bound and spanked on the bottom.

Madonna got the Bad Taste Attention Award again and rubbed it in by going on the Arsenio Hall talk show to say how much she likes to receive an erotic spanking. Taste? There was also the song 'Now I'm Following You', which had the line, 'Dick ... that's an interesting name/My bottom hurts just thinking about you.' It was Stephen Sondheim who collected the Best Original Song Oscar for his 'Sooner or Later (I Always Get My Man)', which, remember, was provocatively performed by Madonna at the 1991 Academy Awards at the Shrine Auditorium in Los Angeles.

But the Oscars were still just a possibility when Beatty and Madonna slipped – 40 minutes late, which is early for Beatty – into a Hollywood screening room to see a rough-cut of Sandra Bernhard's film, *Without You I'm Nothing*. In the film of her stage performance, Bernhard imagines a sex session with Beatty and tells him to put on two condoms: 'Oh, baby, it's no reflection on how much I care about you. We all know you've been around.' Beatty and Madonna, in his lap, laughed together.

Madonna was also thinking about another man – Freddy DeMann. It was his 50th birthday in 1990 and she arranged for a lavish party for the man who had great entertainment-business plans for them. The invitations folded out like a movie invitation and announced the Madonna and Candy DeMann Production of Freddy's 18,250th day on the planet. Madonna's name was in larger type than Candy DeMann's.

Also in 1990, *Dick Tracy* was being filmed. Costume designer Milena Canonero wanted Madonna's Breathless to represent the night, the moon and sex. He put her into midnight–blue, silver and black. And that was *tight* midnight–blue, silver and black dresses. They flashily displayed Madonna's every exercised curve – one dress was cut so low, her breasts spilled out of it during rehearsals. Watching, Beatty smiled and said, 'She's dressed in every way that accentuates her good health...' – which she was very much in. And needed to be in. Madonna suggested she could promote *Dick Tracy* with a tour, which was to become the Blonde Ambition Tour.

'Disney didn't come to me and ask me to market the movie. Let's just say I was killing twelve birds with one stone. It's a two–way street ... most people didn't associate me with movies, but I knew I had a much bigger following than Warren. A lot of my audience wasn't aware of who he was.'

Madonna, not backward in coming forward, whom David Geffen called the 'superstar sex goddess of the video generation', was about to jump into action, and get emotionally hurt again.

CHAPTER FOURTEEN

MADONNA RULES

'Sex is only dirty when you don't take a bath.'

MADONNA, 1987

As the 1990s roared in, Madonna Incorporated was a smooth-running machine, just like the boss of the company. She surrounded herself with experts, in everything from music and hair-dressing to stage construction. And what links them all is the Madonna Secrets Act, which works exactly like the British Government's Official Secrets Act, or that of the British Royal Family. Those who join 'the Firm' do not talk on the record. Even platitudes. Usually. All the team work on the Madonna image, but such is the confidence in the product that they have now opened up about how they get that package ready for the road.

In just a few years, Madonna has been so many different people – the Material Girl of 1985, all Marilyn in hot pink and strapless gowns; she was one of the boys in 1986 with chopped hair and black cap and her 'Open Your Heart'; in 1989 it was the androgynous look, the man's suit and no shirt; 'Like a Prayer' was black lingerie and a cross and chain; by 1991 she was Marilyn Monroe incarnate bumping and grinding at the Oscars and belting out 'Sooner or Later'. That night, the talk dwelled not on Kevin Costner's Oscar wins for *Dances with Wolves*, but on Madonna and her extravaganza appearance with Michael Jackson. They were a couple setting down to business. The other top topic was Madonna's figure. It was the one she got for the Blonde Ambition Tour, the sinewy, sleekily muscled body. And you don't just wake up looking like that. Madonna's secret was Robert Parr, a former baseball player with a crooked grin and a degree in exercise physiology. She recruited him to the team in 1987 and, although he also works with Theresa Russell and Tatum O'Neal and, in 1991, O'Neal's former husband, tennis great John McEnroe, his number-one client and advertisement for his California-based 'Up To Parr' personal-trainer business was Madonna.

Theresa Russell said, 'Madonna is a friend of mine. She eats, breathes and sleeps everything in her career. It must catch up with her, even though I think she realises ittoo, in a way. I don't know what she is going to do. When I compared myself with her, I used to think how lazy I was, and then I realised how much I prefer my life.'

Parr is, of course, more positive: 'She challenges herself more than I ever could. Our workouts often start at five in the morning when she is filming. We work on stamina and endurance for her singing and dancing and we work on the shape of her body. This transformation is not an overnight thing. Madonna realises how important her health and fitness are to her performances. She knows how she wants to look and she works hard at it. Our workouts are very focused.

'Doing different combinations of exercise is what creates muscle balance and avoids injuries by building up overall strength. The cardiovascular training also helps Madonna's singing by enabling her to achieve a more efficient use of oxygen. We wanted to incorporate the sinewy look. We wanted strength and endurance instead of mass and power.

'The advantages of working out are not only physical, they are mental. We go running or biking and then she does thirty minutes on the Lifecycle or Versaclimber – it simulates mountain climbing with the legs and arms in motion. We cool down by running stairs. Madonna then works out with ten to twenty-pound weights. Her upper-body definition comes from weight repetitions, the flat stomach is from a combination of sit-ups and pike-position lifts that work the upper, lower and oblique abdominal muscles. The sinewy look is created with workouts and also with low body fat. Madonna is a vegetarian, and she travels with a vegetarian cook. And she drinks gallons of water to replace lost body fluids. My biggest problem is that she has enough complex carbohydrates and protein so she doesn't get too thin because of her workouts and her performances. We finish the workout with fifteen minutes of stretching – first the large muscle groups and then the smaller upper-body muscles.

'Madonna has the genetic potential to achieve what she has and truly enjoys challenging herself. Not everyone could look like her, but with the right, intelligent workout, everyone can look better. But it takes time and dedication to build the endurance and stamina to then create muscle tone and shape. You change the routine for the look. Warren Beatty wanted a softer-in-the-shoulder look for *Dick Tracy*, and we did that. Then you change the intensity level a little. When we're on tour, I go out about 6.00am and find a running course, a mix of flat and hills close to where we're staying. Then we'll run up and down the hotel stairs. I'm kinda her sounding board while we run.'

Former British commando Tony Toms joined the European leg of the Blonde Ambition Tour in the summer of 1990. By now, Madonna's exercise regimen had taken control of her – she was addicted to it. Onlookers were sent flying as she and her entourage ran through London's Hyde Park. But they weren't the only ones to get battered – so was Madonna's image. But she could not stop running. Toms reported, 'She works harder than an Olympic athlete. It was frightening to see just how fit and strong she is. She had to get rid of some minders because they couldn't keep up with her. The security people think it is just a minding job until they have to go out running with her. It's then they find they can't stand the pace. We were all as fit as fiddles, but working with her still tired us out. We were knackered at the end of the tour.'

She is just a complete perfectionist over everything, and that includes her figure. But it is not just vanity. A Madonna concert lasts two hours and she belts out the songs non-stop while dancing around the stage. So she certainly has to be super-fit. Everything and everybody has got to be perfect for a Madonna concert. She will not put up with any slacking. If someone does something wrong, she bawls them out. But equally, she is a kind and caring person.

In Barcelona, during 1990's sweltering 100°F summer, her hairdresser broke her leg in a nasty fall. Madonna was full of concern for the young girl, often bringing her presents to the hospital and sitting by her bedside. She didn't have to. The girl could have been easily replaced, but Madonna isn't like that.

'She's also funny. I was at the front of group of minders surrounding Madonna and trying to push her through six and a half thousand fans at a stadium in Barcelona. She was directly behind me hanging on to my trousers when the belt snapped and they fell down. I had nothing on underneath. But Madonna leaned forward and said sweetly, "Tony, you're supposed to hit 'em, not fuck 'em." '

Australian Peter Chaplin looks after the inside of Madonna's body. He fed her 'performance food'. Chaplin prepared a high-energy vegetarian diet and said, 'Madonna is a professional and takes her fitness training and her diet very, very seriously. To keep her vegetable-fat level up, I feed her lots of avocados. I also make her drink fresh-squeezed juice because the vitamins in the juice are readily absorbed. On one tour, I thought up the ideal dish for her – Athlete's Answer. It's pasta with herb sauce and nuts and seeds – real training food. On a concert day, Madonna has dinner at 4.15 pm and I try to include recipes that give a complete protein and carbohydrate base to help her cope. She's very up front and honest. You know where you are with her. If she doesn't like something, she'll tell you.'

She likes Chaplin's food. He said she had three favourites, each of which serves up to four people, and revealed the recipes:

FITNESS NOODLES

Pick your favourite noodle for this dish. The best are 10–12oz plain noodles. Cook them according to package directions. Be sure to keep the noodles warm while making the vegetables. Heat 4tbls of vegetable oil in a large frying plan. Add 1lb mixed fresh vegetables (such as carrots, celery and red peppers) cut into matchstick-thin strips. Then add 4tsp of crushed garlic, 1tsp freshly ground black pepper and 5oz unsalted cashew nuts. Stir rapidly for 2 minutes. Place 4tbls soy sauce in a measuring cup and fill with water up to

9oz. Add to vegetable stir-fry ingredients. Mix well, add drained noodles. Garnish with chives or carrot strips.

AEROBIC APRICOT CURRY

In large frying pan, cook I diced onion in 1tbls oil. Add 2 diced carrots and 1 diced parsnip. Add 1.5tbls curry powder, stir for 1 min. Or try Madonna's favourite spice mix – tiny amounts of lemongrass, chilli, fenugreek, coriander, five-spice powder, brown and yellow mustard seeds, caraway and ginger. Add 2 large chopped tomatoes, a few matchstick-thin slices of ginger and natural juices from a 15oz can of apricots. Simmer for 10 min, add apricots, simmer 10 min. Thicken with a little cornflour mixed in cold water. Garnish with fresh coriander, lemon juice and tofu cubes cooked in a small amount of curry paste.

ATHLETE'S ANSWER

On a baking sheet mix 5oz each sunflower and pumpkin seeds and 2.5oz unsalted peanuts. Bake in 325°F oven for 15 min. Mix again, back in oven for 10 min. Remove, add a dash soy sauce, set aside. In saucepan, boil 4oz potatoes. Drain, rinse, set aside. In large pot, boil 12oz bow-tie pasta for 10 min. Heat 1tbls olive oil in small pan and sauté potatoes 3–4 min. Add 2tbls supermarket pesto sauce and 2tbls bouillon cube vegetable stock. Drain pasta, toss in 1tbls olive oil, return to pot. Add potato mixture. Mix well, stir in nuts and seeds. Garnish with basil.

The 21st-century Madonna remains careful about her diet. It reflects her California days – her grocery list is like a menu from a Beverly Hills restaurant. Her fridge is always packed with broccoli, beets, carrots, apples, lettuce, mushrooms, artichokes and oranges. She uses free-range eggs and soya margarine and sticks to rye bread to avoid yeast. She enjoys pasta. She snacks on papaya and apricots and often indulges in a bowl of organic whole-grain cereal and dried fruit such as sultanas. Her treat is Italian biscuits. She also drinks two glasses of freshly squeezed orange juice following her six-days-a-week (Sundays are her day off), two-hour morning yoga sessions with her personal trainer. She does not eat red meat or chicken, so her diet is centred around all sorts of fresh fish – but not shellfish. She is not a lobster lady.

Madonna is careful with her body – and outrageous about what she dresses it in. Her favourite designers are Jean-Paul Gaultier and Franco Moschino because she enjoys their sense of humour.

'I like to cross the boundaries between men and women. That can be frightening, but things I'm most affected by are things that frighten or challenge me. I like to nudge people, to break through stereotypes. There are too many stereotypes. Even liberated women stay in certain categories – no one is too threatening.'

She is not easy to work with. Or for. Hairstylist Victor Vidal says, 'She knows she's difficult, but her saving grace is that being difficult is part of being honest, for her. She complains for a reason. It might be after fourteen hours of rehearsal and she'll say, "Let's get this done." '

Vidal bleached, chopped and cropped Madonna for her *True Blue* video. 'I told her about this vision I had of her. I wanted her to bleach her hair almost white and cut it short. She thought for a moment and then said "Yes", picked up a magazine and never looked up until I was finished.'

Francesca Tolot and Joanne Gair from Hollywood's popular (with the stars) Cloutier Agency do her professional make-up. There are only two basic rules; use deeper shades of colour when the hair is dark, paler shades when she is blonde.

'She's aware of her face – *she* knows what looks good and what does not,' said Gair in a rare remark. The Cloutier Agency have signed the Madonna Official Secrets Act *en masse*.

Photographer Herb Ritts met Madonna in 1985 when she marched into his studio dripping with rubber bracelets, crucifixes and other trinkets. 'Her attraction isn't about her hair or make-up or clothes, it's about her evolution as a person.' Or as a celebrity chameleon?

For the Blonde Ambition Tour, the plan was for Busby Berkeley to meet Anthony Burgess' *Clockwork Orange*, with costuming by naughty Frederick's of Hollywood. The world was going to 'Vogue' – 'I know a place where you can get away, it's called a dance floor/It makes no difference if you're black or white, a boy or a girl ...'

What *does* make a difference is Madonna. She has transcended all the rules of entertainment. It is that old chestnut about the telephone book – if she went on stage and read it, people would pay to see her. It is her. It is the Celebrity. Did anybody ever hear the music at a Beatles concert? We went to *see* Elvis, to *see* Michael Jackson; the Celebrity had overtaken the performer. And that was so clear by the time Madonna strutted out on stage in conical bras and sci-fi bustiers on the Blonde Ambition Tour. High Style. High camp. Electric red lips. Dark eyebrows, the fountain of fake-blonde ponytail. Costumes by Gaultier and her long-time friend Marlene Stewart. Coiffed hair. Plunging necklines. Old Hollywood. Neon Las Vegas. And the corset with the pointy – back in fashion – heavily stitched bra. They went to hear her sing? Getouttahere! Madonna – number one with a bullet bra.

The last incarnation of Madonna, a 21st-century sex siren, a Barbarella, sent Madonna into the 1990s. She had messed with every taboo in the 1980s from sex and sacrilege to cross-dressing and crucifixes, so let's get going. Mimed masturbation? Yes, with 'Like a Virgin'. And there were the topless chaps and their foot-long pointy brassières. A touch of discipline with 'Hanky Panky' and Madonna chiding, 'You may not know the song, but you all know the pleasures of a good spanking.'

'She said, "Let's break every rule we can." She wanted to make statements about sexuality, cross-sexuality, the church and the like,' recalled Blonde Ambition choreographer Vince Paterson, enthusiastically adding, 'The biggest thing we tried to do was change the shape of concerts. Instead of just presenting songs we wanted to combine fashion, Broadway, rock and performance art.' A snappy, irreverent mongrel of a show. Paterson remembers an early conversation with Madonna.

'Are you the one who had Michael Jackson grab his balls in the *Bad* video?' she asked.

'No,' said Paterson, 'he was grabbing his balls before I got on the *Bad* video.'

'Well, maybe I should do it,' said Madonna.

'Well, you should, because you have more balls than most of the men I know,' Paterson says he told her.

The tour began in the spring of 1990 in Japan. Everyone learned from the first moment who was in charge. A sound check was being taken in Tokyo and Madonna decided on a certain volume level. A technician questioned her decision and she made it clear: 'Listen. Everyone is entitled to *my* opinion.'

The Blonde Ambition Tour was all part of the Madonna masterplan. She knew she had to be pragmatic about Beatty. The closest he was to her at present was the seven show dancers in their yellow *Dick Tracy* overcoats and very non-Dick G-strings. Beatty's fingerprints were elsewhere. Madonna was also enjoying a quiet, comfortable love affair. Workers on the tour say she was happy and content. There were only hints as to the identity of her lover during the four-month Blonde Ambition Tour.

'*Genk, Desu ka*,' shouted Madonna from the scaffolding of the Marine Stadium in Chiba as her tour of Japan began. 'How ya doin?' she followed up with as she started her tour and simultaneously baptised the outdoor stadium, which is also the site of Tokyo's Disneyland. There was nothing Mickey Mouse about this enterprise.

After 3 weeks in Japan, the tour moved to America – 18 songs in 90 minutes of sell-out controversy. Jean-Paul Gaultier maintains he took 350 aspirins to prepare the costumes for '*the Madonna*'. One costume was a beaded, acid-green body suit – something Cyd Charisse would have sparkled Fred Astaire with – and Gaultier said he was advised by a Folies-Bergère dresser to wash it in a 'non-aggressive detergent'.

In Canada, there was a problem. Police were called to the Skydome Stadium by parents complaining about Madonna simulating masturbation during 'Like a Virgin' while lying on a red-velvet, gold-brocade bed tilted towards the audience. 'Morality was never involved and there was no prosecution,' said the Toronto Mounties. They did admit that, following complaints that the show was lewd, they had agents watch it through binoculars. There is a lot of dedication involved when you always get your man.

Dick Tracy was going into cinemas with a great fanfare. And the publicity machine was still trying to push the Madonna/Warren Beatty romance. But this was one man, as Shirley MacLaine told me, that Madonna was not going to hang on to. Beatty did not want to change. At 53, he was happily in control of his life. There was Jack and Dustin and Diane and all the others he could speed-dial on his touch-tone phone when he wanted company. Madonna, the self-admitted 'hopeless romantic', thought she could change him. When you have succeeded at everything else, it must have seemed a safe bet. But Beatty was doing what he did best, being Beatty. He spent nights with other women. He made elaborate excuses. Madonna wanted a commitment. So did the world's media. She hit back at Beatty and bombarded Jellybean Benitez with calls. He was staying at a West Hollywood hotel but, before midnight, he was up in the Hollywood Hills to spend a long, happy night with Madonna.

She remained friends with Beatty. She sat on his lap at Swifty Lazar's party at Spago after the 1991 Oscars. But she was hurt. She was angry that she could not control her men – her father's actions; Sean Penn's; Warren Beatty's. She could not take control. She did not want wimps, but she could not ride herd on the ones she did want. She resolved then that she would change the mating rules if she was forced to, make her own arrangements, for she admitted, 'It's really a hard thing to accept in life that no matter what you do you can't change a person. If you say, "I don't want you looking at that woman," they're going to do it anyway. It doesn't matter what you say. You want to think if this person is in love with you, you have control over them. But you don't. And to accept that in life is next to impossible. Then again, I want to be a fly on the wall for all Warren Beatty's conversations, but I don't want the reverse. I'd go, "Warren, did you really chase that girl for a year?" and he'd say, "Nay, it's all lies." I should have known better. I was unrealistic, but then you always think you're going to be the one.'

In the future, she planned, she would ensure she was the one in control, calling the shots, but she could not legislate for happenstance or love and vice versa.

CHAPTER FIFTEEN
ROMAN HOLIDAY

'I am attracted to a thug. I like that quality,
but I like the other side of it too. There's a difference
between my ideal man and a man that I'm sexually
attracted to. Therein lies the rub.'

MADONNA, 1999

If a week is a long time in politics, it can be an eternity in the world of entertainment. Audiences, especially Madonna's video generation of fans, want instant gratification. And they want it *now*. Madonna was seeing her psychiatrist two or three times a week. She seemed to have everything – and nothing. She likes everything neat like her closets; she was a symbol of the Filofax generation, her appointments and even her telephone calls were scheduled. She knew it was close to obsession, like her exercise routine, and that there is a catch-22. She exercised to stop being depressed and, if she did not exercise, she would be depressed about not exercising. She did not sleep much. In the early hours she would make lists, plan ahead. As the 1990s arrived, she had taken three holidays in a decade and was bored by the second day of each of them. She admitted that if she had slowed down more, she might have held her marriage together and her relationship with Beatty.

Interestingly, it was Penn, who in 1991 wrote and directed

Charles Bronson in the film *Indian Runner*, who pinpointed Madonna as a woman of the times. The traditional role of the male in society was being openly questioned and the new men's movement had grown out of – because of or in reaction to – women's liberation. Penn, a man of the Marlboro-mould of masculinity, appeared to have mellowed in his view and accepted that women, too, can have 'balls'. His film debuted well at the Cannes Film Festival in 1991 when Madonna was also promoting *Truth or Dare* (they even shared the same hotel, if not a room). Penn explained that it was about a returning Vietnam vet trying to start a normal life in the American Midwest.

'The film is the story of an American male's struggle. In America today, there is no specific place for masculinity. There is no need to go out and hunt for food or kill the guy from the other tribe. But we've hung on to that concept and almost every guy in the US has some need to live up to that tribal rite. There is nothing of value that men can do that women can't, so we are in a period of transition – trying to accept what has happened. This movie is about issues that I am trying to work out in my own life. A mature life requires responsibility and that means cutting your losses, the art of compromise.' Sean Penn on the art of compromise – certainly something completely different.

Madonna held differing views, however: 'When I lived with Sean, he loved to ball up his clothes. I'd say, "You've twisted a Versace suit into a ball and *I can't bear it*." I would follow him and take his things and hang them up. He'd say, "Leave me alone. I want to do it this way." But I just couldn't stand it.'

Freddy DeMann said of his former number-one client, 'Madonna is the biggest star in the universe. And she likes the view.'

She admits she is stubborn. 'I'm the boss. Quite frankly, a lot of things I've wanted have met with adversity. There's always this preliminary shit that's thrown and then there's my shit fit and then I do what I have to do. And they like it.'

Dead-Eyed Dick was over. So was the Blonde Ambition Tour. Madonna wanted to make music. She was releasing *The Immaculate Collection*, a best-of compilation of eleven hits and two new songs, 'Rescue Me' and 'Justify My Love'.

Madonna went to Paris to film a video to accompany the release of 'Justify My Love'. While she was there, she visited the 1990 fashion shows and dismayed the world's fashion editors by sitting opposite them without wearing knickers. They found it a little distracting.

Herb Ritts was there taking pictures. At Thierry Mugler's third show, Madonna sat in the front row wearing a black plastic coat with fake-fur trim and a bare midriff. Two burly minders kept away photographers. Madonna cheered Lauren Hutton on the catwalk, but she also complained at the fashions: 'Tired, tired – Gaultier's done that.'

Diane Brill got the comment, 'She's soooooo fat.' The celebrity crowd got to their feet at the end to give Mugler, arm in arm with Diana Ross, an ovation. Madonna stayed in her seat. Maybe it was to save her energy. She was going to need it, proving that, like her idol Marilyn Monroe's biggest film, 'Some Like It Hot'.

For three days at the Royal Monceau Hotel in Paris, she began to film the video for the release of 'Justify My Love'. Appearing with her was Tony Ward, a muscled 5ft 7in-tall model with a Roman nose who had been Madonna's 'birthday present' from her brother Mario. Ward, three years younger than Madonna, had done nude modelling and was seen wearing only a smile and an ankle bracelet in

Hollywood's gay magazine, *In Touch for Men*. He has also featured in Herb Ritts' book, *Men and Women*, and was known at the Edelweiss nightclub in Manhattan, a spot for non-gay businessmen who like to relax by slipping into something comfortable after work – a cocktail dress, wigs and make-up. Jayme Harris, a former girlfriend of Ward's, claimed he was a keen cross-dresser. She also said he liked whips and chains and was 'quite forward about it'. Now, he was about to get real exposure. Maybe it was a lesbian kiss. Or the men in the fishnet stockings. Or Madonna's all-but-naked bouncing bottom. Or the hints of bisexuality, cross-dressing, group sex, voyeurism, S&M and the full racy gamut of leather-and-lace sex. Or Madonna, in her skyscraper heels and scant black lingerie, cavorting with Ward or kissing and nuzzling European model Amanda Cazalet. Or the insinuation of oral sex or the woman in suspenders, her nipples exposed, grasping a man's crotch.

Probably most of that made MTV ban Madonna's 'Justify My Love' video. (In Britain, the IBA said it could not be shown before 9.00pm) The video is populated with surreally androgynous performers. There are echoes of Visconti's *The Damned* and Cavani's *The Night Porter*, or the work of the late photographer Robert Mapplethorpe, a controversial tableau. The message said any fetish was welcome. Madonna was a great fan of *The Night Porter*, especially Dirk Bogarde's co-star, Charlotte Rampling.

'She is a genius. Images of women dressed in Nazi Gestapo uniforms – the vulnerability and fragility of a female but the sense of playing that out and performing, doing some sort of cabaret. The confusion – what's male? What's female?'

But the video was not on MTV. Instead, it became the

first video single ever released, selling for $9.98 for five minutes of entertainment. A major hit is around the 50,000 sales mark – 'Justify My Love' was shipped out by the quarter million. In Saudia Arabia, black-market copies were selling for $200 a time. Normally, performers do not earn from videos – often they pay to make them. Madonna had made other arrangements. She had negotiated a 17.5 per cent share of any sales, before it was even decided to sell the video just in time for Christmas 1990.

But it was the other business that had people talking. Who was kissing Madonna as Ward watched? Amanda Cazalet, seven years younger than Madonna, was employed by the Marilyn Gauthier Modelling Agency in Paris. She was a friend of rock-video mastermind, Jean-Baptiste Mondino, who directed the video. 'It was a natural,' said Robert Farrel, who was Cazalet's 'booker' at Gauthier, adding, 'Everyone knew that once Madonna met Amanda, it was going to be her.'

Cazalet would speak only briefly about the video and Madonna: 'After seeing it, the first thing you want to do is make love. She knew exactly what she wanted. She had this inner power, which is incredible.'

No one at MTV believes that Madonna could have thought they would screen the video. American television has tough double standards. It will titillate to get ratings but it will not challenge the boundaries. More extremes of sex, violence and language were still a decade away from even cable television. The contradictions of 'safe-violence' and 'safe-sex' are what MTV practised. Standards are like nipples, even in Madonna videos. Normally, everyone has two of them.

Madonna went on national television in the USA, on

Nightline, a heavyweight discussion programme that is broadcast at 11.30pm. The show was born during the Iranian hostage crisis and built an admirable following. With Madonna on the show, the ratings were the second-highest in its ten-year history (fallen evangelist Jim Bakker's wife Tammy breaking down live topped Madonna), but she was not in control. At times she was inarticulate. Yet she was as bouncy as Mae West in her heyday. 'You're going to wind up making more money than you would have,' *Nightline* host Forrest Sawyer told her. She cheekily replied, 'Yeah, so lucky me.'

Of course, as Miss West knew before her, luck had absolutely nothing to do with it. Or goodness. 'She gets as much out of her talent as anyone ever has,' said John Branca, an entertainment lawyer who has represented the Rolling Stones and Michael Jackson. 'Her major assets are controversy and sex appeal and great music.'

As Branca said, controversy was an asset. Even Madonna's garden got attention. Her neighbour Donald Robinson went to court arguing that her untrimmed trees ruined his view of Los Angeles. She claimed people were looking into her property. Her brother Christopher, a bodyguard, a gardener and one of her assistants testified for her. She did not go to court in person because of death threats, probably from some obsessive crank. Nevertheless, the Sheriff's deputies screened everyone going into the Los Angeles Superior courtroom of Judge Sally Disco, who later ruled that Madonna should trim her trees. She had lost. But she was going to win the big one, the film role she believed was going to make her the greatest star in the world.

Madonna likes to talk, but she is careful about doing so because she feels that when she does she reveals too much

In 1998, Madonna stole the show once more at the MTV Europe Music Awards by bagging awards for Best Female Artist and Best Album.

Another breathtaking performance at the Brit Awards in 1995.

Madonna as Eva Peron in the film *Evita*. She is pictured below with Jonathan Pryce, who starred as Juan Peron.

Madonna is always at the cutting edge of style with her ever-changing image. Here, she performs her hit, *Frozen*, at the San Remo Music Awards.

Sibling harmony: with brother Chris at the *Vanity Fair* Oscar Winner's Party.

Madonna, Guy, Rocco and Lourdes in 2007.

Madonna and Guy enjoying her 50th birthday celebrations.

Madonna with Lourdes and David Banda at the Kabbalah Center in New York.

of her personality. She does. Over the years she has not been able to resist and, brought together, her words give a new insight into how the self-styled little girl from Michigan became a champion of the so-called slut-feminism and one of the world's most famous people.

'From when I was very young, I just knew that being a girl and being charming in a feminine sort of way could get me lots of things, and I milked it for everything I could. I think your parents give you false expectations of life. All of us grow up with completely misguided notions about life and they don't change until you get out into the world. It's like someone telling you what love or marriage is; you can't know until you're there and you have to learn the hard way.

'When I was a child, I always thought that the world was mine, that it was a stomping ground for me, full of opportunities. I always had this attitude that I was going to go out into the world and do all the things I wanted to do. Sometimes I travel through people, but I think that's true of most ambitious people. If the people can't go with me – whether it's physical or emotional love – I feel sad about that. But that's part of the tragedy of love.

'Every time I reach a new peak, I see a new one I want to climb. It's like I can't stop. Maybe I should rest and admire the view, but I can't. I've got to keep on pushing. Why, I don't know. I don't know what motivates me. I just know I've got to do it. You have to be patient. I'm not. The more money you have, the more problems you have. I went from making no money, when I just barely survived.

'There have been times when I've thought, If I'd known it was going to be like this, I wouldn't have tried so hard. If it ever gets too much, or I feel like I'm being over-scrutinised, or I'm not enjoying it any more, then I won't do it. America is really a "life-negative" society. People want to know all the underneath stuff, your dirty laundry, which isn't to say all the stuff the press has been getting on me is negative or dirty or whatever, but there's always a hope, for them, that they'll uncover something really scandalous.

'You can't sit around worrying about people disliking you because they're going to be there. It can't stop you. I could never have imagined that success could be like this, which was a surprise but I can handle it. I can still laugh about it, so I guess I'm right. I think the ultimate challenge is to have some kind of style even though you haven't got money, or standing in society, or formal education. I had a very middle-, lower-middle-class sort of upbringing, but I identify with people who have had, at some point in their lives, to struggle to survive. It adds another colour to your character.

'I don't like violence. I never condoned hitting anyone, and I never thought that any violence should have taken place. I have chances to vent my anger in other ways other than confrontation. I like to fight people and kind of manipulate them into feeling like they're not being fought. I'd rather do it that way.

'Music is still very important to me, but I always had a great interest in films, and the thought that I could only make records for the rest of my life filled me with horror. Ultimately, I want to direct films.

'They thought they would wake up one day and I'd go away. But I'm not going to go away. It's more than ego. It's an overwhelming interior light that I let shine without control. I am guided by my instinct – it's both my faith and conscience. I hate polite conversation. I hate it when people stand around and go, "Hi, how are you?" I hate words that don't have any reason or meaning. Also I hate it when people smoke in elevators and closed-in places. It's just so rude.

'I have to listen to the criticism that I get when it's dealing with my work. It's beneficial, I guess, I don't take criticism very well but it's getting better. If I do something and there's a hundred people in the room and ninety-nine people say they like it, I only remember the person who didn't like it.

'I laugh at myself. I don't take myself completely seriously. I think that's another quality that people have to hold on to – you have to laugh, especially at yourself. I do it in most of the things I do, and most of the videos that I make and most of my performances. Even in my concerts there were so many moments when I just stood still and laughed at myself. I am ambitious. But if I weren't as talented as I am ambitious, I would be a gross monstrosity. I am not surprised by my success because it feels natural. I'm very indecisive: yes-no-yes. In my career, I make pretty good decisions, but in my personal life I cause constant havoc by changing my mind every five minutes.

'My image is a natural extension of my performance, so my songs may not be deliberately sexual, but the way I achieve them could be. Women with blonde hair are perceived as much more sexual and much more impulsive – fun-loving but not as layered, not as deep, not serious – the artifice of being blonde has some incredible sort of sexual connotation. Men really respond to it. I like to leave the impression that Marilyn Monroe did, to be able to arouse so many different feelings in people.

'I always acted like a star long before I was one. If people don't see my sense of humour, then I come off as being expensive, but I always endear myself to people when I find their weaknesses and they acknowledge it. It's the people who try to hide everything and try to make you think they're so cool that I can't stand. I think if someone becomes hugely successful, the public becomes disgusted with them and begins to wish the star would slip on a banana peel. That's the basic aspect of human nature.

'I think women are intimidated by women who are incredibly ambitious or competitive because it's easier to deal with girls who aren't. But I never really think consciously of the fact that I'm a girl or anything like that. In fact, I think I've had advantages because I'm a girl. People have this idea that if you're sexual and beautiful and provocative, then there's nothing else you could possibly offer. People have always had that image about women. And while it might have seemed like I was behaving in a stereotypical way, at the same time, I was also masterminding it. I was in control of everything I was doing, and I think when people realised that, it confused them. People say I've set back the women's movement thirty years – but I think that women weren't ashamed of their bodies in the 1950s. They luxuriated in their femininity and believed whole-heartedly in it. Women aren't like men. They can do things that men can't, mentally and physically. If people don't get the humour in my act, then they don't want to get it.

'The good life is just to stay in music, where I've already established myself and it's easier. I will continue to write music as long as I'm inspired. I'm inspired; I feel inspired. Just to believe in the goodness of life and to believe in yourself. That may sound silly, but that's what it really comes down to, because you can get pretty cynical about life – it's nice to be able to sit back and think that there is innate goodness in people in the world despite all the crazy bullshit that you see presented in front of you every time you read the newspapers.

'I have this feeling that I'm a bad girl – and that I need to be punished. I am what I am, and I do what I do. I never set out to be a role model for girls or women, and I don't conform to any stereotype. You know the idea: you need to be a chainsaw or an army tank to play in a man's world. Well, I don't act like a man, yet I play in a man's world. Irony is my favourite thing. Everything I do is meant to have several meanings, to be ambiguous. I knew I was up against a lot. I'm from a world they have no respect for. It was a really good experience for me to prove myself in that context.

'There was a point in my life when I wanted to be a Peggy Guggenheim, a patron of artists, have a gallery and a great art collection. When I'm really, really old, that's what I want to do. She had a wild life. I like that. I've basically gone wildly out of control. My manager gets insane about what I spend. But it placates me to put my energy into that work. I could be buying a Ferrari, but I'd rather spend it this way. I think the public is tired of trying to figure out whether I'm a feminist or not. I don't think of what I'm doing as gender specific. I am what I am, and I do what I do.

'There is a wink behind everything I do. The public shouldn't think about this. Part of the reason I'm successful is because I'm a good businesswoman, but I don't think it is necessary for people to know that. All that means is that I'm in charge of everything that comes out. Gold! People say "No" to me all the time, but I guess the balance is tipped in the "Yes" direction. If they do say "No", you can be sure there will be a tantrum to follow.

'I admit I have this feeling that I'm a bad girl and I need to be punished. The part of me that goes around saying, "Fuck you! Fuck you! I'm throwing this in your face!" is the part that's covering up the part that's saying, "I'm hurt. And

I've been abandoned and I will never need anyone again."
So, here – have a stereotype! I don't make fun of
Catholicism. I deeply respect Catholicism – its mystery and
fear and oppressiveness, its passion and its discipline and its
obsession with guilt. I hate waste and I hate to waste money.
I don't see the point of having more than one car. And I hate
to waste food.

'Nothing that happened to me was a bad thing. Maybe
I've had moments of frustration or felt that I was being
misjudged or felt that I had painted myself into a corner. But
in the end, everything that happened to me was good. I get
letters from guys in jail all the time too, but they just want
to have a date with me. Most people who don't like me are
people who are fanatically religious.

'No one can ever just play themselves in a movie. That's
ridiculous. Obviously there can be a lot of things in the
character that are like you, but you've got to be a little bit
inventive or imaginative. I mean, there are certain things in
the character that I can relate to, but I'm not playing myself,
for God's sake!

'It would also be nice to play some unsympathetic
characters … but I've never been offered one. God knows, I
have my bad side. I'm sort of naturally a pain in the ass. I
naturally like to do things that rub people up the wrong way.
No, that's wrong. Let me rephrase that, I just like being
controversial, I guess. Even that doesn't sound right. Hey,
well, you know how they always say things are this way?
Well, they're not! Or they don't have to be.

'I believe someone is protecting me. Otherwise I'd be
dead. Otherwise that guy tonight would have gotten out
of his car and beaten the shit out of me. Believe me. It
would have happened if I weren't protected, because I

can't resist mouthing off to people when they curse me.
One time a guy did that to me and I said, "Fuck you,
motherfucker." I wasn't in my car; I was standing on the
kerb giving directions to my girlfriend. And this guy got
out of his car. It was in the Valley. It always happens in the
Valley. This big guy got out of his car and walked over to
me and I was thinking, Oh, my God, he's going to beat the
shit out of me. I was cowering. And I turned into a person
I've never been in my life. I said, "I'm sorry! I am truly
sorry!" So I think someone is protecting me. I don't know
if it's an angel. It could be the Devil. He could have his
own hidden agenda.

'I think most sensitive people have psychic power. I think
a lot of innate psychic power has to do with just being
really observant. My psychic powers show up in dreams. Or
in knowing when people are going to call, or what people
are going to say, or what they are going to do next. I just
had dreams about being murdered all the time. The only
remotely entertainment-orientated dream I ever had was
one where I dreamed I kissed Robert Redford. I was in the
sixth grade. And it has not come true. It was weird. I don't
think I ever had any real fixation on him. But the dream
was so vivid. I was really turned on. You know how you
have a beauty spot that's sensitive or powerful? There's one
for each sign. Mine is my back. I have a great back. It's
beautiful, I can say that. I am not a scholar. I'm a sponge. I
just soak things up.

'Maybe because everyone shits on me so much they felt
sorry for me. I get a lot of bad press. I get ripped to shreds.
I've got everybody waiting to tear me down. I'm a good-
for-nothing, no-talent has-been, and they can't wait until I
drop dead.

'Do I know what to do with my money? Yes, I do. Buy art, and invest money in writing good scripts, and give it to people who need it. Having money is just the best thing in the world. It gives you freedom and power and the ability to help other people. I know what to do with my money.

'Since I was seventeen and moved to New York, I haven't needed my father's help. We're the closest when I'm in a very vulnerable state. The great thing is that when I am, he's there for me. The rest of the time I roam around the world like a miniature tank. The end of the 'Oh, Father' video, where I'm dancing on my mother's grave, is an attempt to embrace and accept my mother's death. My mother had a lot of us in the same month. She kept getting pregnant at the same time every month.

'I had my chart done once. I remember only two things from it. One was that I should eat more cooked vegetables. The other was that I was going to meet an older man who was going to be a great influence on me. And then I met Warren Beatty. I love candy, as you can see. I'm a sugar junkie. It's because I was deprived of love as a child. I'm just kidding. I wasn't deprived. But I wasn't allowed to eat candy. That's really the reason. I've been gorging ever since I moved out of the house.

'You know what religion is? Guys get to do everything. They get to be altar boys. They get to stay out late. Take their shirts off in the summer. They get to pee standing up. They get to fuck a lot of girls and not worry about getting pregnant. Although that doesn't have anything to do with being religious. Well, I moved to New York and went after my dreams. It takes a lot of devotion and discipline and I think the combination of that and the upbringing has helped me to be as productive as I am.

'You know, I can think of isolated moments where I could have given in and it would have made things better. But, all in all, I'm not with any of the people I'm not with for a much larger reason; we just weren't meant to be. If I'd changed and given in – or what I perceived to be giving in – to certain concessions that people had asked of me, maybe the relationships would have been successful, on the one hand, but then I would have had to give up other things in my career. And then I would have been miserable. So it's hard to say.

'I mean, I do look around and go, God, it's great to have fame and fortune, but then I see Mia Farrow on the set with her baby, and I think she seems absolutely content. She has a huge family and that just seems like the most important thing. And, you know, love and everything, I don't really have that, but time hasn't run for me yet. I'm not exactly sure who I'm looking for. I wish I knew – I wonder if I could ever find someone like me. I would probably kill them if I did.

'I love performing, but it is very taxing to go on the road and travel in a bus. Video has made it possible to reach the masses without touring. I don't think about the work I do in terms of feminism. I certainly feel that I give women strength and hope, particularly young women. So in that respect, I feel my behaviour is feminist. But I'm certainly not militant about it, nor do I exactly premeditate it. So I think sex is equated with power in a way, and that's scary. It's scary for men that women should have that power – or to have that power and be sexy at the same time. I like to have control over most of the things in my career but I'm not a tyrant. I don't have to have it on my album that it's written, arranged, produced, directed and stars Madonna. To me, to have total control means you can lose objectivity. What I like is to be surrounded by really talented, intelligent people you can trust. And ask them for their advice and get their input. But let's face it, I'm not going to make an album and not show up for the vocals or make a video and have nothing to do with the script.

'Music is the main vector of celebrity. When it's a success, its impact is just as strong as a bullet hitting the target. Most of my lyrical ideas come from everyday life. Some are more fantasy motivated along the lines of ideal relationships. In general, my songs are a bit of both. When you are singing a song you are making yourself very vulnerable. It's almost like crying in front of people. Acting is like that too. It's just a different way of doing it. Everything inspires me – a great book or movie, an expression in someone's eyes, children or old men walking down the street. You know what I like to do when I go to parties? I like talking to the butler and the janitors and stuff – they're the funniest, they inspire me.

'I think people have too many pretentious ideas about music – what's artistic and what has integrity and what doesn't. They think if it's simple and accessible, then it's commercial and a total compromise. And if it's masked in mystery, not completely understood and slightly unattractive, it has integrity and is artistic. I don't believe that. I'm sure that each record I've heard influenced me in some way, just like every person you ever meet influences you.

'I do, in a way, feel it would have been great in the old days [of Hollywood]. The studio system really nurtured and cared for you in a way it doesn't now. On the other hand, your life was not your own. Now you have more individual freedom, but you don't have anyone looking after your career in the way they did then.

'So many times, I drive around in my expensive car and just think, God, I'm just a girl from Michigan. It all seems so strange. Because I could never imagine it when I lived there. Those are the times I feel like I'm just a girl from Michigan.'

CHAPTER SIXTEEN

NO TEARS

*'You can have all the success in the world and, if you
don't have someone to love, it's certainly not as
rewarding. The fulfilment you get from another human
being — a child in particular — will always dwarf people
recognising you in the street.'*

MADONNA, 1991

Madonna, the control freak of the 1990s. She said the
perfect time of day, the time when she was happiest,
was when the maids had gone. The bed was made up
perfectly. The glasses were clean, the dishes stacked away.
Everything was in its place. There was holiness in orderliness
for Madonna. She could not, however, put on the telephone-
answering machine. She needed to answer the phone.

A personal assistant travelled everywhere with her;
Madonna, like Cher and other popular icons, were treated
like babies. They may have been tough, don't-fuck-with-me
gals, but don't ask them to boil an egg. When a hand is held
long enough, when an ego is stroked so much it shines, the
routine of normal life gets lost. And with it vanishes a
certain humanity. Those who believe they can have
anything they want make their own often dangerous deity,
as Madonna's British butler Eric Martin-Ienco was to
discover a decade later.

Eva Perón created her deity. She is someone, like Monroe,

who has always fascinated Madonna. And Madonna has understood the incredible screen potential of *Evita* since the success of the stage show. She fought hard to win the role.

Eva Perón went from being a peasant brunette to an upswept platinum-blonde and the heroine of her *descamisados* – 'the shirtless ones' – of Buenos Aires. She, like Madonna's mother, died early from cancer. 'Evita' Perón was 33 when the disease finally killed her in 1952. In 1976, Andrew Lloyd-Webber and Tim Rice turned the lady of the Casa Rosada, the lavish Pink Palace in Buenos Aires, into the unlikely subject of a rock opera. First, there was the record album and 'Don't Cry For Me Argentina' became a European hit single. By 1978, Australian entrepreneur Robert Stigwood and director Hal Prince – who had produced Lloyd-Webber's and Rice's *Jesus Christ Superstar* – staged the show in London to sensational reviews. Elaine Page became an overnight star. As did Patti Lupone when *Evita* arrived on Broadway. It had been the most coveted and demanding role on Broadway since Barbra Streisand appeared as Fanny Brice in *Funny Girl*.

Oh, what a movie it would make! A dozen actresses have flirted with the title role since 1979. Stigwood hired Ken Russell to direct a film version in Spain for Paramount Studios. In *Enfant Terrible*, Russell decided Liza Minnelli should star and not Elaine Page. Minnelli flew to London to make a test recording. 'Calling it a disaster would be one of the great understatements,' said Bill Oakes of RSO Films. The tape was destroyed at Minnelli's insistence, but Russell continued to want her as *Evita*. RSO Films and Russell later parted company on the project in 1991. Video director Keith MacMillan then suggested doing *Evita* by 'shooting in a surrealistic soundstage environment'. There would be *interesting* guest-casting like Boy George playing the Pope. 'We entertained the idea for about ten minutes,' says Oakes, who said MacMillan saw the film like The Who's rock opera *Tommy*. In the meantime, a completely separate project was going on and Ronald Harwood wrote a screenplay, which director Marvin Chomsky, a master of the television mini-series format, turned into the 1981 film *Evita Perón*. The title role was taken by Faye Dunaway. Pebbles make more waves than that film did.

In 1982, *Evita* went from Paramount Studios to Twentieth Century Fox, which was then headed by Sherry Lansing, the first female to attain such a position in Hollywood and the one woman who, in 2001, could compete with Madonna for power and status in the entertainment world. She and director Herbert Ross saw the film as 'a swirling decadent fandango' and the star would be ... Streisand or Ann-Margret. Herbert Ross then left the project (he wanted too much money) and Streisand was not really interested. She knew she was too old for the role. It was Jon Peters, the former hairdresser and now Hollywood superpower, who was then her boyfriend, who had wanted Streisand to play the power-mad prima donna. Stigwood was interested in Meryl Streep but found 'unacceptable' the condition that Mike Nichols (*The Graduate, Working Girl*) be the director. Directors like the late Alan Pakula, Francis Coppola and Luis Puenzo were talked to and about. Then the Weintraub Entertainment Group (WEG), headed by superbly connected Jerry Weintraub, struck a deal over financing and distribution of the film. Oliver Stone was to direct and, in the summer of 1988, scouted locations in Argentina.

He went to the birthplace of Maria Eva Duarte: 'It was a lonely spot on the immense *pampas* where she grew up and

I talked to people that still remember her. I wanted to do a film which would be beyond all political resentments and demagogic speculation.' Stone said he was considering several actresses to play *Evita*. They were an eclectic bunch: Streisand, the Australian singer and *Grease* actress Olivia Newton-John, and Madonna. Stone would not say if he was considering Patti Lupone.

Madonna had meetings. And meetings. She and Stone are both big egos and there were plenty of seismic tremblers from the talks as their egos snagged like the subterranean plates grinding on an earthquake fault line. Stigwood wanted Hector Babenco, the director who had won an Oscar nomination for *Kiss of the Spider Woman*, to guide the production. And he wanted Madonna as the star. Babenco was frustrated by the negotiations and moved on to other projects.

Stone did not like that. And that thinking had linked Madonna and Babenco. That did not sit well with Stone who was now into the mainstream with projects like *Platoon* and *Wall Street*, and was about to start work on *Born on the Fourth of July*. Christ, he was making a movie starring Tom Cruise (even before the *Mission: Impossible* movies), the biggest star in Hollywood at that time. Madonna? Hell, who needed the aggravation?

'We decided on certain things before production,' says Bill Oakes. 'We wouldn't dub the voice. It had to be somebody who could act and sing. Madonna asked us if she could be considered and she remained under consideration until she and Stone fell out. It would have been difficult to conceive of them working together.'

Madonna felt she was being kept away from the facts; was it going to be an operetta? A straight drama? A musical with dialogue? She felt she had made enough mistakes in movies.

But, although she and Stone disagreed, she was determined to get her way. Madonna went on the record saying, 'I've decided that if anybody is going to do it, I'm going to do it.' Events were to prove the strength of her willpower.

Stone and Streep met in the summer of 1989 and, in August, the Oscar-winning actress, who is also a classically trained singer, sang much of the *Evita* score. Streep, like Madonna, a hard-working perfectionist, was taking twice-weekly diva and tango lessons with singer-choreographer Paula Abdul. Stone had completed the script, which was described as 'a politically charged love story'. The original score was intact apart from one song. In Hollywood parlance, 'the package' of Stone and Streep was complete. Streep's tape was sent to London. Lloyd-Webber and Tim Rice were not totally convinced. An RSO source said the praise was not lavish but along the lines of 'she can carry a tune'.

Jerry Weintraub's company was having its own problems after a string of Hollywood flops like Kim Basinger's *My Step-mother is an Alien*. Oliver Stone moved on to his Jim Morrison biopic, *The Doors*. Streep also went through the revolving *Evita* door. She was disgruntled at 'wasting' a year on the project.

And after Madonna got what she wanted – the title role of *Evita* – Streep said, 'I can sing better than she can if that counts for anything.'

Madonna had won by maintaining her stance. While others argued, she kept advertising her interest at meetings with the men that matter – the moneymen known as 'the suits'. They sit in tower blocks and decide how to spend millions of dollars. A wrong decision and they have to find another game to play. Madonna as Evita. Certainly bankable and certainly worth a gamble. Especially for Jeffrey Katzenberg, the great

Madonna fan at the Disney studios. Since *Dick Tracy*, he and Madonna had maintained contact. Officially, the studio called it 'a continuing creative agreement'.

Stigwood, Lloyd-Webber and Co. were now involved with Glen Gordon Carron, the creator, and often writer, of the successful Cybill Shepherd–Bruce Willis television series *Moonlighting*. Carron would direct the film from his own screenplay, which, by Spring 1991, was being called 'great'.

Disney, keen to keep the budget under $30 million, were having more meetings. But the project was 'hot'. Cingeri Productions, led by Andy Vajna, who made a fortune with the *Rambo* films, wanted some of the action. Cingeri's films are distributed in America by Disney, but early in the talks it was clear Katzenberg was carefully monitoring Disney's interests in *Evita*. And so was Madonna. Britain's Jeremy Irons, an Oscar winner for his wicked portrayal of Claus Von Bulow in *Reversal of Fortune*, was the actor wanted for Juan Perón. When Glenn Gordon Carron met with Irons, his leading lady was also present. Not only had Madonna won her role, she had negotiated conditions which gave her a say – some control over the final film. Her time with Warren Beatty had not been wasted.

Madonna was also happy publicly to display her enthusiasm. She agreed to present Andrew Lloyd-Webber with an award saluting his work at the Los Angeles Music Center Benefactors' dinner at the Beverly Wilshire Hotel. A politically correct crowd as well as celebrities attended. Madonna arrived 15 minutes late wearing a black sheath of a dress and platinum hair, and with a crowd of bodyguards snapping, 'Get back!' at preying paparazzi. On stage, she livened up the mainly staid audience by calling up Lloyd-Webber with, 'Andrew? Where are you, you bad boy?'

Lloyd-Webber was bemused by his *Evita* star: 'I think I'm going to have an interesting and remarkable collaboration. My goodness, she's a good girl.'

Goodness, as we know, had nothing to do with it. It was hard-headed business. And Madonna was not putting all her film hopes in one production basket. She had not wasted her time waiting to get the *Evita* title role. While the negotiations were going on, she was playing an acrobat in an, as usual, as yet untitled Woody Allen film. It sounded as though they were getting on well. He called her 'prima donna' and she called him 'little twerp'.

There were other film projects. In the autumn of 1991, she began work on *A League of Their Own*, a film described by the producers as 'about a worldly ball-player with a sharp tongue and a fast reputation'. The project first involved Debra Winger but then Madonna took the role of Mae in the story about a female baseball team in the 1940s. The director was Penny Marshall and Madonna's co-star was the future double-Oscar winner Tom Hanks, who had starred in Marshall's enormously successful film *Big*. Madonna decided to make *A League of Their Own* while waiting for a starting date for *Evita*. The Disney Studios chairman, Jeffrey Katzenberg, had made a vow of film-budget austerity and the $30 million price tag for *Evita* seemed too much for him. But the Lloyd-Webber/Robert Stigwood/Glen Gordon Carron/Madonna package remained intact. Madonna was wide eyed, like a child in a candy store.

Madonna continued to cast her net around other movies. Freddy DeMann said that Madonna wanted to star as the late Martha Graham, the mother of modern American dance. She also has the rights to *Little Odessa*, about a Russian girl in Brooklyn. And she and Demi Moore, hot from *Ghost*, were going to be Leda and Swan in an action film along the lines of *Lethal Weapon*. Madonna and Moore spent the early part of 1991 working on the script. Producer Joel Silver, who made the *Die Hard* movies with Moore's husband Bruce Willis and also the two successful *Lethal Weapons* with Mel Gibson and Danny Glover, planned two *Leda and Swan* film sequels before the first film was even shot. Madonna as Mel Gibson? If you follow the formula, she must eventually play Lady Macbeth. On stage in London?

And, given her Scots connections from her second marriage, she probably will. She was determined to be a major box-office movie star, a screen idol. And she was quick to voice her ambitions: 'I haven't been a failure so far. And the reason is that I simply haven't put a lot of thought into it. I haven't honoured or respected a movie career the way I should have. I didn't approach it the way I approached my music career. I'd had a lot of success in music, and all of a sudden people are going, "*Here's a movie.*" And I didn't think about it. I just took it. I underestimated the power of the medium. It's been a good lesson for me. *Dick Tracy*? You could say I have a lot of unresolved feelings about it. I remember being very upset that all of my big music scenes were cut up the way they were. I learned a lot about film-making from Warren, but obviously it didn't make me a big box-office star, did it?'

She would do everything to make sure *Evita* did, including what amounted to corporate creeping. 'There's a lot of business stuff,' said Madonna about the long negotiations she says she turns into a little voyeuristic fun for businessmen. 'I live for meeting with the suits. I love them because I know they had a really boring week and I walk in there with my orange velvet leggings and drop popcorn in my cleavage and then fish it out and eat it. I like that. I know I'm entertaining them and I know that they know. The best meetings are with suits who are intelligent because then things are operating on a whole other level.'

The suits saw Madonna as a female Stallone–Schwarzenegger of the 1990s. At the Oscars, she looked like Marilyn Monroe. She and Michael Jackson were the oddball sensation. He had worn collagen-pumped lips while signing his billion-dollar contract with Sony Records. She wore the Hollywood full-lipped look in her controversial 1991 *Truth or Dare: On the Road, Behind the Scenes* (also known as the *In Bed with Madonna* documentary). Madonna had something to sell at the Oscars as well as herself. Jackson wore two gloves, gold-tipped cowboy boots and a dazzling diamond brooch at his throat, his hair hanging down his back and around his regularly-sculpted face. Madonna was a peroxide picture in a low-cut, pearl-encrusted, Bob Mackie, shimmering white gown. The $20 million in diamonds – borrowed for the evening from legendary New York jeweller Harry Winston – included a 34-carat pink diamond valued at $14 million, which was reset for the evening into Madonna's ring size. The baubles added extra twinkle to what headline writers were the next day calling the 'date of the century'. Imagine if it was a *real* date – the genetic possibilities of little Madonnas and Michaels? Twinkle, twinkle little stars. But who would grab whose crotch? No. No. It was business.

Madonna and Jackson took the two front-row seats in the aisle, centre stage at the Shrine Auditorium. Madonna was perfectly positioned as Jeremy Irons was named Best Actor for *Reversal of Fortune*. As Irons made his way to the stage, she leaped up with a congratulatory hug and kiss, eager for the celebrity audience to see how close she and the man she wanted to be Juan were. A billion people watch the Academy Awards on television; this was heavyweight public relations. As Madonna worked this worldwide 'room', Michael Jackson gazed merrily into space.

There was little space a few hours later at Spago, the then obligatory Oscar-night hangout. Wolfgang Puck's restaurant is a star spot all year, but on Oscar night the late agent Irving 'Swifty' Lazar took it over and it was invitation only. In 1991, Donald Trump could not even buy entry. Madonna and Michael waltzed in to the A-table watched by Israeli security guards. They sat with Anjelica Huston and Michael Douglas and his then wife Diandra. Al Pacino nodded to Madonna who showed him some cleavage. Jack Lemmon stared. Jeremy Irons found *Reversal* co-star Glenn Close for a chat. Jodie Foster arrived in a breast-baring Armani jacket. Actors. Popular and honoured ones. Madonna liked the company. Warren Beatty – his *Dick Tracy* took three Oscars – sat with the late French director Louis Malle and his wife Candice Bergen. Beatty's new lover, model and 'Victoria's Secret' favourite, Stephanie Seymour, was not with him. In a moment, Madonna was over and sniggering with Beatty and then sitting in his lap as he fondly fondled her. Madonna squealed, 'It's so unbelievable. What a night!' She sounded like a girl from the Midwest. Steve Bray, the loyal, longest serving soldier on the Madonna racing team, smiled and said, 'She was always like this. She wanted attention – now it's her job.'

Truth or Dare got attention (the London première, with the more provocative title *In Bed with Madonna*, was shown to packed audiences in July 1991). This was a home movie like *Sex, Lies and Videotape* is to *Bambi*. The beautiful Alek Keshishian – 'handsome' is redundant for the long-haired, brown-eyed man – directed the film. Madonna allowed him, his cameras and microphones access to almost all her waking moments, but she did not fall for his charms: 'I found Alek quite attractive, but I kept my distance because I never like to have a crush on somebody everybody else has a crush on.' It didn't inhibit her. She demonstrated her artfulness at oral sex by showing her gulping style on a plastic bottle of Evian water. She sang a song about farting. She ogled as two men kiss and shouted, 'Oh God! I'm getting a hard-on.' Later, she would reveal, 'That's my favourite scene in the movie. I love that people are going to watch that and go home and talk about it all night long. I live for things like that.'

There are other things to talk about. For the first time since her father's remarriage, she visited her mother's grave. In the film, she lies on top of her mother's grave and wonders if her mother is 'just a bunch of dust'. In an unedited three-hour black-and-white tape, she frolics with one of her male dancers on the Blonde Ambition Tour and he rips off his clothes as she shouts at him, 'Your cock is big.' In another sequence, another ambitious dancer is reprimanded: 'Get out of my bed and don't come back until your cock is bigger.' She calls Warren Beatty 'a pussy man'. She appears topless. Kevin Costner appears backstage after her Blonde Ambition appearance in Los Angeles and tells her, 'You were great. We thought it was neat.' After he goes, Madonna puts her finger down her throat and says, 'Anybody who says my show is neat *has* to go.' Bootleg copies of the unedited documentary sold in Hollywood for between $8,000 and $40,000 depending on film quality.

Warren Beatty wanted some scenes of him deleted before the film went into the world's cinemas. He did nothing naughty on film – he just did not want to be associated with it. But Madonna's graveyard 'meeting' with her mother and most of the other incidents remained when the film was released in the High Street cinemas. One of the Beatty scenes that remained was one of the most intimate. Madonna is being examined by a throat specialist at her New York apartment. As the doctor is at work, Beatty is off camera and muttering about the insanity of filming the medical team. When the doctor turns and asks if Madonna wants to talk off-camera, Beatty loses his cool: 'She doesn't want to *live* off-camera! What point is there to existing?'

Beatty made a point of avoiding the Hollywood première of Madonna's indulgent *Truth or Dare* in May 1991. He clearly did not want to be in a situation where he might be asked to comment on the film. The special–invitation-only screening at the Cineramadome was to benefit the AIDS Project Los Angeles and the AIDS Action Foundation. The post-screening party was held at the Arena nightclub, one of Los Angeles' most popular gay clubs. It was quite an evening. Madonna appeared and, at first, was not recognised. Gone was the Marilyn look. In its place was something close to Morticia from the 1960s black-and-white cult television series, and a British favourite of the time, *The Addams Family*, which in 1991 was revamped as a big-budget feature film starring Anjelica Huston as Morticia and Raul Julia as her husband. It was so successful that a sequel, *Addams Family Values*, was made. Madonna wore long, brown hair, a Jean-Paul Gaultier catsuit and black eyeliner almost to her ears. The snake had slipped another skin. Marilyn one moment, Morticia the next.

Things were more familiar at the Arena where many of the 700 invited guests gathered later. Her brother Christopher was there along with David Geffen and actress

Mimi Rogers, the former Mrs Tom Cruise, Barry Manilow, Steven Seagal, Matthew Modine, Rosanna Arquette, super-producer Joel Silver, Vanilla Ice and a host of enormous drag queens. So was Sandra Bernhard. Madonna was mostly a good girl. Bernhard was her outrageous, suggestive, uninhibited self. The two girls rubbed up against each other suggestively to the delight of the Arena audience.

Truth or dare? At the 1991 Cannes Film Festival, Madonna hosted a small dinner party where the guests played truth or dare, the game that gave her film its title. Designer Jean-Paul Gaultier dared Madonna to French kiss actress Anne Parillaud, the star of *La Femme Nikita*. She did. Madonna was having fun publicly playing her game. But what was even more revealing in 1991 than the film *Truth or Dare* was an interview Madonna gave to the New York-based gay magazine *Advocate*. It quickly became known as the most faxed article in Hollywood. Mainstream Hollywood was amazed at what Madonna had to say. She was asked, 'How big is Warren Beatty's dick?' And the shock was not her answer, but that she even acknowledged the question. But the answer to the big question: 'I haven't measured it, but it's a perfectly wonderful size.'

She admitted her 'agency' was 'freaking' about her being demeaning on the film about Kevin Costner and she added, ''Cause Kevin Costner is like this big hero and everything. But, I mean, come on; people rip me to shreds every chance they get and I can take it so he should be able to take it. Emasculating? Now, look, you can only take the balls away from people when they give them to you. I enjoy expressing myself and if I think someone is being a pussy, I say it.'

She was asked if she was personally kinky. 'What do you mean by kinky? I am aroused by two men kissing. Is that kinky? I am aroused by the idea of a woman making love with me while either a man or another woman watches. Is that kinky?'

She said she has not used dildos or sex toys. 'I like the human body. I like flesh. I like things that are living and breathing. And a finger will do just fine. I've never owned a vibrator.'

In the *Advocate* interview, Madonna set herself up as a feminist heroine. A social politician? No taboo was too much for discussion. Whether it is regarded as shameless or heroic, it got the world talking about issues – and Madonna. She got jumped on and dumped on for her film and for her interview, but emerged as the world's most interesting icon. And the most stimulating.

But by 1991, Tony Ward, who had become her lover during and after co-starring in the 'Justify My Love' video, was out of her life. It seemed she could always – as the Oscar song went – get her man; keeping him was the problem. And Ward – for all Madonna's liberated view of the sexual world – was a little too risqué and risky for her. She had jokingly stubbed a cigarette out on his back at his birthday party, on one of their first 'dates'. He excited her – maybe too much.

Ward, because of his Madonna association, became the focus of much newspaper interest and it was discovered that after he and Madonna had become intimate, he married another woman. The marriage certificate showing Ward and Amalia Papdimos, then 23, a Greek citizen, in Las Vegas, did not please Madonna. Her view then, for all her attitude, was for a traditional family: 'I wish I were married and in a situation where having a child would be possible. People say, "Well, have one on your own." I say, "Wait a minute, I'm not interested in raising a cripple." I want a father there. I want someone I can depend on.'

Madonna believes in fate. A fortune teller told her in 1991 that her heart would be broken, that she would not have children. That upset her. Then the fortune teller told her that she was not suited to her career choices. That devastated her. Madonna got drunk. For the first time in her life, she lost control. But what do fortune tellers know? Mark Kamis, always the loyal friend, remembers the time.

'Whatever happened with Ward, there was a lot of anger in her work, but then things changed – there was more love and I think that's who she really is.'

If, indeed, Madonna could ever be one person. She has always operated as a maverick on her way to fame. Madonna has been called brilliant and blasphemous, a nightmare and a dream. 'What more could she do to shock the world?' asked Terry Press, a DreamWorks executive who previously worked with Madonna on *Dick Tracy* and then begged the question again, saying, 'We've seen her naked. We have seen her with women. She is one of the most self-absorbed people on planet. What's next?'

Oh, just a multi-million-dollar entertainment empire, a little bondage and sado-masochism – and screwing an old man to death. But just in the movies. In real life, Madonna was still desperately seeking the right man or, rather, the right genes. Good genes in tight jeans was not a fantasy but a quest for the best. Madonna was a Nobel sperm-bank sort of girl; it was something which was now more instinctive than calculated or maybe, as some said, vice versa. She is someone who has always been open to options.

CHAPTER SEVENTEEN

THAT'S SEX BUSINESS

'Pain cleanses us, it absolves all our sins.'
MADONNA AS 'REBECCA' IN *BODY OF EVIDENCE*, 1993

Before Madonna began experimenting in other more controversial celluloid entertainment, she enjoyed significant success as a mainstream movie star in *A League of Their Own*, which she had only taken by default while waiting for *Evita*. The film about the Second World War women's baseball team, The Rockford Peaches, was centred on Geena Davis, the Tinseltown 'It' girl of the moment. But Madonna, as 'All the Way Mae', won over audiences and the critics.

It was not long before she started upsetting them again. This icon of outrage wanted everyone to keep talking about her, to keep buying her records, watching her videos and movies. Her concern then was whether her audience was shockable any more. And when you have shown millions just how far you are willing to go for attention – the biographical *In Bed with Madonna* being a prime example – what is next? Madonna created a gold mine digging into the boundaries of what society would accept, but the risk for her was that society would get bored before it got censorious. Nevertheless, the woman who had dressed her career in spandex, lycra and black nylon was still, like her cleavage, plunging into dangerous areas. It was a high-wire act with no safety net.

On 21 October 1992, around 750,000 copies of *Sex* appeared worldwide wrapped in black Mylar plastic so that non-buying, casual shoppers could not flip through the foolscap of top-quality print, which contained Madonna's frolicksome sexual fantasies – 128 pages of naughty photographs and words. With expert photographer Steven Meisel, in the 21st century a glossy-magazine celebrity himself, as her shutter star, she attempted to create her version of female sex fantasies.

For photographic sessions in Florida, she dressed as a Playboy bunny and hired a male stripper and a porno cinema for location work. In *Sex* there is sado-masochism, lesbianism, bestiality and simulated rape. And pages and pages of Madonna's musings on the title subject. The book did not live up to expectations. With *Sex*, she made a mistake. She badly misjudged how far she could take on public opinion, sexual inhibitions and double standards. She lost a lot of the respect her fans, especially women, had previously afforded her. Madonna was disappointed: 'It was meant to be funny, mostly, but everyone took it very seriously – which just showed me what little sense of humour most of us have when it comes to sex. In fact, no one seems to have a sense of humour about it at all, not when it is presented to you by a female. I think that if a male had conceived the idea and I was just a model in the book, it would have had a very different reception. Once again, though, I wasn't suprised by the reaction – everyone rushing out to buy it and yet feigning total disdain. A woman who is rich and famous and intelligent and naked is a very daunting thing for most people. If you are any of these first three things you have to keep your clothes on. You're allowed to be naked if you're stupid or if you are perceived to be a victim or something that can be objectified. But you are not allowed to be naked and empowered.'

That was Madonna's view. Others, less charitable, said that it was not disdain for her but that the market was already saturated with similar sexy offerings. The book – despite thousands of fans camping outside bookshops for its midnight release – was, by her standards, a failure. Friends say this was the moment she began to rethink her image.

'She is very calculating,' said a close friend. 'She scours popular culture looking for the trends that will bring her most success. In the 1980s, it had to be provocative and shocking and she knew that, getting most of what she did exactly right. The book *Sex* was a rare miscalculation. But she got back in the vibe because she realised the 1990s were all about the spirit and self-improvement.'

However, *Sex* was part of a package. With it were the album *Erotica*, which was all about what its title promised – the *Erotica* album video featured Madonna walking naked through Miami. The book received a poor reception, the record did not make waves and then came the movie, *Body of Evidence*.

She started 1993 at number one – of the laughable but now legendary Mr Blackwell's Top Ten Worst-Dressed List. It was a remarkable achievement given how little she, as the diva of daring, was wearing at that time to be worst dressed in. While Mr Blackwell, an ageing, tinted Hollywood dress-designer who had his annual, self-publicising giggle from his turreted home near the British Consulate in the Hancock Park area of Los Angeles, could be shrugged off, it was not so easy being a headliner on a Ten Most Unwanted Stars list.

Madonna was also devastated when audiences found *Body of Evidence* more of a bore than an event. The critics thought of her as a B-movie Sharon Stone and voted the movie one of the greatest belly-flops ever. In the film, she's the rather sexually over-enthusiastic Rebecca who loves her lover to death after binding him with leather straps to the bed. It was an MGM film but from the first minutes it is clear you would be better renting one of their old musicals. Rebecca likes to be hurt and when she has an idle moment she enjoys filling up men's navels with hot candle wax.

'Pain cleanses, it makes us free, it absolves us of our sins,' intones Madonna's Rebecca, who shouts, 'Slap me!' at a lover and, when he does, she bites his shoulder. Kink followed kink, frame by frame. It's revealed that Rebecca as a child would steal strawberries from a neighbour's garden and often fall into the rose bushes and she says, 'The fruit always tasted sweeter because of the pain it took to get it.'

Directed by Uli Edel, who made the controversial *Last Exit to Brooklyn*, the film really did not seem to have much chance, even with Madonna's Rebecca arguing, 'Sex pertains to everyone; it is the universal language. Some people just speak it better than others.'

Chuck Henry, the film critic of ABC TV in Los Angeles, was first with the vitriol: 'It is one of the worst films ever made. It gives new meaning to the phrase "amateur night". If this is supposed to be a big appearance by Madonna, this woman is in big trouble. Watching her act is like seeing an animal in heat. It's celluloid garbage. It's a bomb.' He added, just by way of explanation so that no one could misinterpret his message, 'It's a really bad film.' The late, great *New York Times* film critic Vincent Canby offered, 'Madonna just seems busy, like someone trying to follow directions on how to microwave a twenty-five pound turkey in six minutes. She's a self-made personality of engagingly naked ambition and real, if often raw, wit. She has a sense of humour, also a particular gift for defining the camp sensibility. Forced to play more or less straight, she's at a loss.'

It was a public execution. It was a film that could not satisfy anyone outside the parameters of die-hard Madonna fanatics and the Raincoat Brigade. What seemed incomprehensible was why she, Madonna, one of the richest and most successful entertainers in the world, got involved in such a project. In closed-door offices, executives wondered if the empress had no clothes. Was it all over for the woman who starred in millions of teenagers' disobedient dreams? Madonna was caught in a corner. One group despised her and her sexual poltics – the other was not interested in her. One review of *Sex* suggested, 'It can be a warning about what happens when pop icons become bloated, one way or another. Just think of Elvis in Las Vegas and you'll have an idea where Madonna is heading if she doesn't watch out.'

She had to consider the question of over-exposure – and that did not count her strutting down a catwalk for Jean-Paul Gaultier in his dungaree dress, the straps nestling between her naked breasts. Was Madonna just desperately searching for bigger headlines? And would she get them? Her brand name appeared to be fading but, as always, she was planning the repackaging of herself. Or other people.

When all seemed to be going wrong directly, Madonna was indirectly creating Maverick with the guidance of the intuitive

Freddy DeMann. While she was involved in making and producing records, including 'Bedtime Stories' (a platinum-blonde Monroe lookalike on the album cover in a photograph by Princess Diana favourite Patrick Demarchelier), the company that existed because of her was trying to find some wings. Flying wasn't that easy even with Madonna firmly at the controls. The record label distributed by the corporate major Warner Brothers has generally run on a staff of about 30 people and all have Madonna's personal approval.

Maverick got involved with the rap act group Proper Grounds but they did not flourish. The company also went to Hollywood, making two films using Madonna to headline *Dangerous Games*. *Variety* in Hollywood thought it just a mix of the usual (sex, drugs and husband–and–wife horror) but added the dismissive, 'A confrontational downer likely to appeal to only a marginal audience.' The other film, *Canadian Bacon*, looked much more hopeful with a cast including Dan Ackroyd working with his former partner John Belushi's brother Jim Belushi, Alan Alda and the rotund, loveable John Candy. It was all about the White House going to war with Canada and no one cared. Madonna cared, ferverently; and it was not just the Maverick movies but the music which was not going smoothly. It led to a tremendous confrontation with Courtney Love, for Maverick wanted to sign Hole, Love and Kurt Cobain's ultra-cool grunge band. Very publicly, Courtney Love gave Madonna a big thumbs down. But then they had very good luck. DeMann said on the choices, 'Before we sign an artist, we run them by Madonna and she checks them out.' Alanis Morissette checked out. And sold – in the early 1990s – a lot more music than Madonna, especially with the album *Jagged Little Pill*, which went on to sell more than 25 million copies. Morissette, like Madonna before her, won a host of awards worldwide and broke the template of how hugely popular and critically applauded artists could sound and behave. Another unique woman – and a personal Madonna signing to Maverick – was crop-haired, bass-playing Me'shell Ndegeocello. Madonna felt vindicated by their success and even more resilient because of it. Morissette said of her boss, 'She expresses herself eloquently. Some of that is in response to people questioning her intelligence for a very long time. We had a couple of girlie nights out; we are so intense, we always seem to end up really talking. We're so alike in a lot of ways. We don't have the same taste in men but we have the same philosophies about dynamics with men – the whole concept of creating the grey area when it comes to a man being totally intimidated and freaked out on their knees in front of us, or a man being disinterested because they want a woman they can control.' Not a likely option with Morissette and Madonna.

Control was the point for Madonna but she became increasingly frustrated about not being able to get everything she wanted in the early part of the 1990s. Her game plan was not working out. Her fans would not have realised it. There was The Girlie Show Tour and the Brit Awards and this show and that promotion; there was the video *Take a Bow*, which was just another audition for *Evita*. It was all about her love for a bullfighter, Madonna looking very furtive in 1940s garb and then writhing in La Perla underwear. Alongside this public sex show, she had another project that mattered more than anything. She wanted a child. And, like picking a pop group, picking a project, a movie or a new song, she found a father. It was, for a time, Madonna's most secret romance. The man? Healthy genes in tight jeans which displayed what newspapers worldwide would later label 'The Tackle'.

Madonna also had her other passion to fulfil – the movies, and one she called 'my other baby' in particular. Despite all her success, Madonna had not achieved acceptance in Hollywood. It was illustrated in a legal dispute between former longstanding lovers Clint Eastwood and Sondra Locke. Locke cited Madonna during her civil lawsuit against Eastwood in which she contended that he sabotaged her career. His lawyers said she didn't have a career to ruin. She countered that Madonna had shown interest in one of her projects. Eastwood's people shrugged and said that was further evidence that she didn't have a case.

When Madonna was asked about still trying to 'break into movies' at the age of 38 she snarled, 'Why don't they ever ask *men* that question? I'm a very resourceful person and am creative in a lot of different ways. It's not like I'm in a position where I go, "Oh God, in a couple more years I'm not going to be able to get those parts." I don't get those parts anyway and I wouldn't want them. I'm not insanely jealous of the movies Sandra Bullock and Demi Moore are making. I'm not worried because I don't think the privileges that youth brings are things I want. The lucky, beautiful young people aren't getting things I'm pining for.'

CHAPTER EIGHTEEN

THE CASA ROSADA

'Don't Cry For Me, Argentina.'
EVITA, TIM RICE AND ANDREW LLOYD-WEBBER

Madonna had gone to Hollywood hell and back for the opportunity to star as Evita. When she heard that British director Alan Parker had been given the task of adapting the stage musical to the screen she was at once delighted and distressed. The good news was that Parker had not cast his leading lady. But would he cast her? Would he like her? Would he want her? After all the trouble and time and anguish she had put into the project, it had the ingredients of a nightmare that Christmas in 1994. Parker had two or three women in mind to play Eva Perón but Madonna had no clue if her name appeared on the list: 'I wasn't about to just sit around and find out. I wanted to let him know exactly how I felt and so I wrote him a letter. An impassioned plea, more exactly. I don't remember how long it was or what I said exactly, but I do know I felt as if I was completely possessed while doing it. And it must have been one of my more persuasive efforts because it worked. He called me up.'

They had a handful of face-to-face meetings. She won the role and *Evita* enveloped her life for many, many months to come. It was time to fasten the seat-belts; she was in for a bumpy ride.

Madonna had told Parker that she was willing to do whatever it took to become Evita – to learn Spanish, take tango lessons, have vocal lessons to increase her range. She admits she had become obsessed with Eva Perón, intrigued by her story. It is a dramatic one. Eva Duarte's mother was the mistress of a prominent man in the Indian village of Junin. He died when Eva was six years old. She and her family were initially refused entry to her father's funeral, which is where her rebellion against authority began. She was only 15 when she arrived in Buenos Aires, a striking figure with big brown eyes.

'Her eyes were strong,' says Argentinian movie-maker Victor Bo when recalling her. 'She didn't need to speak. She *looked*.'

By the 1940s, she was her country's most popular radio-soap star. She met and charmed Colonel Juan Perón, dislodging a teenage rival, and when he became President in 1946, the Evita legend began. She became South America's most powerful woman and, by gathering up Argentina's female vote, she guaranteed Juan Perón's Presidential re-election. She became, in effect, Vice-President of Argentina. The nation loved or hated the couple, but Eva Perón's early death in 1952 sent the country into mourning.

'I felt I could understand her,' Madonna gushed. 'Where she came from. The controversy surrounding her life. The extreme reactions she provoked in people. And the more I researched her life, the more I became possessed by her. There's always the danger that you can like someone less, the more you get to know about them. But I fell madly in love with her and her story. I had nothing but compassion for her when I finally understood the poverty she came from, what she had to endure and her illness – just how young she was when she died. For years, she refused to acknowledge she was sick and wouldn't seek help. She was afraid of being injected with poison, thought everyone was trying to kill her, and so she wouldn't take any medicine or painkillers. As a result, she suffered an enormous amount of pain while still working eighteen-hour days. And it really felt as if art were mirroring life when we arrived in Buenos Aires to begin filming and found some people outraged by my very presence in their country, others marching through the streets in support of me. I thought this was perfect, for it was exactly how it was for Evita when she was alive. I had performed in Argentina and I knew how passionate its people are. There's no in-between for them – it's black and white.

'The hostility can be hurtful and at other times I can laugh it off. Particularly when it's the same boring old tripe and you can sense that not even the newspapers themselves really believe what they are saying. It's all just something that sells newspapers and which goes along an established line of thinking, with that misogyny that runs throughout society and says that women who are successful are whores, bitches, immoral, whatever. You do get some solace from thinking, Well, the same thing has happened to this person or that person. I'm not the only one – I'm just one in a long line of women who have been trounced for being individually strong. Eva Perón not least among them.'

When Madonna arrived in Buenos Aires in January 1996 to begin rehearsals and all the rest of the paraphernalia – wardrobe fittings and camera tests, and meetings and meetings and more meetings – she continued her research into Eva Perón. She read books and watched documentaries. She also met an Argentinian film director who had copies of movies Eva Perón had appeared in. Each day, she said, she learned more about her subject.

'People see Eva Perón as either a saint or the incarnation of Satan. I can definitely identify with her. Some of the old men all but foamed at the mouth when they talked about the old days, so it was like we were back in 1942. They still seemed smitten with her. I kept being told how much I looked like her or moved like her. One particular group of Perónists I was brought together with were so vehement about their beliefs that they were thumping the desk as they talked. Then, in the middle of all this drama, one of them said, "Oh, but your skin is so much like hers was." I got a lot of reassurance from all of that.'

But there were many sour deals before Madonna took her place on the balcony of the Presidential Palace in Buenos Aires where, in 1951, Eva Perón tearfully told thousands of her people that she was dying. After nine months of talks with Argentinian President Carlos Saul Menem, it was agreed that the crucial balcony scene for *Evita* could be filmed on that very spot.

One meeting has never been revealed. Madonna was secretly flown by helicopter to an island to meet Menem, and tried to enlist his support for the film: 'Up to that point, everyone had been crticising our intentions and obviously the President had to keep his own people happy. But I knew that if I could reassure him that I would approach the character in a very respectful way, he would be turned around. That made it exciting; in fact, it was so hush-hush I felt I was going down there on some espionage mission.'

There had been open hostility towards the film and the stars and crew, from Perónists who feared the movie would dishonour the memory of Evita. Graffiti on the city walls read, '*Chau* [goodbye] *Madonna*' and '*Fuera* [go away] *Parker*'. That so many of the film-makers were British did not help as the memory of the Falklands War was still a volatile issue. Menem had originally called the project 'a disgrace' and then around Buenos Aires it was being gossiped that Parker's script portrayed Eva Perón as a prostitute.

Alan Parker, famed for movies like *The Commitments* and *Pink Floyd – The Wall*, had wanted to make the *Evita* movie ever since he first heard the double album in 1976: 'Within a week of its release, I asked about filming it but Andrew and Tim wanted to see it on stage first. In 1979, I was approached about making it but I was just coming off *Fame* and I didn't want to follow one musical piece with another. Normally, I never regret turning down work but I felt resentful I let it go.'

Nearly two decades later, he got his chance and recalled soon afterwards receiving that letter from Madonna. He remembered it being eight pages long: 'She doesn't do things like that every day. She said that no other person could play the part; that she'd sing, dance and act her heart out. And she did. She really put her heart into it. This work was not like spending two days on a pop video – a huge amount of vocal training was needed to strengthen her voice and extend its range. She went out of her way to do her homework, arriving early in Buenos Aires to meet people who knew Eva Perón. She's not gone about this frivolously at all. This was a new film genre – not opera, not MGM musical with people speaking and then bursting into song. I felt today's audiences wouldn't take that, so if it was to be all sung it had to be sung well. Madonna and the others had four months of vocal training and recording before filming began.'

It was an epic enterprise and that balcony scene was crucial, said Parker. 'We wanted to use the balcony of the Casa Rosada, or the Pink House, which is what they call the Presidential Palace for the scene where Eva addresses the crowd and sings "Don't Cry For Me, Argentina". I went to meet Menem twice and talked films and politics with him. I explained that the story was through-sung. He couldn't get his head around that. The British Embassy were fantastically helpful. They would point me in the right direction, use this person, not that one. Memem finally realised there were not that many people against it. I already knew this. I'd seen the graffiti. Knowing a bit about typography, I guessed it was one person's work. Also the phrase *"English tast force"* was spelled wrongly every time. So I came to think our only opposition was a dyslexic Perónist. We shot the balcony scene in the days before we left Argentina. It was wonderful using the very balcony where Eva Perón had stood. There were thousands of extras, all Perón supporters. It felt like being part of history, not just recreating it. It was an electric moment.'

The busy British actor Jonathan Pryce, who played Juan Perón with wig, false nose and teeth, called the moment magical. Of Madonna he said, 'She's a strong, dynamic force and I can only admire that. I grew to like her a lot. People have preconceptions about her but you soon learn she's a regular person.'

Antonio Banderas, who played the narrator, Che, was as smitten by Madonna as the *descamisados* were by Eva Perón: 'I had never met a harder worker. She focuses completely.'

As the film company left Argentina, moving on to Eastern

Europe and then London to complete the film, she was going to have to maintain that focus. On 19 March 1996, Madonna had arrived back in America for a short break before joining the *Evita* caravan in Europe. She was off to Miami but stayed in New York for a time to shop on Fifth Avenue – and see her doctor. She had no clue she was pregnant. She said she often missed periods when not sleeping, working too hard or travelling and, of course, she had been doing all of that and more. 'There had been moments in Argentina when I'd felt a bit seasick but it was very hot, we were working out of doors, the food was bad and everyone was complaining about upset stomachs. I just thought I was feeling the same as the rest of the team. Then I went to see a doctor. Yes, you could have knocked me down with a feather.'

Now she had two 'babies' to worry about. Her child, which she had witnessed 'tap dancing' on the ultrasound, and the film, which she was praying – literally – would not be affected by her condition. She wanted to be great as Eva Perón and not disrupt any schedules. She said she fell in love with her child the moment she heard the heartbeat. So much happiness and so much concern: 'It scared the shit out of me. I certainly wasn't planning for it to happen when it did. I had more than enough things to worry about, just getting through the movie. On top of all that, to take on board the reality of motherhood. I was like, "Oh God, this is the last thing I need, I don't want to do anything that could sabotage the film." But everyone involved was so supportive of me and I was so prepared for what I was doing in my work that, in the end, it had to work out.'

Nevertheless, initially, she kept the news of her pregnancy to only a handful of friends and family. And the father. She was fearful of the news leaking out in the press, correctly certain that she would be hounded. Pregnant Madonna was news — and it was a photograph the world would pay obscene amounts of money for. Later, a diary she kept throughout the filming of *Evita* was published in *Vanity Fair* magazine. In it, she wrote, 'I was stunned when I saw on the ultrasound a tiny living creature spinning around in my womb, waving its tiny arms around and trying to suck its thumb. I could have sworn I heard it laughing. The pure and joyful laughter of a child.' Crucially telling is her entry on Mother's Day: 'I long to know the sensation of having a mother to hug or call up and say conspiratorial things to about how difficult men are...' Later, only a few days before her pregnancy became public, she explained, 'I feel like a fourteen-year-old who is trying to hide the fact that she is pregnant from her parents. I keep looking in the mirror expecting to see that glow of pregnancy and all I see are dark circles under my eyes and acne. I should be happy and excited but instead I'm scared...' It was not too-long before she was advertising her happiness.

CHAPTER NINETEEN
LITTLE MIRACLE

*'The worst thing written about me? That I was
having a baby for attention.'*

MADONNA, 1998

The good and the grateful were all in attendance. Once
again, the politically aware AIDS Project Los Angeles
were hosting their Commitment to Life Awards. The ninth
annual fund-raising event – by the end of the evening, $3.5
million had been pledged – was at the celebrity-crowded
Universal Amphitheatre beneath the stars and the
Hollywood sign. The next-door Universal Studios film lot
had been taken over and turned into New York's Central
Park with colourful hot-dog stands and carriage rides and a
carousel. The late summer theme was a Salute to the Movies
and the Music of the 1960s, and present were some survivors
of that decade including Michael Douglas, Raquel Welch
and Neil Diamond.

There were also current stars present, like the cross-
dressing, best-selling author and American bad boy,
basketball star Dennis Rodman. Attention antennae on alert,
he was flouncing around with customary camera-fatiguing
flamboyance when his former girlfriend arrived.

Madonna was unexpected and very expectant. A pin-up of America's AIDS charities, she was there to do a job, to wave the flag and introduce her provocative protégé, performer Me'Shell Ndegeocello. While Rodman sashayed, she made her remarks in out-of-character, expletives-deleted, subdued style. She was, for once, playing down the image. Outrageousness and her provocative personality were put on hold. In a whisper only magnified by the elaborate sound system, she asked the audience, 'I beg you to stop sending baby gifts to my home. I beg you...'

Madonna was in Budapest – the Hungarian capital was doubling for 1940s Buenos Aires – in April 1996, with six weeks of filming still to be completed on *Evita* when she announced she was pregnant – three months pregnant. She had had to go public – her costumes were becoming tighter by the day. Madonna's pregnancy was just another hiccup and the permanently upbeat director Alan Parker said, 'She's been splendid throughout, utterly professional and giving the performance of her life. Personally, I'm very happy for her.'

But he could not match the joy of Madonna. It was a combination of all she had worked and hoped for. Her child, she believed, would give her the personal fulfilment she had been so anxious for and, she fervently hoped, calm her fears about early death from cancer and not seeing her child grow up. She had been in therapy for a decade trying to deal with her own mother's death.

Professionally, *Evita* offered her a chance to become, like her idol Marilyn Monroe, a movie superstar. Since 1984, when *Like A Virgin* was released and she began work on the film *Desperately Seeking Susan*, she had been chasing Hollywood fame and acceptance. It had been a long haul through a miserable mire, including *Shanghai Surprise* and *Body of Evidence*.

Her search for a father for her long-wanted child had mirrored her attempts at a movie career – turbulent and unpredictable. It had included such unlikely father figures as seemingly non-committal lover-boy Warren Beatty and love 'em and leave 'em Sean Penn – both of whom, in 2001, were married with children they had after separating from Madonna. She said the former lovers and their *babies* aggravated what she called her 'longing, a feeling of emptiness'. Peter Shue, a well-known Manhattan man-about-town asserted, 'It's like she wants me to just stay with her and just do nothing.' Dennis Rodman said, 'She had ways of making you feel like King Tut. But she also wanted to cuddle.' Rodman says Madonna asked him to give her a child during their relationship: 'She said be in this hotel room in Las Vegas on a specific day so you can get me pregnant.'

Madonna admitted she was pining for a child, and seeing her former husband and lover become parents made her more despondent. She talked about her loudly ticking biological clock to anyone who would listen. On American television, she told good-natured reporter Forrest Sawyer that she was considering placing an advertisement for a 'sperm donor'. She laughed about the need for someone to take on the 'fatherhood gig' and added, 'I'm sure I'll meet the right guy.' What she didn't say was that she already had. The father of the heiress to Madonna's then $347 million fortune was Carlos Manuel Leon, whom Madonna first spotted when she was jogging through New York's Central Park in 1994. He was 28 years old when Madonna first met him. Nicknamed 'Carlito' and later 'The Tackle', he was lean (7 per cent body fat), tall (5ft 11in), a former bicycle messenger, competitive race cyclist and fitness trainer with brown eyes and a goatee beard. And, according to gossip, something of a sex machine. But with Madonna involved, they would say that, wouldn't they?

It was a package that clicked for Madonna. When they met in Central Park, she admired his sunglasses. He became her personal fitness trainer and then things became more intimate. Officially, from 13 September 1994, he had been her boyfriend. That's the date he emblazoned in a heart tattoo across his left shoulder. Until he met Madonna he lived at home and his mother wouldn't let him have a tattoo, or an earring. Cuban-Americans Armando and Maria Leon, who have turned into doting, stereotypical grandparents, found out on 8 April 1996 that Madonna was their son's girlfriend – and that she was going to have his baby. Armando Leon, then 51, who owned five financial outlets in New York (they make commission cashing social security and payroll cheques for workers without bank accounts) and his wife Maria, then 49, a social worker, married in 1962. They loved Madonna. At the time, Mrs Leon, apparently without irony, said, 'She is just like you and me.'

Mrs Leon was less worried about Madonna than about her son and her future grandchild: 'She loves Carlos very much. Everything people say about her is not true. Will they marry? There are no plans at the moment. As long as they stay happy – that's what is important.'

Not long before, she thought her son had brought a Madonna lookalike to her apartment on West 91st in New York. 'When he told us about her I said, "Sure, sure, sure, you are dating Madonna." And then Madonna called me and said she wanted to meet me, to come up to the house. She walked right in front of me and I didn't believe it was her.

Now, I cook her black beans and we listen to Cuban music and talk. I think she likes being part of a family. She loves Carlos and we love her. Carlos has always been hard working and quiet. No matter what was going on, he would contact us every day.'

Maria Leon may have got over her initial shock, but Tobias Nunez, who went to Hallows High School with her son, had not: 'I still can't believe it. He was a nerdy guy; he was very strait-laced. He came to a party at my house but he didn't get into it. He never used to talk about girls and he sure as hell didn't have a girlfriend. He was interested in going to college. He wasn't stupid. He got good grades. He didn't play hooky. We wouldn't play hooky in Catholic school or we'd get into trouble. And we stayed away from drugs. I can't remember if he listened to any of her music. He was more into hard rock like The Who and Led Zeppelin. Club music, house music – that's what he liked. He was shy and innocent – well, I guess he's not so innocent now.'

The odd couple romance flourished before their daughter Lourdes was born. Madonna, that Scarlet Pimpernel of the music world, found that she could not disguise her growing shape. It seems then she was at her most maternal and allowed Carlos to play his manly role. He didn't like being pushed around. And, according to Madonna, he was monogamous. 'Carlos was very jealous. When I was looking through a magazine, I was careful not to comment on attractive guys.'

But who really wore the trousers? Carlos Leon's aunt Daisy Alvarez says she has, with hindsight, pinpointed the situation: 'She liked to boss him around. She was used to doing that to people. I don't think he liked that much.'

His brother Armando Junior said, 'I teased him about it.'

Carlos Leon had found himself in a strange world. It was not just adapting to money that can buy almost anything; if you want it, you have it. You want to fly to the West Coast, you go. Hungary? Fine. Argentina? Get to the airport. Already, there were echoes of Elizabeth Taylor's romance and then marriage to construction worker Larry Fortensky. At first, he had tried to lead a 'normal' life by going to work on construction sites and taking a packed lunch and a flask of coffee with him. With permed hair and designer suits, Fortensky looked uncomfortably out of place. A talking point at dinner.

Madonna's friends talk of Carlos Leon being 'sweet' and her publicist Liz Rosenberg called him 'lovable'. They could have been talking about a pet. While he had his Warhol 15 minutes, the focus was mostly on the mother-to-be. Except at the World Gym at the Lincoln Center in New York where there was a different perspective: 'It's not that Madonna's going to be a mother, but Carlos is going to be a father!' said Gina Makowski, the manager of the fitness centre. But even she added, 'He's very sweet.'

From the moment Madonna's pregnancy became public it was widely suggested that Carlos was simply a sperm donor and would be discarded with the nappies. Although their relationship did not last, Madonna has finally answered the questions over whether he signed over his patnernal rights to her: 'It is just one of those nonsense things that people who don't know anything about it like to invent about something which is quite truthfully none of their business.'

In 1999, Carlos was quoted as saying he saw his daughter 'as often as possible'. Three years earlier, he was the father-to-be in an event which was treated in Hollywood like a royal birth. Madonna and Child was big business. US newspaper helicopters were on alert. American *Vogue* magazine of October 1996 devoted an unprecedented 15 pages, including its cover, to Madonna. Of course, in the you-stroke-my-back cynical culture, it was also a useful box-office launch pad for *Evita*.

For Madonna, the baby was a plus. Whether it was ever going to add up to baby making three only Madonna will ever know for sure, for with his donor duties a success, Carlos did not remain in the happy family picture for long.

Although he proved more than a Central Park himbo, he had no illusions about business with – or marriage to Madonna. He is, say his friends, devoted to her and proud to be the father of her child. He would have been happy for it to be more official – legal – than that; nevertheless, his name appeared on the birth certificate when Lourdes' arrival at The Good Samaritan Hospital was registered at the County of Los Angeles offices in downtown Spring Street. He did not pressure for more than that.

Madonna was anxiously seeking a nanny; she wanted someone aged under 40 who was bilingual and able to speak Spanish to her baby's father and paternal grandparents. She was also desperate for security. Her 'bachelor mansion' overlooking the Hollywood sign was well known. There had been incidents there and, in January 1996, she had gone to court in Los Angeles to keep a stalker at bay – and faced Robert Dewey Hoskins who was accused of threatening to 'slice her throat from ear to ear'.

The confrontation took place after a judge ruled that Hoskins could stay in court as Madonna gave evidence against him. Subdued and nervous, she took the witness stand reluctantly, dressed in a black knit suit. Asked by a prosecutor how she felt about being in the same room with Hoskins, she closed her eyes and said, 'Sick to my stomach … I feel incredibly disturbed that the man who threatened my life is sitting across from me and he has somehow made his fantasies come true. I'm sitting in front of him and that's what he wants.' When asked about her reaction when she was told of the threat to cut her throat, she said, 'I guess I felt incredibly violated.'

With some irony, as the hearing went on, the court complex was besieged by fans hoping to catch a glimpse of Madonna. Her lawyer, Nicholas de Witt, had tried to get Hoskins sent to the cells while Madonna gave evidence. But Judge Jacqueline Connor refused the request along with a plea for her to appear on videotape, saying the impact on the jury of such moves would be so prejudicial it would jeopardise any verdict they might reach.

Mr de Witt had argued that Hoskins hoped to intimidate Madonna: 'He wants to look in her eyes, he wants her to know he's had some kind of effect on her. Mr Hoskins really wants one thing in this case more than anything else. He wants to see the fear he's instilled in her.'

Hoskins's lawyer, John Myers, said his client had a constitutional right to confront his accuser: 'He's entitled to be in the courtroom, just like in any other case.'

Hoskins was charged with one count of stalking, three of making terrorist threats and one of assault. He had been shot and wounded by a security guard at Madonna's Hollywood estate in May 1995. Prosecutors said it was the third time he had been to her mansion in two months. But Madonna had tried to avoid any court confrontation, saying her schedule and security concerns made it impossible. The courts threatened a

$1 million fine if she did not appear. She did – as did her bodyguard Basil Stephens, who described how he shot Hoskins because he seemed 'fearless' and threatened the singer. Stephens said he confronted Hoskins because 'he was definitely the kind of character that would carry though with his threats' to 'slit her from ear to ear'. Jurors were shown a security camera videotape of a man approaching a gate to leave a note, and twice scaling a wall and wandering through the grounds. Stephens said he twice told Hoskins to leave before the third visit led to the shooting: 'I've had many people come up to the estate, but none was as credible a threat as this. The look in his eyes, the refusal to leave. He didn't seem to be afraid of anything. He seemed to be very determined.'

Stephens said he first spoke to Hoskins on 8 April 1995, when Hoskins left a note at a gate. The night before, he had scared off an intruder and he said Hoskins admitted that he was that man: 'I confronted Mr Hoskins and told him to take his note and go away. He said, "Give her the note or I'll kill you." I walked towards him and he said, "Tell Madonna I'll either marry her or kill her." I said, "What did you say?" And he said, "I'll slit her throat from ear to ear." '

Stephens said he called police, got a gun and chased the man but lost him. Madonna hired an extra security guard to patrol the estate and the trespasser apparently did not return until 29 May. Stephens said he was alone when he confronted a mumbling, swearing intruder on that day. 'Then he lunged at me. He said he was going to kill me. I drew my weapon and said if he didn't stop I'd shoot. He lunged at me again and I fired. He didn't go down. He spun around and lunged at me again and I fired again and he went down. I was upset. I thought I had taken somebody's life.' He said he called an ambulance. And Madonna.

Hoskins showed no emotion when he was convicted on five counts of stalking, assault and making terrorist threats and was jailed for five years. Prosecutor Rhonda Saunders said Hoskins was no ordinary over-zealous Madonna fan: 'He was determined to have her marry him or have her throat slit.'

Madonna was fearful enough for herself but now that she was going to have a child she was determined to take action. Apart from Hoskins, there had been incidents with other interlopers. She had had disputes with neighbours over security walls and camouflaging hedges. Also, her property was a highlighted attraction on tourist 'maps-to-the-stars-homes'. Her solution was to buy a smaller property – 3,586 square feet of living space compared to 7,800 square feet – in the Los Angeles suburb of Los Feliz. For $2.7 million she got a main house with five bedrooms and a two-bedroom guest house. She said it would be 'easier' for her and her family. There was round-the-clock security as well as live-in help. Cher, who had helped her close friend Michelle Pfeiffer with the arrival of her two children, her adopted and then natural daughter, was constantly telling Madonna to 'sleep now – for that's it for life! They keep you awake whatever age they are!'

Madonna attended Thursday evening (7–9.00pm) Lamarr's classes at Cedars-Sinai Medical Center in West Hollyood with Carlos but he was not included in the interior decoration plans. The 'girls' – Madonna's sister Paula, Donatella Versace, Debi Mazar and Rosie O'Donnell – all presented their nursery ideas before and after the Californian baby shower at the beginning of August 1996. But Madonna's thoughts were already on her own childhood and *Romper Room*, a 1960s American television series. It was an updated version with hand-painted wallpaper – nursery rhymes and cartoon paintings of *Gilligan's Island* characters – as well as assorted wall hangings, mobiles and music boxes, and cuddly toys from FAO Schwartz in New York and the children's department at Neiman-Marcus on Wilshire Boulevard in Beverly Hills. She had three changing tables and cupboards packed with the paraphernalia of life with nappies. There are also walls of pictures in primary colours – the *mood* educationalists said it was best – and a sound system with shelves of classical CDs – music Lourdes listened to in the womb.

Madonna was and is a believer in the methods developed by doctors in northern California, which say babies can hear sounds in the womb. Following their instructions, she placed loudspeakers on her tummy and played music and talked and sang to Lourdes. She tried not to shout or even raise her voice during her pregnancy. Everyone around her was banned from swearing. She told aides a minor curse word would incur a $1,000 'fine' – and she was going to collect.

While Madonna – some of her make-up people called her 'Hitler Mom' – prepared to give birth, her daughter's dad – whom Madonna presented with a crown-shaped, diamond-studded ring on their first 'anniversary' – was making plans for an exercise empire. With Tony Schettino who owned the World Gym in New York, he had plans for fitness centres in Florida and California. One would compete with exercise entrepreneur David Barton who ran the 'in' keep-fit spot at the Delano Hotel on Miami's South Beach. It's a small world. Madonna was co-owner of The Blue Door restaurant – the 'in' South Beach eating spot – at the Delano Hotel. Madonna, who feels she has been 'used' by men in the past, was comfortable with her Carlito. He was another example of her eclectic taste in men. For Madonna he was the right man – at the right time. It is an intriguing irony that a woman so in tune with her body and the fitness of it should become pregnant by her personal trainer.

'Some days are great and you feel really good and have the best feeling about how you look. Then, on other days, you just look in the mirror and go, "I'm a whale." It's so temporary though and what you get for a small amount of suffering is quite worth it, I'd say.'

She explained, 'You have to look at your lifestyle and ask, "Am I at a place in my life where I can devote a lot of time to being the really good parent that I want to be?" None of us wants to make mistakes in that role and I imagine a lot of us look at the way our parents raised us and say, "I definitely wouldn't want to do it quite that way." I think you have to be mentally prepared for it. If you're not, you're only doing the world a disservice by bringing up a child you don't want. Things happen when they are meant to happen and if the chance of being a parent comes along again and you're ready, you'll do it. I was ready because I felt more ready to be a good mother than any time in my past. Absolutely ready.'

As was Lourdes Maria Ciccone Leon when she arrived on 15 October 1996. It was a fitting entrance. Photographers were camped outside, a personal publicist waited at a Beverly Hills hotel, and security guards patrolled every entrance to the Good Samaritan Hospital with extra platoons on the eighth floor where Madonna, at 38, had given birth. Lourdes weighed in at 6lb 9oz. The announcement of the arrival of Madonna's child was made, in a lavish Hollywood twist, by Dr Paul Fleiss, father of the convicted Hollywood madam Heidi Fliss. The paediatrician said Madonna had asked him five months earlier to care of her baby.

LITTLE MIRACLE

Madonna remained in hospital but after 36 hours she and Lourdes – from that moment always Lola to her mother – went to their new home. Madonna's baby was born by Caesarean section – leaving her with a 7-inch scar – after she had struggled for several hours to give birth naturally. She had wanted no drugs but took the advice of her obstetrician Margaret Banks for her own and her daughter's safety. Madonna was conscious for the birth and was able to watch the procedure in a carefully angled mirror. Carlos Leon held her hand during the labour but did not watch the final moments of birth.

Madonna's first public thoughts on motherhood were given in a radio interview in Los Angeles and she was in grand humour: 'I feel like Dolly Parton. My breasts enter the room before I do. She only gets a couple of more months of me feeding her then I want to be able to fit back into my shirt. Nursing is a very big sacrifice but it is a great experience. I had a twelve-hour labour and it was bad for me. Some people have short labours but mine went on for ever. It was long and arduous. A trip to the dentist is nothing in comparison but I had a really easy pregnancy so I guess it had to get tough somewhere.

'When I was pregnant I had cravings. I wanted poached eggs every day. And oranges. I also had haemorrhoids and back pains; for most of the time I was pregnant, I did not want to go out in public. I felt very self-conscious being the size of a house. Some women find pregnancy very sexy but I for one had no desire to strip off and show my big fat tummy to the world. I spent most of the time feeling ugly, fat and lonely.

'Lola is great, having a baby agrees with me. I play music for her non-stop. When she was inside me, I was in the recording studio blasting the *Evita* soundtrack. That's what calms her down when she's crying.'

Madonna began then and continues to document Lola's life in an elaborate scrapbook with her framed birth certificate, mementos, medical details like height and weight and body fat, and photographs. Of all the changes Madonna has made in her life, of all her Pimpernel disguises or attention-grabbing outrageousness, motherhood has had the most startling effect. Madonna, for a time, turned into a hippy. An earth mother. She was still spending more than £40,000 a year on personal health, fitness and beauty and around £50,000 on her wardrobe but she was about to go through a long period of flowing dresses, wavy, darkened hair, henna, Indian tattoos and an ongoing fascination and belief in yoga. It was reminiscent of The Beatles and their maharishi. Somewhere in the forest of success, you have to find yourself.

But one of Madonna's associates whispered that this was no fad but from the heart: 'I think having a baby made Madonna feel more vulnerable, wondering what Lola would do if her mum died and so she needed to make peace with herself over her mother's death. It's a side of herself she has rarely talked about, but it affects her deeply. She has some of the strongest maternal instincts I've ever seen. When Lola is around, she lights up like a Christmas tree. It unlocked a vast reserve of love in her. The two of them play in Madonna's closets. They love going through her jewellery and shoes. Lola goes around the house wearing twenty necklaces and bracelets, walking on her tippy-toes like she's wearing high heels. It's very sweet. She's a real girl's girl. Madonna looks completely transported when Lola is around.'

And, for a time, Carlos Leon was also around. Madonna

had snapped at suggestions that she had used him as a donor: 'There is speculation that I used the father as a stud service, implying that I am not capable of having a real relationship. These are comments made by persons who cannot live with the idea that something good is happening to me. It's just all part of the view the media likes to have of me. That I'm not a human being. That I don't have any feelings and I don't really care for people. That I'm just ambitious, cold and calculating. It's all just part of the image that unhappy people like to construct for me.' What devastated her most were suggestions that she had given birth to get attention: 'Some people have suggested that I have done this for shock value.' It was a remark she was to repeat many times. It genuinely upset her that anyone could think that of her.

But as far as Carlos was concerned, it was only a matter of time – a short time. He was with her at the American première of *Evita* where she outraged the fashion police by wearing a garish red velvet suit with a giant flower at the waist, feathers and flowers above, and spike-heeled shoes, beneath a towering red hat fringed with a black veil. Madonna, who could have had the help of any designer in the world, had chosen her friend Susan Becker to advise her. Madonna got attention for her audacity and arguably that was the point in the first place, for she – and her movie – made the front pages worldwide, even if Eva Perón, a devotee of Christian Dior, might not have approved.

But just a month later, at the Golden Globe Awards, when Madonna – 20lb slimmer after Lourdes' birth – was spilling out of a black bra-top gown and collecting her Best Actress honour, Carlos was not around. Madonna did not need her hand held; she felt secure in her reviews. *Variety* wrote, 'Madonna gives her all to the title role and pulls it off superbly.' Another critic offered, 'This is her role: a Material Girl seeking sainthood.' Another saw the movie as 'an *objet d'art* that evokes serious viewer admiration more than passionate excitement'. Generally, Madonna was said to have triumphed in *Evita*. It was a personal vindication to the doom-sayers whom she believed were just another type of stalkers and, sometimes, more damaging.

Business was good that January in 1997. Maverick had also signed The Prodigy, which was another example of Madonna's growing interest in Britain – and her business acumen. Many record companies were desperate to have a financial arrangement with The Prodigy following the tremendous reception for their album *Firestarter*, and it was Madonna's personal attendance and attention at meetings at Maverick's white-painted, anonymous offices near the Beverly Center in West Hollywood that helped secure the deal. Like Alanis Morissette, the British group were a hit-making, lucrative asset and, by the turn of the millennium, her company – which also has divisions in movies, publishing and merchandising, all contributing revenue to Madonna's personal fortune – was easily approaching its first £1 billion worth of sales. That's impressive arithmetic and maybe why she became passionate about an accountant's son from Britain's Shakespeare Country. She's always liked good figures.

It was in 1997 that the Material Girl from Michigan, the Boy Toy, the disco tart, the rock diva, the star of *Evita* finally declared herself an Anglophile: 'I have some excellent friends in London and have thought about sending my daughter to school there. I think British people are more intelligent than Americans.'

Madonna had become good friends with Paul McCartney's daughter Stella – a maid of honour some years later at her second wedding – and hosted a wonderful if private party for Stella when she won her role as designer for Chloe. It could have been the influence of Alan Parker – he called her 'M' during filming – but more likely the need to escape from the feverish atmosphere of Los Angeles, where the ethos involves not how much you succeed but how badly your competition fails, had enthralled Madonna with the UK. Even in 2001, she could not explain the attraction. It was a 'gut' thing, she said. She had been overwhelmed by English chic. She spent more time in London than Los Angeles and talked about buying a house in the British capital. 'Now she wants to be calm and cool at the same time and that is more London than New York,' explained Ray Kybartas, a personal trainer and good friend.

Madonna decided to buy a house in London and, luckily, money was not a concern. Although, like Cary Grant, instinctively careful with her finances, Madonna kept repeating that she would fight being 'ripped off because of who I am'. She viewed a home in Hampstead Garden Suburb and Spaniard's House with a built-in four poster bed and electronically-controlled waterfalls. There was a £4.5 million property in Little Venice that caught her interest and the Earl Terrace developments in Kensington where homes started at about £3 million. And there was a house in Warwickshire, which Prince had rented during a UK stay in 1997. Madonna was desperately seeking – *roots?*

Back in America, it was acknowledged that the romantic relationship with Carlos Leon was over. But he would always be Lourdes' father and part of her life. However, he and Madonna would go on with their own lives. Despite all the cynics, it was, as far as the principal players were concerned, a loving and fulfilling answer.

Times were changing for Madonna. She was enchanted by the fashions – the floaty chiffon numbers of Albert Ferretti – and visited Voyage, the self-elevated as exclusive boutique in Fulham Road, London, favoured among others by Patsy Kensit and Jemima Khan.

But Madonna was not concerned with the ladies of London. She had tea with Hugh Grant, an eventful dinner with actor Rufus Sewell, who famously left before pudding. She got involved with Mungo Tennant, a cousin of Princess Margaret's friend Lord Glenconner. Closer was her time with curly red-haired Tim Willocks, an accomplished novelist and psychiatrist. Men, it appeared, were becoming, like her collection of handbags, something to be seen with. This was a *Sex and the City* time and the city was London. Madonna suddenly had the freedom to feel she could do as she pleased; she had proved herself both personally and professionally. There was no longer the need to shock to get attention as she was, other than Diana, the Princess of Wales, the most photographed woman on the planet. She believed she could also indulge her inner self.

CHAPTER TWENTY
A BIRD IN THE HAND

'Rejection is a great aphrodisiac.'
MADONNA, 1998

Motherhood, understandably, changed Madonna for ever. She dwelled more on the meaning of life and the future; on mysticism and the increasing belief that the answer to her many questions was in devotion to certain disciplines, including yoga. She began putting down the foundations for the future. Her friends said the change in attitude was in preparation to sustain her iconic status for at least another couple of decades.

'People underestimate how smart she is,' said Ray Kybartas, adding, 'Her talent gives her this enormous energy and with each year that passes she has got better at directing it so that she can be more creative and get more done.' Kybartas said Madonna had become much less frivolous: 'The way people made fun of her book *Sex* made her feel like a clown. It upset her. She wanted to lose that, to be taken seriously again.'

Her success with *Evita* had given her great gravitas as Alex Keshishian, who directed *In Bed with Madonna*, said: *'Evita* was one foundation stone of the new Madonna. The other was baby Lola. I think she finally felt she had respect, that she didn't have to prove everything any more. In *Evita* she felt like a movie star, which is what she had wanted her entire life, even more, I think, than being a pop star. And then with Lola, she finally found somebody that she felt was more important than her own self.'

Record producer William Orbit, who collaborated with Madonna to create the distinctive psychedelic feel to the album *Ray Of Light*, which she recorded in 1997 and was released early in 1998, said he was surprised by how almost turn-of-the-century Madonna was, so far from being a superstar diva.

'Madonna's a sleeves-rolled-up kind of girl. You can't really reconcile all those things you've seen with any person you're working with. She didn't have any airs and graces. She drove to work. She was very civil and polite to everybody. And she is a genuinely clever songwriter in that larger-than-life, Broadway musical kind of way. I was more impressed by her as a producer, musician and songwriter than as an icon.'

By now, the British Press were calling her 'Maddie' and 'Madge', indications they were adopting the world's most famous woman. She felt she had been wooed this way before, as some of the lyrics of *Ray of Light* showed: 'Had so many lovers/Who settled for the thrill of basking in my spotlight.' The words appeared to reflect her true feelings, for she said of the lovers in regard to the lyrics, 'Well, it's not to say that they were only attracted to me for that, but I realise that that was a big part of it. Power is a great aphrodisiac and celebrity is a great aphrodisiac. And rejection too.'

Madonna, of course, is a veteran at mastering things. She had arrived in Manhattan with pennies to work as a waitress.

A BIRD IN THE HAND

It was three years before anybody took her ambitions seriously and it was DJ Mark Kamins who provided her big break. Later, much later, he reflected on his friend reaching the age of 40.

'I think Madonna has slowed down, in a good way. She was once the wildest person I knew. There was really nothing she wouldn't do if she thought it would be fun. Lola helped kill a lot of Madonna's pain; there was a lot of anger in her early work, now there's more love and I think that's who she really is.'

Old friend Steve Bray argued that Madonna changes because she is always trying to grow: 'She's just this free spirit. She opens herself up to experience and anybody who does that is going to be changed by their life. It's not phoney; she's a genuine chameleon, always looking to fit in but never committed to staying in one place.'

Nevertheless, British screenwriter Andy Bird appeared to have Madonna grounded. Bird was a struggling actor and writer relying on friends' sofas for overnight accommodation in London when he was introduced in Los Angeles to Madonna through their mutual friend, the movie-maker Alex Keshishian. It was lust at first sight. Bird, educated at Kiniton High School in Warwickshire, had worked as a fitness instructor – he's tall, lean and long-haired – and immediately Madonna was smitten by his looks, manner and British accent. He was *cool*. And, as the British tabloid newspapers would announce, she was *tweet* on Bird. He was a dozen years younger than Madonna but that did not appear to matter in the heady days of 1998. It was a difficult romantic involvement for them both. They were all over each other and London; at the Metropolitan Bar, at Nobu, and went hand in hand to yoga classes at the Inergy

Centre in Kensal Rise, North London. Bird was to discover that, when Madonna becomes involved with something, it can take over. Madonna is happy to road test everything in advance – even if it is a stretch. He went on yoga 'dates'.

Ashtanga yoga in 2001 was one of the fastest-growing health and fitness practices, and leading teacher John Scott, who has helped Madonna and her friends like Sting and Trudi Styler, believes anyone can benefit from it.

'This is different from other forms of yoga where you move slowly and hold positions. Ashtanga yoga is fast flowing and aerobic. You move from one posture to another with dramatic speed. But the most important aspect is the breathing technique, which is through the nose. The breath and time of inhalation and exhalation is synchronised with the movements. The reason it has taken off so dramatically is that previous health and fitness exercises haven't included the breath. If you are running on the treadmill, your body is working and your mind is somewhere else, for example on the video screen. With Ashtanga yoga, your breath links your body and mind together, resulting in a meditative, spiritual practice. Many celebrities endorse its benefits. For them, Ashtanga yoga is far more than mere exercise – it is responsible for their stamina, focus, feelings of well-being, their toned physical bodies and peace of mind.'

New Zealander John Scott discovered Ashtanga yoga working as a commercial designer at a holistic health and fitness centre on the island of Skyros in Greece. He was drawn to it as a form of exercise to keep a toned physique developed through surfing: 'It blasted away all my misconceptions about yoga being dull. This was dynamic and strenuous.' He teaches with his wife Lucy at their yoga retreat in Cornwall, and travels every year to India to join the living guru of this form of yoga, Shri K Pattabhi Jois, known fondly in the Ashtanga community as Guruji. There is a set sequence of tough movements known as sun salutations that are done at speed, synchronised to fluid, steady breathing. They are followed by a routine of tough standing and sitting postures.

Breathing is done through the nose and concentrated in the chest, not the stomach, and controlled through the back of the throat. Done properly, the movement/breathing system helps to heat up the body, producing sweat and increasing flexibility. John explained, 'The sweat is cleansing and purifying, initiating the release of toxins retained within the superficial fat layers of the body. As students progress, toxins held in the deeper layers of muscle tissue and internal organs are also released, resulting in a healthy, toned and flexible body.'

Madonna happily talks about her discipline: 'I've been practising Ashtanga since my daughter was born. I stopped working out the way that I used to and it's a very visceral, disciplined yoga. There's so many different kinds of yoga – it's not one of the easier ones and it doesn't come easy to most people, including myself. I usually practise an hour and a half, five to six days a week. I'm more relaxed and less rushed. It's all the yoga. It's changed my life. It gives you a lot of clarity and softness. I'm not as aggressive as I used to be. And I'm a lot more patient.

'Ashtanga yoga is the hardest thing that I've ever done, but it is really focused and there is a great simplicity to it as well. I'm a total perfectionist who beats myself up when I don't get things right. And so I had to learn not to judge myself and to let go of the idea that I had to accomplish this and master it in one day.'

After Lourdes was born through Caesarean section, Madonna wanted exercises that would tighten up her stomach muscles. Friends pushed her towards Ashtanga and she became a student of Florida yoga teacher Wayne Krassner. Lola went along to sessions. Krassner vividly recalls the first time he met Madonna. She has one of the best-known faces in the world, yet he did not recognise her until halfway through the class he was giving for eight students in a friend's dining room.

'She seemed so humble and polite. I thought she was just another student. That's how she wanted it. I learned the truth when I was introduced to her personal assistant, who wanted me to do private sessions at Madonna's mansion. She says she's been unable to return to her previous gym workouts. She can't walk inside a gym, she gets horrified by it, like an addict who's overdosed. I think she had reached a burn-out level or something. It felt wrong emotionally and mentally, and it felt wrong physically for her.'

But stretching with Andy Bird was comfortable for Madonna. She had greatly matured, professionally and personally. The Princess of Wales had asked Madonna's advice on how to handle the press when Madonna visited Kensington Palace in November 1996. Princess Diana had sought her out and invited her to afternoon tea – then a novelty refreshment for Madonna and at the time she became a tea addict. They talked about many things – Diana's infamous *Panorama* interview was broadcast on the BBC only eight days after Madonna's return to America.

'We had met at an art gallery, and I had a little chat with her,' recalled Madonna. 'She wanted to get together with me so I could tell her how she could have a thick skin and not be bothered by what everybody writes. I said I had always sympathised with her position and made some joke how the only person who seemed to get more attention than me was her. She said, "I think you handle the press better than I do." I replied, "You will have to get a skin as thick as an armadillo."

'I broke down when I heard she had been hurt in the car crash in Paris. I was crying, "Please, God, let her live." I had been chased down that tunnel so many times I have lost count. If there weren't such large offers of money, then these people wouldn't go to such extremes to take pictures. Then you have to look at the editors and ask who is responsible for this. But even that does not dig deep enough. As much as I would want to blame the press, we all have blood on our hands. All of us. Including me. I bought those magazines and I read them.

'I understand the extremes they will go to for pictures – photographers have paid children to lie under my car so it would look as though they were trapped beneath the wheels. People had the same fixation with Princess Diana that they have with me. You are never allowed to make mistakes without being hanged in the public square. Then there was this idea that neither of us could have a relationship with a man; that we could never find one we could connect to because our marriages had failed; that we were unlovable. The bravest and most dignified thing about Diana was that, while she exposed herself to the public, she also said, "I'm not perfect, I have my problems." I am not saying I agree with everything she ever did, but what we need are not role models who say they are perfect but ones that say they are flawed and vulnerable, and are going to try and change and be better. We need people like that more and more because everywhere we look – television or fashion photography – we see the glamourising of death and violence and drug addiction. I sensed a kind of desperation from Princess Diana – I realised she did not have the same kind of support from friends that I enjoy.'

Madonna was not always a people person but, as she approached her 40th birthday, she had realised that although she could achieve so much – in a fame sense she ruled the world – she was mortified that she had not established a family unit. For all the rebellion, she was someone who needed the traditional; if not a white picket fence and strawberry dessert on Valentine's Day – as her father had provided for her mother – she yearned for a stable family unit for her and, especially now, for Lourdes. Andy Bird looked and, more importantly, *felt* like a contender. When they first met in 1997, he was living on the dole in West London and relying on the kindness of friends while fantasising about film-making. Madonna adored him – he could have been *her* in New York all those years earlier, eating discarded McDonald's fries out of garbage cans, huddling around a small electric heater. Andy Bird – 'the blackbird', as he always dressed head to toe in black – was a habitué of the restaurant called 192 at that address on Kensington Park Road in London. His clothes were not new and he adored his aged motorcycle boots held together by tape. He did not drink but chain-smoked Gitanes.

'Andy is charming company, but never had any money,' said a friend, adding, 'If you had lunch with him you almost inevitably paid, but found yourself not minding very much.'

Alex Keshishian met Bird in London and when, in 1997, Bird flew to Los Angeles with a screenplay for a London gangster film – what else? Keshishian contacted Madonna and told her that there was a 'great guy' in town she might want to meet. They did, at a dinner in a restaurant in the Hollywood Hills. There was an immediate connection. And Andy Bird was very flattered. Madonna was enraptured. She hauled him off his friends' couches and installed him at her home. Her friends were amazed at how fast Bird became an essential part of her life. And lavish reporting followed.

'Her circle of friends, which included rich, young female socialites and a lot of creative gay men, felt Andy wasn't good enough for her,' said one of the London set, adding, 'They were suspicious and, I guess, a little jealous, although Madonna didn't know or care.'

Andy Bird admitted, 'I just can't get my head around the situation. Why is she so into *me*?'

Madonna and Bird travelled to England for a long visit as a couple in late 1997. It was also the first time that both sets of their London friends had the chance to see and assess the relationship at first hand – at a birthday party thrown at Momo, the modish bar and restaurant off Regent Street, by Madonna's English *feng shui* expert Gary Hawkes. In her inner circle that night were Madonna's veteran friends Ingrid Casares, Victoria Fernandez (a Colombian socialite), fashion photographer Mario Testino and his brother Giovanni (who also acts as his picture agent), and interior designer David Collins. 'Madonna was all over Andy that night, very physical and tactile,' said a guest. 'She was hanging on to him as if he was about to fall out of a train. He didn't look very comfortable and I know that he thought some of the people in the restaurant were sycophantic and pretentious.'

Bird went to a London fashion PR friend of Madonna's who provided him with a new wardrobe of trendy Japanese Evisu jeans, Jeffrey West shoes and coat, trousers and jumpers from the J Linde-berg line – all in black. During the same trip Bird took Madonna to where he felt most comfortable, to meet his own friends at the 192 bar. When Madonna walked in with Bird, there was a stunned silence, followed by a scramble for autographs. Madonna did not enjoy the reaction, particularly the lack of 'cool'. Before they returned to LA, Andy took Madonna to meet his parents, Horace and Kathleen Bird, who live in the Warwickshire village of Clifford Chambers. Madonna and Andy Bird arrived there in a Range Rover leased by Madonna. There was a newspaper fuss, but Mrs Bird tried to help. 'She was a lovely girl and seemed to be fond of our son but then mothers are very biased. What matters to us is if our son is happy, and if his girlfriend is making him happy, we don't mind who it is. She might be Madonna, but they are just like any ordinary couple. She's a really smashing girl.' Her son flew back to California with Madonna on a private jet.

Madonna had an ongoing attraction for Andy Bird but, understandably, the imbalance of their achievements and lives was not going to allow the relationship to succeed. For a long time, Madonna would phone Andy Bird in the middle of the night saying she could not live without him. During the day, she could. Their fast-track romance soon led to regular and more intense, heated rows. Eventually, Madonna moved Bird out of her mansion. She gave him $30,000 and told him to find an apartment to rent close by. When he found an unfurnished one, Madonna, her Old World frugality showing, gave him some of her old office furniture. 'It wasn't like she wanted to break up with him, but she wanted her space. Andy hated the situation too. He felt very uncomfortable about the money disparity and the fact that she was subsidising him, due to her lifestyle and his lack of income,' a friend of Bird's said, adding, 'The dynamic of their relationship began with him saying, "I don't want to be seen to be living off you." But, in the end, it was Madonna who lost patience and was telling him, "It doesn't help us to keep paying for you. You've got to do something. I want you in my life." '

They split up – somewhat. The relationship continued long distance with Madonna in America and Bird on the sofa of the Notting Hill flat he shared with a 192 waitress friend and her mother. It was not satisfactory for either of them. He would be invited to wherever Madonna was, be it one of her houses in Los Angeles, New York or Miami. He found this increasingly oppressive although enjoyed the pleasant sex. Other matters niggled too. Madonna, he said, wanted to know where he was and who he was with. When he was in England, she would phone him at his Notting Hill gym, or at 192, or the Met Bar. This organisation was clearly displayed at his birthday when he was in Los Angeles. Madonna organised a surprise dinner for him at the exclusive Indochine restaurant. 'Madonna arranged for Ben Pundole, the manager of the Met Bar, and his deputy, Martine, to be flown over from London for the party. They were given first-class tickets and booked into the Mondrian Hotel. They were the English acquaintances whom Madonna found most acceptable…'

When Madonna celebrated her 40th birthday in New York in August 1998, the always dishevelled-looking Andy Bird was with her. He said there was a 'deep, mutual love … a lot of pride has to be swallowed on both sides'. It never got much better although there was contact – sometimes initiated by Madonna – on the telephone. In one call, she told him she had written the song 'Beautiful Stranger' for him. And in letters, she repeated her telephone remarks about loving and adoring him. He had lived – and survived – a long lesson in Madonna's need for control.

But Madonna was confused. She had met the director Guy Ritchie and saw in him a man who could look after her – and her family. He was more Sean Penn without the downsides than Andy Bird or Carlos Leon could ever have been. More (without getting too close to the psychiatrist's couch) like her strong, principled father Tony Ciccone. She was smitten with Ritchie and found herself in that full flush of love where everything and everyone is sensed as a threat. Madonna did not want any upset in her friendship with Guy Ritchie.

She had met him at the home of Sting and his wife Trudi Styler, who had produced Ritchie's name-making movie *Lock, Stock and Two Smoking Barrels*. It was a garden lunch party at Sting's Wiltshire home and Trudi Styler had placed Madonna next to Ritchie. Later, Madonna described the scene: 'You know when people say, "he turned my head" – my head didn't just turn – my head *spun* around on my body.'

Guy Ritchie looked and acted as though he could have walked out of his own movie. Madonna was bewitched, if a little bewildered. At first. She felt this man, a decade younger than her, was a real *geezer*. Nevertheless, more of a chap than a geezer who for his own reasons talked his social pedigree down rather than up.

CHAPTER TWENTY-ONE

LOCK, STOCK AND...

'I cry when I see the Wizard of Oz. *Every time.'*
MADONNA, 1989

Madonna had done the rainbow tour as *Evita* and now she was on a British run. Her California connections were a weak link. What was a girl to do? Her did-they-or-didn't they/Do-they-or-don't-they? association with actress and performance artist Sandra Bernhard was also on the rocks. Madonna had apparently paid too much attention to Bernhard's other lady friend, Ingrid Casares; and it had been Casares who had caused the final bust-up between Madonna and Carlos Leon. He 'blew his top' when he learned she had been out on the town with 'the girls' and that Casares had been her 'date'. He cooled down a little when Madonna explained to him that it was like him going to a baseball game and to a bar with his friends. Leon wanted to understand that, but still didn't follow the thinking. The understanding was that, clearly, he would always be the father of Lourdes but, as far as Madonna was concerned, that was it.

She had been involved with other men – most

devastatingly with Andy Bird – but that extraordinary, special relationship eluded her. And she was 40-something. She embraced the Jewish mystical tradition, *Kabbalah* – a completely different form of spiritual expression from Ashtanga yoga – a mix of philosophies comprising a 3,000-year-old Indian medicine, a 2,000-year-old Jewish religion and an ancient form of yoga favoured by warriors before battle. Model Christy Turlington and actresses Demi Moore and Goldie Hawn supported this holistic approach to health and beauty, which seeks to promote inner and outer harmony. Madonna was seeking something else as well.

She hoped her new British geezer had it. He certainly had interesting connections. Guy Ritchie is related to Sir Winston Churchill, the Duchess of York (a cousin, two family lines) and the late Princess of Wales (a cousin three times removed). His grandfather, Stewart, was a major in the Seaforth Highlanders who was decorated in the First World War, and was killed in the Second at Dunkirk trying to protect the evacuation. His father, John, was also an officer in the Seaforth Highlanders and later became a successful advertising executive producing the still celebrated Hamlet cigar commercials. John Ritchie and Guy's ex-model mother, Amber, divorced – and she later married a baronet, Sir Michael Leighton, on whose estate near Shrewsbury, Loton Park, Ritchie spent some of his childhood, learning, among other country pursuits, to shoot. It would become the most profitable part of his education. Ritchie was expelled from many schools, perhaps for being unteachable, although he was once quoted as saying he was expelled from the £5,000-a-term Stanbridge Earls School in Hampshire for drugs. His father recalled, 'It wasn't drugs. He'd been caught in a girl's room and he wasn't going to his lessons. Guy says those things on occasion. I think it's rather modern to say it. He likes to pretend he's been a bit of a scallywag, but I don't actually think he was.'

Either way, there was some street-cred in the expulsion. The teenage Ritchie, afflicted by extreme dyslexia, had fallen for the allure of the underworld and had read all the books about and by the Kray twins. He was proud of his family's military background, and fascinated with guns.

'Guy and a mate rented an apartment whose street entrance door you can still see, next to the Pizza Express in Notting Hill Gate,' said one of his former street colleagues. 'Guy was a good kid, but he was a little too full of himself and used to brag a lot. Bought himself a blue Triumph TR7 sports car and drove it around his patch like a lunatic, jumping lights – all bravado; ultimately, he came a cropper with some very nasty people – about a thousand quid, maybe even less than that – who cut him up for their money.'

A scar from his left ear almost to his mouth is a constant reminder of the incident. Ritchie's critics say he flaunts it like a badge of courage when all along he simply and stupidly dealt wrongly with the wrong people. Ritchie is a martial arts black belt, greeting friends with a forceful punch on the arm. If they wince, he laughs and says, 'Don't know me own strength.' For some, it is infuriating. Madonna thought it endearing.

He had a run-in with Andy Bird and also, reportedly, with *Lock, Stock* actor Nick Moran. He also had a punch-up with an over-eager Madonna fan. Madonna liked her action man and felt safe with him. Before Madonna, his longest relationship had been the seven years he spent with Rebecca Green, daughter of Carlton Television chief

Michael Green. Their affair ended around the time he became a success with *Lock, Stock*.

He had a short but intense affair with celebrity model Tania Strecker and a friend of hers told this story: 'Guy was really in love with Tania for a while. Later, Madonna came on the scene. Tania caught them getting into a car together in London. Guy said something to Madonna like, "Er, this is Tania," so Madonna said, politely, "Hi, I'm Madonna," and Tania snarled back at her, "I know who you are." '

It was Madonna and monogamy after that for Guy Ritchie. Madonna accepted that half of her time would be spent in the UK and, living in London in 2000, said, 'There are many days when I feel like a stranger in a strange land and I despair, and I miss my friends. Americans and English people aren't actually that similar. One always thinks about England as being this repressed, tradition-based place, where everyone has this uptight, prim way of relating to each other. But, in fact, Americans, who are known for being boisterous and straightforward, are quite puritanical, so it's strange. On the outside, it seems like everyone in England is uptight but, actually, they're not, they're a bunch of dirty wankers. My God, all you have is naked people in newspapers here. You know, I'm having my cup of coffee and I'm opening a newspaper and tits are everywhere here, but really! And I cannot believe how expensive real estate is in Britain. I'm just too middle-class to throw my hard-earned money away like that. You know, I have a love–hate relationship with England.

'I always, always, always fantasised about living in London, and then it wasn't what I thought and I went through a whole, "Oh, America is so much nicer." I don't really like living in rented houses with other people's things. I miss my things. And it's just a different lifestyle here. At six o'clock everybody goes home and nobody works on the weekends and people go away for a month in the summer. It's a very old-fashioned lifestyle. It takes a lot longer to get anything done here. But there's an appreciation of life here that doesn't exist in America. Culture. Music and art and literature and nature. Everybody always asks you what school you went to here. It's accents and schools. People use them to put other people in categories, whereas in America nobody cares what school you went to.

'I went to one dinner that was fun. I got to sit next to Prince Charles. I had Michael Parkinson on one side and Prince Charles on the other. Prince Charles was very charming. We talked art, we talked the entertainment business, we talked about the media, we talked about travelling and jet-lag. Prince Charles asked me how I met Guy. He was quite a romantic. And he was very down-to-earth. I didn't find him stiff at all. He was very relaxed at the table, throwing his salad around and stuff. Flinging lettuce willynilly. I liked him; he was funny. But I left early because I wanted to be with Lourdes – I like to put her to bed.

'On a normal day, my daughter wakes me, so I get up at seven, and she goes to school and I drink my coffee and look at the naked girls in the paper. Then I spend hours at my computer, e-mailing. I have yoga practice every morning, with my teacher. Then I meditate in silence. By then, my daughter is usually home from school and I have lunch with her, and then she takes a nap, and I go off and do my things for the rest of the day. I have a very small handful of good friends here, but I do miss my friends in America.

'Guy makes up for that. I knew from the start but I didn't tell him how I felt, because he lived here and I lived in

America, and I wasn't interested in torturing myself by having some long-distance love affair. But it happened anyway. Not many people stop you in your tracks. But that's got so much to do with chemistry and timing. It was one of those inexplicable, uncontrollable things. It's very exciting, meeting someone that makes you go wobbly ... Umm ... Bonkers ... wobbly-bonkers. But it's hard work having a long-distance relationship and he's really stubborn and so am I. I was having lunch in the garden of Sting and Trudi's house and he was a guest. He just appeared on the seat next to me. And that was that.'

'It's always been difficult for her to find a man,' said Sting, adding, 'She needs someone powerful, and I'm spoken for. But we weren't really playing Cupid.'

Guy Ritchie always said he would never leave London but he went to Los Angeles with Madonna. At that point, as the 20th century was almost over, he said it was to escape the spotlight on Madonna and himself. Indeed, the media seemed to sense that this was a relationship that mattered and every movement by either of them was recorded.

In Los Angeles, he explained, 'Every time I went out to get a pint of milk there was a drama. That house got besieged, so it made sense to come out here. And there was the fight with a fan. A fanatic. So I had the altercation. Ever since then, we've had no problems. For whatever reason, it stopped. I don't know how people think it's flattering for them to park themselves at your door and never allow the likes of the little one to go out. And the missus could never go out just for a walk, but we sorted that out. It shouldn't have to happen, but there's only so much besieging you can take.' And what about his scar? 'I like to keep 'em guessing. A punch-up I had twelve years ago.'

Guy is also a passionate supporter of shooting: 'My stepfather began it. I was brought up with rough-shooting on his 5,000-acre estate near Shrewsbury. Dad used to shoot quite a bit and we'd go up to Scotland three days a year. We'd have one driven pheasant shoot and a few days rough-shooting. Wouldn't tell anybody, unless they could understand the whole of it. It's a really complicated issue that you'd need to understand fully. If I was an outsider looking in, I would not approve. I've gotta tell you, I would not approve. I would think everything about it was Machiavellian and slightly macabre. We had a *Lock, Stock* versus the Purdey boys, down at West London Shooting School. Good boys, the Purdey lot – terrible shots though. Our team won, I'm pleased to say, then it was off to their gun factory. I've never seen anything like it – the craftsmanship is totally second to none. It's like going back a hundred years, and the history. I can see why they cost what they do – they are literally hand made. I love all of that. We did a couple of days in West Yorkshire. Fantastic birds – a hundrend and fifty feet high, at least. We were stood in this deep valley. These birds were seriously high – fucking fantastic shooting. But I'm out for the *craic* as much as anything. All I want is seven mates to go and have a scream with. If I can have a few drinks in the morning, a few drinks in the afternoon, and enjoy a few hours of shooting, I'm happy.

'I've got a Browning B3, 12-bore. I changed to an over-and-under once I'd got introduced to clays and because everybody else seemed to be using over-and-unders. It seemed that all the top guns had them, so I thought there must be something in it. There are times when you've got to evolve, haven't you? I like high pheasants or driven grouse but I do love rough-shooting. I used to shoot a lot with a pointer – my step-dad had them. We used to shoot over a pair of pointers, and I can't think of anything more exciting than that. I loved that – mad about that. And you never knew what it was going to be until it bolted, that's what I remember most as a kid. You were all geed up, once the dog was there, and your heart's going like mad, and you've no idea in which direction it's going to go until the dog flushes it. I used to love it.

'I really enjoy the clays. I like them because they've helped me really improve. I do about eight hundred clays a week, no problem. Well, I have been shot more than once. But I don't know how funny I found it. Yeah, I've been shot about three times. I've got the marks to prove it too – got shot through my foot once with a .22 rifle whilst out rabbit shooting; straight through, fractured the bone. And I've been peppered about two, three times. In actual fact, I'm always being peppered.'

Ritchie was 25 when he found a job as a runner for Island Records, and worked on and off for film companies. He had worked as an antiques dealer but that ended when he delivered a table to France on the roof of his van and drove through a low tunnel – it was smashed to bits. He made a five-year plan. First year, learn the film business. Second, make pop videos. Third, commercials, fourth, a short film. At 30, he met Matthew Vaughn, the estranged son of Hollywood actor Robert Vaughn, who was the main *Man from U.N.C.L.E.* and has made countless, and some classic, films including *The Magnificent Seven*, and made appearances in the 2001 television series based on that movie. Robert Vaughn has had limited contact with his son for nearly 30 years following his divorce from Matthew's mother, Kathy Saigol.

Together, Ritchie and Vaughn made *Lock, Stock And Two*

Smoking Barrels for £960,000. Vaughn produced his first film, *The Innocent Sleep* with Michael Gambon and Rupert Graves, when he was 23.

Vaughn remembers, 'I was bullshitting beyond belief. Sitting on a set with all these people twice my age who were saying, "What should we do now?" and I was rushing off to ring friends in the States to ask them. I had no passion for the film, so I learned that lesson. The next film, I knew I had to be passionate about. Then I met Guy. Guy loves to punch people, and the first sign of violence I'm out of the door. I've never hit anyone in my life. The common ground is that we love films that are entertaining and commercial. My gut will tell me within twenty minutes whether or not something's worth taking a risk. But I made *Lock, Stock* so cheaply that it wasn't even a risk. If you make a film for two to three million pounds, you're going to get it back from television and video around the world. On a creative level, I think Guy is a genius, or a moron sometimes, but whenever it has taken a big step of faith, he's delivered like a genius. He gets the ultimate say on the creative level, and on the business side he puts it back to me.'

And now, of course, Madonna was in the frame – long-term, as it turned out. Ritchie found himself a little astonished at how events had unfolded: 'I'm not a typical Madonna fan, I've got to tell you, but everyone's been exposed to Madonna's music for, I mean, it's impossible to avoid it. She is a good dancer. It's actually hard for me. If you'd seen me dance.'

Madonna was happy to show him all the moves. That was clear in July 2000, on Pantelleria Island, 50 miles from Tunisia and black pearl of the Mediterranean, where they call romping in the ooze of the resort's volcanic mud 'doing the fandago thalaterm'. Madonna was gloriously pregnant and showed it in pictures broadcast worldwide.

'She just let it all hang out. I think it's just a wonderful image for all females at forty-something,' said her long-time friend and agent Liz Rozenburg. Madonna larked around, not at all self-conscious about her 'big bump', cavorting in a thermal pool that can be as hot as a hundred degrees Fahrenheit, but which has just the ingredients a pregnant woman wants; a warm bath that leaves the skin soft, reduces stress and relaxes just about every muscle. All body toxins, islanders boast, vanish in a thirty-minute splash. Madonna stayed in a rented villa on the island near Sicily, with Guy Ritchie, her daughter Lourdes and a group of friends. She had happily paraded out on the streets in a T-shirt and jeans, totally happy to show her big, naked stomach. Then, in a black bikini, her wallowing really enchanted the tourism bureau, so much so that it announced on its website, with a series of photos of her fully clothed, walking the streets, 'Madonna in Pantelleria!'

The secret of the magic of Pantelleria is that it is exclusively made up of two kinds of volcanic rock. Early visitors were entranced by the abundance of obsidian, a black shiny glassy mineral, and the fertile volcanic soil. The rich black mud contains high levels of sulphur for a youthful and clear complexion. Absorbed in the bloodstream, it helps to relieve severe skin ailments, among them psoriasis and acne. Arthritis and rheumatism sufferers also use the mud for relief. Madonna followed many celebrities in discovering the marvels of mud. Giorgio Armani has a villa on the island and Eric Clapton and Michelle Pfieffer are regulars, as are Sting and Trudi Styler, who had originally recommended the island to Madonna. It has a series of fresh-water craters, as well as prehistoric tombs and, as Madonna spotted, a single lake, Spechio di Venere, or the Mirror of Venus.

Madonna always planned to have her baby in Los Angeles and then return to Britain. And when Madonna and Guy Ritchie's son Rocco – named after one of her uncles, and meaning 'rock' in Italian – arrived, it was dramatic. The little boy was delivered by an emergency Caesarean section two weeks early. Madonna had spent most of her pregnancy in London but returned to Los Angeles for the birth, labelling British hospitals as 'old and Victorian'. Ritchie said he rushed her to the Cedars-Sinai Medical Center in West Hollywood – she had been there 48 hours earlier – after she woke in pain and losing blood. She said she immediately summoned Ritchie from a Los Angeles screening of his film *Snatch*. He said he half-carried her to their car. (Madonna stated later, 'He met me at the hospital, though he likes to think that he carried me inside.') She was white-faced, crying and distressed on arrival. Ritchie was at her side as doctors carried out the procedure. Madonna had intended to have Rocco at the Good Samaritan Hospital where Lourdes was born, but plans changed at the last minute.

Much, of course, was made in Britain of her decision to have her son in California. Logically, it all made sense – but not to the British press. She was reported to have upset health workers when she criticised British hospitals in the lead-up to the birth by saying she did not want to give birth in an 'old, Victorian' building. She was also concerned about the efficiency of British health services if any complications arose during labour. She was asked about her decision to have the baby in America and sounded shocked at the thought of staying in England, telling the interviewer, 'Come on now!' He asked, 'Have you been to hospitals in

England?' She answered, 'They're old and Victorian. I don't know. It's always strange to be in hospitals and go to see doctors in foreign countries because everybody has a slightly different way of dealing with things.' She then qualified her criticism by saying she did not like the thought of complications when giving birth away from home, adding, 'I like efficiency.'

She needed it. Madonna had been diagnosed with placenta previa, a complication that develops in about 1 in 250 pregnancies when the placenta covers part or all of the cervix, causing the mother to haemorrhage and the baby's blood supply to be cut off.

'Because you can haemorrhage, they tell you that they don't want you going into labour,' she explained. 'So I arranged to have a C-section two weeks before my original due date.'

Madonna showed up at the hospital two weeks before her appointment, in no condition – or mood – to wait: 'When I went in they were like, "You can have your hair done, your nails done." And I'm like, "Are you kidding me?" I don't care about that, no. Just give me some morphine." '

The nurses complied and so did Rocco, who was born just before 1.00am, about three hours after Madonna entered the hospital and, because he was a month premature, he was placed in intensive care to make sure his lungs were sufficiently developed. Madonna was released from the hospital after two days, but Rocco stayed for the rest of the week with his mother turning up every day to feed him. 'I sat in a little room next to intensive care reading books and running in there every three hours,' she said. On 16 August 2000 – her birthday – Madonna and Ritchie took Rocco home. Later that night, some close friends and family joined them, along with Rocco's big sister, for a small birthday dinner. Madonna said, 'The whole week was emotional, as you'd expect; the day we brought him home was a very happy one.'

She had already decided to name him after one of her uncles: 'I went through all my relatives – Guido, Gatano, Silvio and Rocco. Guy kept going, "No, no, no, that's way too fancy." Finally I said, "All right, he can have your English last name – it's actually Scottish – and an Italian first name which also means rock." '

At Cedars-Sinai, Madonna recovered in some style – aromatherapists, manicurists, a limousine service, tastefully reproduced 18th-century furnishing, original art and 24-hour room service are all on offer in the hospital's deluxe maternity unit, in addition to a well-stocked fridge, cable TV and video and lap-top computers. For new fathers recovering from a tough night holding hands and mopping brows, a massage therapist is on hand. The hospital also offers a romantic post-delivery dinner for two. For an extra charge, a mother's help or 'doula' can assist with the baby and give advice on breast feeding, burping and how to change a nappy. But that was not Madonna's reason for giving birth again in Los Angeles: she wanted Dr Paul Fleiss to handle the delivery and obstetrician Margaret Banks, whom she trusted, to be present for the after-care. She wanted the familiarity of Dr Fleiss and to be near her sisters in Los Angeles – 'they'll look after me'. Family, as always, mattered. As did Guy Ritchie, who was overwhelmed by the arrival of his son. He cut the baby's cord.

'The baby was only 5lb 9oz and then started losing a bit of weight and I got worried. He was only a little fella but gorgeous. He was small and came out early, but not alarmingly small. He was sweet small. He was healthy, as good as gold and put on weight quickly. He was in hospital for a few days, which is natural when a baby is premature. He showed absolutely no sign of doing anything dodgy and he smiled like a bastard. When he was born he had a huge mop of black hair and I was thinking, Where did he get that from? He was hairy and dark and I'm neither – he looked just like my dad. Fatherhood does change you. It is unlike anything else I've experienced and it's so hard to articulate the emotions. It's like a huge wave of love but much stronger. His mum is pretty good with him. There doesn't seem to be any jealousy from his sister and we're a big happy family. Lourdes is a real character and I love her to death. I can't get enough of her and we've got a real family unit going. The missus is incredibly inspiring and we seem to work very well together.'

Ritchie said in 2001 that he and Madonna will always have a home in Britain although they get less attention in Los Angeles: 'She gets hassled less in Los Angeles. She can live her day-to-day existence over there, which is a release. She is happy there and she's happy here. The pair of us love the countryside here. You'd be hard pushed to beat that anywhere in the world. We'll always have a home here but we'll always have a home there and go between the two. I would like to relocate to Hollywood but not completely. Britain is all I know. I feel my priorities changed with the baby; it puts things in perspective.'

Photos of Madonna wearing a silver necklace spelling out 'BABY' were published to promote her album *Music* a month after giving birth to Rocco. She was not sure it was a good move, explaining, 'I can't wait to get home and cuddle him. It's great being a mother again. Rocco's changed my life.

We're a family now – I feel complete. It is hard to be apart from him for a minute. I always thought you couldn't tell whether babies are boys or girls when they're young but Rocco's got blond hair and blue eyes just like his dad. He's so obviously a boy and he even flexes his arms like Guy. It's hard not to wish their lives away, but I can't wait until he grows up. Lourdes is great with him, although she's a bit jealous sometimes. But we've let her hold him and she seems to adore him. It's beautiful to see and it completes me. Lourdes loves her little brother and I know she'll make a great babysitter one day. She seems very grown up next to him and is so affectionate. She's always kissing him. It's certainly weird to think that I'm the mother of two children.'

Of her son's father she said, 'He has changed my life and put things in perspective. Guy sometimes gets a bit miserable when he has to change nappies. But I tell him, "Oi, it's your turn," and I make him do it. But he's a proud dad and I'm so happy we all feel part of a real family.'

But as always with Madonna, only a month after Rocco's birth there was business to take care of; the album *Music*. She said it was based on her immediate experiences: 'Some of the songs reflect my melancholic and thoughtful side, while others take the plunge into reckless abandon. I didn't put limits on myself other than to make sure there was plenty of club-orientated, dance-friendly material because I enjoy that myself.'

Nevertheless, Madonna the control freak admitted that having a baby in the house involved a big adjustment: 'I wake up every morning and try to have a really scheduled day, but I can't. It's really hard when you're breast-feeding. But there will be life after breast-feeding.'

Time moved quickly on and it was clearly going to be a

different life. 'Ten years ago you'd ask her to recommend a personal trainer,' said her backing singer Nikki Harris in 2001, adding, 'Now you call her with any ache or pain, and she'll have the perfect doctor. She's grown up. Motherhood has definitely calmed her.'

Madonna herself confronted the 40-something pop-star issue: 'Yes, there are those moments when I can't believe I'm as old as I am but I feel better physically than I did ten years ago. I'm doing more. I'm more fulfilled. And I don't have those moments when I think, Oh, God, I'm missing something.'

Ritchie appeared to have fulfilled Madonna. 'I feel like he's my equal, and that's hard to find. Even Leon likes him. It's shocking how civilised they are to each other. Guy gives me a run for my money. He's smart, he's busy and he's got a career. He keeps me on my toes. Like when I came home from hospital with Rocco. I had absolutely no idea it was coming. I had just sat down in front of my breast pump when I spotted a paper bag on the table. It was all crumpled up and I almost threw it away. Then I noticed something in it, a little box. Then I saw a card. In it was a really sweet letter that Guy wrote to me, about everything we'd been through, and my birthday, and the baby, and how happy he was. I thought he had bought me some really nice earrings or something. Then I opened it up. It was a diamond ring and I screamed. It was shocking. I've never had a diamond ring! Even when I was married, I had a simple wedding band. I never liked big rocks on my finger – well, I do now.'

It was clear that she and Ritchie would marry. Madonna's roots were showing and not just on her head. 'I wouldn't say it's an engagement ring. We talk about marriage, but we can't decide whether it's something that's necessary. I know that I can't have a proper relationship, have a child with someone and share a life with someone unless I'm willing to make changes in my life. And I started doing that in England. We already live like we're married.'

Madonna had set up house with Ritchie in Kensington when she began work on her new album. She would go to the recording studios in her silver Mercedes, an immaculate car with tinted windows to stop people staring in traffic snarl-ups. 'Compared to when I wrote *Ray of Light*, I was completely unfocused, not sure of the direction or the sound I wanted,' she explained. Recording an album of her own outside New York for the first time in her career, Madonna admitted, 'I was intimidated by the cool, creative vibe of working in a studio where street life was visible outside the windows. I just kind of threw myself into it – I felt really connected to the world. Once I found my way, I wanted everything simple, direct and meaningful. I've never written as many good songs and not used them before. But if it wasn't new, if it wasn't important, I wasn't interested.'

Becoming pregnant during recording – just as she had done during *Evita* – Madonna tried to conceal her condition for as long as possible from the Fleet Street photographers who trailed her whenever she stepped outside her house: 'All the people in the studio couldn't figure out why I never took my coat off. I used to say, "Oh, I've got the chills." '

Madonna is a tough mum and there are echoes of her own childhood. She sets limits and enforces them. 'Rather than threaten a time-out or rationalise something to Lourdes, she's one of those moms who can give her kid a look and they immediately know what's up,' says Nikki Harris.

Lourdes takes French, karate and art classes and isn't allowed to watch any TV – not even a Disney video – at home. 'It's more work not to allow them to watch, believe me,' said Madonna. 'But I feel like TV turns them into passive creatures. I want her to develop her imagination. She'll get that with commuting. We'll just be going back and forth a lot. Guy really wants his son to have an English education, so we'll see what happens. And I intend to work New York slowly into Guy's repertoire. But it was hard enough getting him to come to Los Angeles. So one thing at a time.'

'Madonna has worked very hard for this life she has,' said her friend Debbie Mazar. 'At the same time, she knows it's like a fairytale. And there's even a Prince Charming. Only one chapter is missing, and Lourdes picked up on this just the other day. Aware that, in many of the stories which have been read to her, the heroine meets the love of her life and gets married, Lourdes asked, "Mom, are you going to get married before I get married?" '

CHAPTER TWENTY-TWO

HER MADGE

'Madonna is a genuine chameleon.'
FORMER LOVER STEVE BRAY, 2001

Madonna was enraptured by Guy Ritchie and all things British but still, understandably, she missed *home*. Britain had welcomed her and even designer Ralph Lauren took advantage of that combination in 2001. At the New York fashion shows he, according to the expert Suzy Menkes, had moved from 'Malboro Country to Madonna Country'. She enthused that the curvy jackets and jodhpurs from Lauren were sexy country chic. 'The same tweedy English style that Madonna favours was given a racy sexiness by fitting it tight and making skirts short and perky.'

Madonna felt the same in 2001: 'I'm having a major love affair with England. I love London. It's an exotic place for me. You get a feeling when you go to another country that you can sort of start all over again. I don't want to say the word "reinvent" because that's so boringly over-used on me, but for me Britain is a different culture. It's exciting. I like how formal everyone is. I couldn't take it all the time because I wasn't raised that way. I like the eccentricity that is bred with all that British repression and formality. It makes for good creativity. I love going to a pub and sitting there with friends and having a drink. There is much more of a feeling of community in England.'

Madonna made Britain accommodate her lifestyle, but she got into some very British habits. Her newspaper, the *Independent*, was delivered at 7.00am to the £2 million home she shared in Kensington in London with Guy Ritchie. Madonna felt more relaxed in London, but some of her Los Angeles habits helped: she is always around early in the morning and, even in California, the hours before the sun starts its proper day shift are chilly. Her tartan pyjamas travel the world with her and she wears them as she watches over Lourdes and her daily bowl of Cheerios. Madonna loves to watch her daughter have breakfast. It is a peaceful time and she lets no one intrude as she sips her Bustello Cuban coffee with organic milk and brown sugar. Lourdes eats and Madonna reads the *Independent*. Both of them finish quickly and Madonna would play Barbie dolls with her daughter before Lourdes went off to nursery school at 8.30am. Madonna the businesswoman with a head for figures would then kick in. With fresh coffee and, sometimes, a milk chocolate McVitie's Digestive biscuit, she goes directly to her computer and her immense world opens up before her. She was making a grand success of it.

London life for Madonna was a good omen – she had achieved a great hit with her cover version of Don McLean's 'American Pie' – and another attraction for her was British actor Rupert Everett, who had suggested the song as part of the soundtrack for the movie in which he and Madonna starred in 2001 – *The Next Best Thing*.

It brought them even closer together. In it she played an

ashtanga teacher, and that was perfect casting for yoga teacher Liz Lark, who is an expert in the discipline: 'It was an obvious choice of exercise for Madonna; it's a very challenging yoga, which is tremendously popular among creative people in the arts and high-powered professionals. I'm sure Madonna loves it, because it is a choreography of movement and breathing, which will appeal to her as a dancer. Ashtanga is a fast-moving activity that bears little resemblance to lotus-position meditation. Explosive breathing makes it noisy and in a two-hour session people find themselves sweating as much as they would in a conventional workout. The result is powerful, lean muscles, without the bulk associated with weight-training. Students rave about the mental agility and clarity they achieve. You have to give a hundred per cent when you practise ashtanga, which focuses your concentration brilliantly. It's very much mindful, not mindless exercise.'

Whatever her critics have said, Madonna has never been mindless in her attitude to life – and especially her career. She sensed the advantages of working with Rupert Everett and enjoyed the idea of their movie.

'It's not that my career has been based on surprising people. My creative instincts have been to challenge myself and constantly to do things that are going to broaden my own mind and, in the process, hopefully the minds of other people. First, it has to interest me. OK, is this going to take me to another place? Am I going to learn something? Is this going to inspire me? That's where I always start, whatever it is, whether it's music or film or whatever. Hopefully, the manifestation of that is work that has some effect on the audience. I didn't need *Evita* to give me confidence in my acting ability – I needed some good roles and time with a really good acting teacher. I don't think it was necessarily *Evita*. The film critics have always been difficult for me. I wouldn't say it's a question of them paying more attention, but I do think they're much more judgemental. That goes for anybody who has been really successful in one area and then wants to go off into another area and take it very seriously.'

In *The Next Best Thing*, Madonna and Rupert Everett play Abbie and Robert, best friends, who end up having a child together. It's not a terribly uncommon scenario, except that Robert is gay. The two happily raise their son, Sam, but the bliss ends a few years later, when Abbie falls in love with the understanding, handsome Ben played by Benjamin Bratt. Madonna was not initially convinced.

'My first impression was that it was too much like a sitcom. I liked the idea of the friendship between Rupert's character and my character, but that was it. I thought it needed some rewrites. And that's when Rupert came in. The more it was worked on, the more I liked it. Even though I had nothing to do with the writing of the storyline, I have found myself in situations with a man where I've said, "Wait a second, you mean if I had less to offer you, I'd have a better chance in a relationship?" I didn't exactly say it like that, but there have been many situations in my life where I felt that my accomplishments and my success actually hindered certain relationships. So I could relate to that.'

Rupert Everett is gay in real life and and it has worked for him on screen, especially when he played Julia Roberts's confidante in the film *My Best Friend's Wedding*; all agreed that Everett stole the show. So, being the gay father of Madonna's child in *The Next Best Thing* appeared, on paper, perfect casting. Off screen, it was exactly that as well. They are intimate fans of each other. Everett explained, 'Madonna's very sexually attractive, across the board, whether you're gay or straight. She is a gay man trapped in a woman's body. I had had a major crush on her for years when I first met her. I've proposed myself as a sperm donor and been turned down. Besides, she doesn't want a sperm donor, she wanted a live-in lover, and that I can't be. I'm too free-spirited.'

Madonna responded, 'I don't think Rupert is really ready to have children. I adore Rupert as a person and as an actor – gay men love to go shopping and throw dinner parties, and do all the things I like to do.'

They were introduced by the always intriguing Sean Penn, who did not like to go shopping or attend dinner parties at the time of the 'Like a Virgin' success. Then, Everett was the star, basking in the critical glow of his movie *Another Country*, about a tortured homosexual public schoolboy, but he has never stopped being an admirer. 'Madonna can be tough to work with. She's a real gem but she's a stickler for perfection. I think that's the difficulty. She works very hard. She wanted to rehearse our dance routine every day for fifteen hours. I'm much lazier. I intended to use my two left feet as part of the performance. I'm not as obsessed with details as she is. She's as tough as she needs to be. Women in showbusiness – either you succumb or you become as strong as men on their own terms. And that can sometimes be extremely tough on the outside. I think she's not all tough, but she certainly is a very formidable woman. She has a lot of vulnerability, but it wouldn't necessarily be directed at you. She also listens to ideas – I suggested she do "American Pie" as part of the movie soundtrack. Madonna was kind of nebulous about it at first, but she and her producer William Orbit came up with a fantastic version. I loved it.'

Madonna has always been a supporter and friend of the homosexual lifestyle but Everett deliberately distances himself from any gay-rights politics or evangelism: 'Being out is not about anything political for me. I'm out because I can't be bothered being in.'

It is an essential attraction for Madonna: 'I don't find that gay men are intimidated by my strength and intelligence,' and she says she loves his sense of humour, and the fact that Rupert's gorgeous, but there are plenty of gorgeous gay men that women don't fantasise about being with. 'I wanted to go a bit deeper. He just has that certain something. He's not obviously gay and he's got a really macho vibe about him. He seems genuinely interested in women, and on top of that he's really smart and very funny. We like a clever boy.'

But Rupert Everett was not clever enough to conquer the British weather on his best friend's wedding day – that would be asking too much, even for Madonna. She, of course, made it to the church on time.

CHAPTER TWENTY-THREE

HIGHLAND FLING

'Here's to us, wha's like us, damn few and
they're all deed.'

<small>TRADITIONAL SCOTTISH TOAST</small>

Love − ain't it grand? Madonna thought her wedding to Guy Ritchie might be worth £2 million. Or maybe £3 million? But even in our celebrity world, the magazines *Hello!* and *OK!* thought that a little too rich. For all her instincts and business acumen, Madonna had not learned one thing about Britain − Christmas and New Year is a sacrosanct holiday and the 'dead' time for sales of magazines and newspapers. There was no way either of the big-paying magazines could do the arithmetic which would allow them to do a multi-million-pound deal for exclusive coverage of the wedding. But they were terribly tempted.

Of course, why would Madonna care about being paid to get married? It is quite simply in her nature. Every deal must have a contract, every arrangement must have a pay day. And she was anointed at the Grammy Music Awards in February 2001. She shook her hips performing but was not awarded any honours; but she did get a 'goody bag'. Organisers of the Grammys hired Distinctive Assets, a Californian company that deals with Hollywood and has on file the shape and shoe size of most of the names in town, even the neck sizes of their pets. Jaimsyne Blakely, who founded Distinctive Assets, said the value of the 2001 Grammy gifts was around £10,000. It is a marketing game; designers who want to get their goods to the stars give them for free to Blakely's company. As Madonna is the star most designers want their clothes on – if she wears a Stetson then cowboy chic is on the high street – her 'goody bag' was a Tumi suitcase packed with £20,000 worth of merchandise – the haul included a soft leather jacket and crocodile cowboy hat, crystal-encrusted Swarovski flip-flops, jewellery, mobile phone accessories, a mini camera, an Easel bikini, free gym membership, hospitality at top hotels and a customised condom case. Her children also benefited at the Grammys – Lourdes got a miniature version of her mother's necklace and a leopard-print Hello Kitty handbag. Rocco received a cashmere carriage blanket and matching hat. Material Girl? No – just treats.

Madonna has come to expect such treatment, so it was testimony to her love for Guy Ritchie that she was willing to spend *their* money on their marriage. Cynics, of course, point out the value of the publicity – she was, at that time, negotiating a 40-date European tour for summer 2001, which would pay her £1 million for *each* concert. Madonna had wanted to marry at Althorp House where Princess Diana is buried but, concerned about security, Earl Spencer, Diana's brother, turned down the request and a huge sum of money. He did so reluctantly, as it would have been a public-relations triumph for both sides; the idea was to use the house and chapel with, perhaps, pheasant shooting for the guests afterwards. Earl Spencer's office confirmed that such talks had taken place but did not work out. Instead,

Madonna could afford to indulge Guy Ritchie and his haggis-bashing and bagpipes inclinations.

Skibo Castle in the remote vastness of the Scottish Highlands is a pink granite concoction and an accolade to the power of self-promotion; it was built by Andrew Carnegie, the Scots-born steel tycoon who began life as an unemployed weaver in Dunfermline. Carnegie, barely more than 5ft tall, sailed to America at the age of 13 in 1848. He worked as a telegraph messenger, became superintendent of a railway company (where he introduced sleeping cars) and made some shrewd investments in steel companies. Along with the Rockefellers (oil) and JP Morgan (banking), he was part of the clique of ruthless industrialists dubbed 'the robber barons'. When he returned to Scotland in 1898 with his American wife, Louise, he brought a fortune with him, totalling £11 billion. He wanted to be a Scottish laird and bought the 7,000-acre Skibo estate near Dornoch, Sutherland, for what he called the 'reasonable' sum of £85,000, the equivalent of £4 million in 2002. He gained a lot of history for his money. The name is derived from Schytherbolle, the Celtic word for fairyland or 'place of peace'. Carnegie was determined to create his own past. What was left of the castle was razed and a Gothic folly built in its place – a gaudy, turreted fantasy. The staircase was of Sicilian marble, the indoor swimming pool was a vast room with a sliding floor, which doubled as a ballroom, and there were stained-glass windows depicting Carnegie's triumphant progress from hovel to castle. In imitation of the royal custom instigated by Queen Victoria at Balmoral, a piper was hired to play guests into dinner. The door knobs were set very low so that the diminutive Carnegie could easily reach them.

On Carnegie's death in 1919, the castle passed to his only daughter, Margaret, who used it as a summer house. When financier Peter de Savary bought it for £5.5 million in 1990, he spent £11 million on refurbishing Skibo, which recreated Carnegie's sumptuous, oak-panelled, mock baronial luxury. He put in a championship golf course and turned the castle into a private health and country club which cost £3,000 a year to join. A night in the cheapest of the 21 bedrooms costs £580, excluding VAT but including a four-poster bed.

Carnegie had played host to composer Edward Elgar and author Rudyard Kipling. De Savary had attracted Prince Andrew, Michael Douglas, Sean Connery and Jack Nicholson. Butlers have been on drunken rampages, cars have been driven into the marble swimming pool. A chef has been awarded £3,400 compensation after being shouted at by de Savary for serving a platter of processed cheese and ham. And a piper plays the guests into dinner where everyone, including strangers, is expected to mix as if they were at an intimate dinner party.

Madonna's first marriage to Sean Penn was held on that faraway bluff in Malibu. This was another Hollywood wedding – Highland style. Nevertheless, Madonna was given yet another celebrity perk when she was allowed by the Head Registrar of Scotland to bypass rules that state either the prospective bride or groom must appear in person to collect their marriage schedule, a legal document to make the ceremony official. The registrar of Dornoch, Lesley Connor, delivered it to Skibo Castle in her white Toyota car. But before the wedding, there was to be the christening of Madonna and Guy Ritchie's son, Rocco.

To the strains of a Highland piper, Madonna appeared out of the mist, wearing an elegant three-quarter length cream coat, her hair tied in a chignon, and hurried into the church in Dornoch. With her, Guy Ritchie cradled four-month-old Rocco in a white christening robe. Around a dozen of Madonna's friends arrived on a scheduled British Airways flight from Gatwick that had to be diverted to Inverness because of fog. The congregation included Sting and his wife Trudie Styler, Gwyneth Paltrow and Stella McCartney. Rupert Everett, showing his devotion to Madonna, was dangerously delayed by the weather, and arrived just before the end, dressed in white jeans and a black leather jacket. Ritchie's father, John, and Madonna's family sat on pews carved from oak from the Skibo estate. No strangers were to be allowed in for the christening. But Scottish Church law rules that the ceremony must be witnessed by non-family members, so a few local people were allowed inside. The christening was carried out by the Reverend Susan Brown, who would also marry them the next day. Rocco was carried from the cornucopia-etched font, down the nave and around the congregation as 'an introduction to the family of God'. After the 30-minute ceremony the couple emerged from the church to wild cheers from the crowd and the drumming of 4 Highland bandsmen. But it was Rocco who received the biggest reaction. Ritchie, smiling broadly, bounced him into the air so that the crowd could get a better view. The local council set up spotlights in the trees. Celebrations continued late into the night. Calum 'Spud' Fraser, the piper who had greeted Madonna at Inverness Airport, entertained the crowd with 'Highland Cathedral' and 'Like a Virgin'. He said, 'I was there when Madonna arrived and it was very important for me to be here and play for her at the christening of her son.' William Sutherland, a fisherman from Brora who brought his two children to see Madonna, said, 'We've come to be part of the whole experience. Madonna has put Dornoch on the map and we just thought it was important to turn up. I suppose it's a historic moment. You certainly wouldn't get this sort of turn out for royalty.'

The police had organised Madonna and her family's arrival like a military operation. Officers finalised the arrangements over tea and biscuits in the Great Hall of Skibo Castle. One officer said Madonna had been 'ever so sweet to us'.

Constables were out at dawn blocking roads to the church after erecting steel barriers around the sandstone building. Madonna's car was escorted by police motorcycles. A police spokesman said, 'We took no chances in making the arrangements. Madonna is entitled to as much help as we can give to her.'

Everyone wanted to help — especially the retailers. A special consignment of haggis arrived at Skibo Castle from Cockburns of Dingwall, langoustines and salmon from Wester Ross and mussels from the Dornoch Firth.

There are many customs associated with weddings: throwing the bouquet, wearing something old, new, borrowed and blue — and the traditional first row. Madonna and Guy Ritchie were no exception — as she organised the last-minute details of their meticulously planned nuptials, her husband-to-be went shooting with his friends. One of the wedding party revealed, 'Guy seemed almost bored with the actual wedding details and just wanted to get out shooting. He told Madonna how he'd have her out on the moors by the end of the week. She put him down very neatly by saying the only objects she'd ever shoot would be clay. No way did she plan to murder small birds.'

Ritchie, who made shooting a condition of the wedding venue, spent every day hunting partridge on a neighbouring estate. But it did not stop what some dubbed the 'royal wedding'. Certainly, the media circus around the ceremony – and the week before – reflected coverage of a national event. And the level of security would have made a Prime Minister or President blush. And that was how the couple exchanged their personalised vows.

At exactly 6.00pm on Friday, 22 December 2000, Madonna, wearing a £30,000 white lace gown designed by Stella McCartney and on the arm of her father, Tony Ciccone, walked down the red-carpeted rose-strewn staircase leading to Skibo's Great Hall to marry. Flanked by dozens of 4ft-high church candles, she listened to 'Nessun Dorma' as she walked towards Guy Ritchie waiting for her on the half-landing in full Macintosh hunting regalia, with kilt inspired by the costume of 18th-century Scottish gentlemen. Madonna was, at times, in tears during the ceremony. With film star Gwyneth Paltrow and Donatella Versace as bridesmaids and Lourdes as an enchanting flower girl, Madonna plighted her troth, but omitting 'obey'; she vowed to 'cherish, honour, delight in family and always keep and hold to one another'. She and Ritchie exchanged rings made by designer of-the-moment, Stephen Webster. Gathered around and watching were 50 friends and family. It was an eclectic mix. Chief guests were Trudie Styler and Sting, Jean-Paul Gaultier, Rupert Everett, Kelly Brook with actor boyfriend Jason Statham, Matthew Vaughn and Stella McCartney who was Maid of Honour. Ritchie's father and step-mother, Madonna's sister Melanie and manager brother Chris, and a handful of friends including Piers Adams of the K Bar chain, singer Debi Mazar, Ingrid Casares and film-maker Alex Keshishian comprised the rest of the party. Madonna's rule was that only the wives of male guests or girlfriends to whom Madonna had been introduced and knew, should be allowed to attend.

As they had waited for the bride's traditionally late entrance, pianist Katia Labeque and local harpist Jennifer Port played classical pieces, joined by organist Stewart Anderson for 'Nessun Dorma'. As the newly married couple descended the castle's main stairs after the half-hour service, kilted staff served vintage champagne. Before leading their guests into dinner, the Ritchies disappeared to their suite in the West Wing to change, reappearing in a Jean-Paul Gaultier dress for her and a midnight-blue suit for him. Piped into the oak-panelled dining room, the guests gasped at the sight awaiting them. Thousand of pounds' worth of flowers, mainly red roses and Christmas poinsettias, filled the vast room. They were the gift from Donatella Versace and had been used at four-month-old Rocco's christening. Ivy wreathed around floating candles trailed along the centre of the 45ft-long mahogany table, draped in burgundy velvet for the night. Maids in Edwardian outfits brought on a succession of courses starting with Waikiki chicken salad, a Hawaiian-style light coconut and pineapple dish, followed by Southern States seafood salad using lobster as its base, and roast beef. Vintage wine and malt whisky was freely available, but many of the guests drank little if any at all. The wedding cake was wheeled in – a 3ft-high concoction of profiteroles and caramel. Back in the Great Hall, a local folk band, Skelbo, played Scottish reels and jigs while in the basement DJs teed up the music in the temporary nightclub created by brewery heir and professional party organiser William Bartholomew. The best man's speech was shared by Ritchie's friends Piers Adams and Matthew Vaughn, who were helped in their rehearsed remarks by producer/scriptwriter Richard Curtis. They used baby pictures of Ritchie as props.

After the wedding dinner, in tribute to her bridesmaid, Madonna changed outfits again. In a Versace number, she started the dancing with her husband wearing his second midnight-blue dinner suit of the night. One guest whispered, 'We all expected a much more raucous affair but right from the start everything has been, well, actually, very tasteful and almost low key. Even Guy's stag night was over pretty early and it was hardly riotous. Madonna was determined that this wedding should have class and style. She was actually quite nervous all day – pacing around checking that everything was just right.'

Madonna had spent a week being pampered in the castle's spa, venturing out only for brief walks and a picnic. Horse-riding, falconry and even four-wheel adventure drives are all included in the Skibo package but, dressed from Holland and Holland in suitable tweeds, the only sport she indulged in was clay pigeon shooting. She had practised a week before the wedding with an up-and-over Purdey shotgun at West London Shooting School in Northolt, Middlesex. She wore a tweed hunting vest by Barbour and leather pads to protect her shoulders, mole-skin Burberry trousers and Hunter wellies. Her teacher had said, 'Her lessons consisted of the safety aspect, gun handling and the correct stance. It's the same for every pupil, famous or not. But she's very nice.'

Although Madonna was keen to capture Scottish tradition at Skibo Castle before honeymooning at Sting's 50-acre Wiltshire estate there were some things that were just too traditional. An early-morning piper who usually plays for guests at 8.30am was cancelled by her. She also asked for the heating to be turned up. Like Sinatra, she likes things *her* way.

And that includes her father-in-law staying quiet. John Ritchie made the awful mistake of telling the press that his son would be wearing a kilt in the family's Macintosh hunting tartan for the wedding. He could not see the harm in it – but that was before he arrived in Scotland. John Ritchie had beaten the Highland weather conditions to reach Inverness Airport and only face a 45-minute drive to Skibo Castle. There was no Range Rover with blackened windows waiting for him, as there had been for many other celebrity guests. Instead, he and his wife Shireen, Ritchie's step-mother, hired a car. Skibo Castle staff had had to sign a four-page confidentiality agreement and some were not allowed to leave the grounds of the castle for the entire wedding week. Mobile phones had to be switched off at all times. It was an oppressive atmosphere and one guest suggested it was like being in prison.

Madonna – the control freak – at work again. Of course, she knew what could have happened if she had not kept tight control. She was also aware of trying to present a mature and classy wedding. She had endured the circus in Malibu with rifle shots and buzzing helicopters. And this time she was not just to become a member of Ritchie's family – she had also married into a Highland regiment and the honorary title of 'Daughter-in-Law of the Seaforth Highlanders'. For more than two centuries, the title goes to women who marry into regimental families. The now-amalgamated Seaforths, a regiment which has numerous VCs, was bemused at having Madonna as an official Daughter-in-Law. Retired Lt Col Angus Fairrie, curator of the Regimental Museum in Fort George, said, 'I know she's some sort of pop star. Regardless, she's now a Daughter-in-Law of the regiment. It doesn't mean that we'll invite her to mess dinners or anything like that. God forbid! But, of course, we're delighted to welcome her to the family. Daughter-in-law is how she'll always be regarded by the men from now on. We've already got Hugh Grant as a son, which is all well and good, but he doesn't get invited either. Put it this way, Madonna's picture won't be going up on the wall. Particularly the one in the conical bra ... is that how you describe it?'

Whatever they say, even retired soldiers really *are* aware of Madonna. Just like the rest of the world. The Marquess of Aberdeen at the age of 80 wrote a memoir for the *Oldie* magazine in March 2001. In it, he detailed his wartime exploits with prostitutes. It was wonderful, eccentric and very British reading. Lord Aberdeen later talked about his love of cricket – and Madonna. He said, 'I've got that very special book by her. It's called *Sex*.'

CHAPTER TWENTY-FOUR

CARRY ON CHAMELEON

'I too have my moments of doubts and weakness.'

MADONNA, 2002

Sex. In 2002 sex – publicly at least – was not such a driving force in the marketing of Madonna's image but there were rumours that she was pregnant with her third child, her second by Guy Ritchie. There were, as always, stories of all sorts of sexual daring-do but by now Madonna was, according to all her friends and associates, more than anything a devoted mother and career woman. She was also very into the huntin', shootin' set ambience of the £10 million country home she and Guy Ritchie established at Ashcombe in Wiltshire in England.

Madonna became a country girl – Hollywood style. Her expensive shooting clothes and gear was customised from Purdey, the company in London's Mayfair which supplies wardrobe and guns to the Queen and Prince Charles. For all of that, it emerged that in her shooting day encounters she was having trouble hitting barn doors, never mind pheasants. In Michigan they like the targets closer up. Nevertheless, despite nasty remarks by local game keepers and residents, she carried on shooting and always looking the part of the landed gentry in Lady Henrietta Palmer's designer range of cashmere field coats (with suede cuffs), shooting caps and knee-length breeches. In fact, as one local wag pointed out, she looked better than the British gentry: there were no frayed cuffs or collars.

For Madonna, who in 2002 took a dislike to being called Madge and wanted to be known as 'M' – perhaps echoes of her James Bond *Die Another Day* recording – her work was still primarily important. Playing country girl with her husband was for weekend relaxation, the career was the business and vice versa.

The big challenge was appearing on the West End stage in London. A string of American celebrities including Kathleen Turner and Kevin Spacey, and the Australian and former Mrs Tom Cruise, Nicole Kidman, had added electricity to London theatre in the past. Madonna wanted to prove it was more than her name – which meant tickets were sold out – that she was selling. And that made her very nervous, which, for a perfectionist like Madonna, can be complicated for those around her.

In David Williamson's play, *Up For Grabs*, Madonna played a manipulative art dealer. Originally the play was set in Australia but Madonna had it moved from Sydney to New York. Distinguished Australian playwright Williamson, who wrote the screenplays for Mel Gibson movie successes *Gallipoli* and *The Year of Living Dangerously*, went with the flow. He was in constant touch with Madonna by phone and email and they also had other compromises including new names for two of the characters and a change conclusion to the play, which in the original had been hailed as 'a brilliantly funny satire on the art world'. Mr Williamson said

Madonna had listened to different opinions put forward by himself or director Laurence Boswell, and added, 'When there were things I disagreed with I said, "No way" '

The play – because of Madonna's appearance – received so much attention that ticket touts asked up to ten times the face value of all tickets, not just the good ones. When it was announced she would be in the play at Wyndham's Theatre, it was only hours before the London *Evening Standard* announced that she was 'The Hottest Ticket In Town', costing at least £150 a seat. That was the stall-seats, which had a face value of £37.50. As you know, Madonna first appeared on stage in David Mamet's *Speed-The-Plow* on Broadway in 1988. There is, of course, a lesson from the legend.

But by 2002, Madonna – although many had shouted and argued that she wasn't – had also become an oil painting. Oil portraits of Madonna were – to some audiences – 'shockingly' exhibited as part of a comeback turn by Glasgow artist Peter Howson. The artist said of the breast bustling, thigh thickening view of Madonna, 'They are highly sexual paintings, but then Madonna is a very sexual woman. She wouldn't pose for me because she said I would make her look too ugly. But I feel as though I have seen her in the nude.'

Madonna owns two of Howson's paintings – she has one, Sean Penn has the other. The painter said, 'When I met Madonna we got on. She told me that the reason she liked my work was the combination of sadness and power.' By the summer of 2002 Madonna had not reacted to the new works but Howson, a remarkably easygoing Scot (who was 60 in 2002), said with great honesty, 'I have offered her first refusal if she wants to buy them. But have no idea what she will think.'

The paintings are extraordinary and there could only have been disbelief if Howson's work was not heralded by such an extravagant art lover as Madonna. Howson said his work – Madonna as a muscular, sinewy, reclining nude on a bed – was a tribute to her powerful personality. Howson was relaxed when the paintings were revealed in 2002, although he joked of Madonna's husband, 'I think he'll probably come and hit me.' More seriously he added, 'If he's a man of wisdom and integrity, he'll be quite pleased, I imagine.'

The controversial painting was priced at £100,000 while another titled 'Death and Madonna', which displays Madonna crouched down in a churchyard, was on sale for £120,000.

Pennies, of course, in Madonna's multi-millionaire world. However, in the Spring of 2002 she was not being too secular. She wanted to lift the spirit of her fans and anyone else who wished to pay attention. She sent an internet message to the world – signed 'M' – which revealed that, despite her strong image, she did have her own insecurities: 'You may look at my life and think I live a charmed existence. I am rich and famous but you would not be looking at the whole picture if that was all you could see. I, too, have my moments of doubts and weaknesses. My moments where I react before thinking things through. My moments where I take the easy road. My moments when I gossip and am envious. My moments of deep insecurity.

'It is important that you know this because we all suffer from the same thing and if I can share any wisdom with you at all it would be this: the only thing that gets me though these hard times is to give. Just give for that sake of sharing and not for what you can get for it. When you feel down and trapped, get outside of yourself and do something nice for someone. Doing something before you are asked to do it, pushing yourself beyond your comfort zone. Helping someone in need, going the extra mile. This is a great cure for sadness, anxiety and self-obsession. Giving is the best medicine…'

Madonna was prepared to give a great deal in her marriage with Guy Ritchie. And, of course, to her family: 'When you have children you look at life differently. You have a much fuller sense of appreciation and for the fragility of life, and how magical we all are as human beings. You're lucky just to wake up. Period. Just to wake up and have a life and be healthy.'

Still, for super-achiever, super-woman wannabe Madonna, the magic word is always *more*. Throughout her life she had always been the driving force and when she confronted the equally dominating Sean Penn, their relationship exploded. With Guy Ritchie it seems their marriage simply ran out of steam. That didn't stop things boiling over.

CHAPTER TWENTY-FIVE

A DANGEROUS AGE

*'The number 'fifty' is not a bad word! I see it
as another excuse for a party.'*

MADONNA, 2008.

The success of *Hard Candy* and her 2008 sell-out tours reflected the ongoing, the enduring, popularity of Madonna. Kabbalah played an ever-greater influence on her during her life with Guy Ritchie: 'I think a big part of the secret of staying at the top of my game, physically and mentally, is the recognition that I am not the owner of my talent. I'm just the manager of it. I know that I've been blessed with many gifts and I think as soon as you think you own what you have, it will go away. The other part of it is that I have a great sense of curiosity and I am always trying to learn new things and put myself in a position where I am working with people who know more than I do.' Kabbalah helped her endure worldwide acrimony over her adoption of David Banda. Reports that she and Guy Ritchie were expecting another child were mistaken. She did want another child but was experiencing fertility problems. She wanted to adopt.

Swept Away was pilloried by the critics and won not

Oscars but five Golden Raspberry awards while relations between Madonna and her husband were not warm. Each, it's said, blamed the other. Yet, they wanted the marriage to work and made a joint decision to go ahead with an adoption. She had taken advice from celebrity adoption veterans Brad Pitt and Angelina Jolie. Having appeared at the Live Aid concert in London's Hyde Park in 2005, Madonna had become more aware of the deprivations in Africa. It was the roots of her incredible support of the Raising Malawi campaign to help orphans in a country where a majority of the population are below the poverty line. A year later she adopted 13-month-old David Banda.

She was vilified for her actions in some circles and had to deal with numerous legal challenges. Much of that was provoked by her visit to the Home for Hope orphanage with Guy in October 2006. She was accompanied by a film crew making her documentary *I Am Because We Are* about the AIDS peril in Malawi. From the outside the adoption seemed to some to be 'too Hollywood' and the situation wasn't helped by a village elder commenting that Madonna appeared to be 'coming from God'. She had yet again sparked an Almighty row, in the middle of which was the little boy who was being given a chance not just of a better life but of having a life. As the criticism became more heated, Guy Ritchie said, 'How dare anyone question her motives? It's so preposterous that anyone would be critical of Madonna for wanting to share her love and wealth.'

Madonna was stung by the furore. She issued a statement: 'After learning that there were over one million orphans in Malawi it was my wish to open up our home and help one child escape an extreme life of hardship, poverty, and in many cases death. Nevertheless, we have gone about the adoption procedure according to the law, like anyone else who adopts a child. Reports to the contrary are totally inaccurate.' Madonna also appeared on television defending her actions. She was asked on the BBC if she felt bewildered by the outcry: 'I'm a detail-orientated person but I don't often have things my way. The world's reaction was quite shocking. There's no way I could have prepared myself for that.' At the end of 2006 at the Kabbalah Centre in London, a ceremony was held to bless David and celebrate his joining the devotees.

The storm over David had brought the couple close again and they renewed their wedding vows at Ashcombe House where Madonna, having become more spiritual, decided to hold no more shooting parties. Afterwards, the family went on holiday to the Soneva Fusi hotel in the Maldives. Ritchie would take the kids to the beach while Madonna, fearful of sun damage to her skin, spent much time in the gym. It was something of a metaphor the separate lives they had once led and would all too soon be leading again.

In the spring of 2008, Madonna was talking about Guy purely in business rather than loving terms: 'We make different kinds of movies. I don't have the technical knowledge he has. He's got a vision and his films are very testosterone-fuelled. Mine are much more from a female point of view, and I can't help but be autobiographical in everything I do. My career? Honestly, it's not something I sit around ruminating about. Who is my role model and how long can I keep this going? I just move around and do different things and come back to music, try making films and come back to music, write children's books and come back to music.' She had certainly kept herself busy. As well as her Malawi documentary she directed short comedy *Filth and Wisdom*. She designed clothing for the Swedish company H&M and linked up in a multi-million-dollar deal with a concert promoter. But she was yearning for New York.

The couple were together at the Cannes Film Festival for the screening of *I Am Because We Are*, but they looked distant, like, someone said, Charles and Diana in the last months of their marriage. Madonna spent more time with her personal trainer Tracy Anderson than with Guy. The marriage became open season in the media. A friend of both was quoted near the end of the marriage as saying, 'No one knows if this is going to be settled easily or turn into an absolute bloodbath. What started out as love has now ended. It's very, very sad.'

Yet, away from the spotlight, it appears their marriage has always been something of a battle. Chalk and cheese come to mind. Not that Madonna would ever eat cheese, far too unhealthy. She's said, 'As a mother, I would fall into the category of a disciplinarian. I make my children tidy up their bedrooms. I do not like them to play video games or watch television, and I make sure they do their homework.' That discipline, it appears, applied to much of Mr and Mrs Ritchie's home life. Take Christmas. The children get three presents each as she hates the commercialism.

Guy Ritchie said that this was enough: 'As long as the kids get three presents at Christmas, everyone's happy.' The highlight of the day was usually a low-fat macrobiotic feast prepared by their chef (neither of them cook). It is highly unlikely to feature turkey, as Madonna has issues with the rearing and slaughtering of poultry, but rather grains such as quinoa and vegetables. Associates indicate that there was always a small amount of unsalted meat for the children and for Guy; but salty, fatty treats such as chipolatas and stuffing were completely out. Indeed, the festive season is seen by Madonna as no excuse to stint on her punishing health regime. She even hired a nutritionist to advise on her children's food. As a result, except for the very occasional ice cream as a treat, they have controlled amounts of dairy food, no cheese, no cream, no salt, no preservatives and no sugar. Although Madonna tries to send out the message that she is not too controlled to have fun, she is far too self-disciplined to deviate from her strict diet. She works out daily, no matter where in the world she is, for somewhere between two and three hours. So why not a workout on Christmas Day? She told an interviewer, 'I'm not going to slow down, get off this ride, stay home and get fat. There are no short cuts to being Madonna.' Turning 50, no matter how she attempted to shrug it off, meant much to Madonna. It highlighted the decade gap between her and Guy Ritchie and, of course, as landmark birthdays do, reminded her of her own mortality.

A visitor to their home for a Kabbalah meeting said that the family seem to lead a very unusual, if luxurious, home life: 'They entertain very beautifully, but it is not what you would call conventional. A housekeeper will set out a great big table covered in stuff, all macrobiotic, which no one dares eat unless Madonna tucks in. They're all terrified of her. A uniformed butler serves the most incredible wines, which Guy loves but, again, Madonna barely touches. Television is all but banned for the children. If they use the computer, they are thoroughly policed and their time on it limited. Nannies who applied for the job of helping to care for Madonna's brood were told that they could not have TVs or telephones in their rooms, as the mistress of the house felt it was an unhealthy distraction from family life. The children are certainly given plenty of educational stimulation. Lourdes (known as Lola) is a bit of a star at the Lycee School in London and is fluent in French. She is said often to speak to David Banda, on whom all they dote, in French, and he is now picking up a smattering of the language, too. Rocco, meanwhile, despite having always lived in the UK, has acquired an American accent.'

They worked hard at integrating David into the family, all of them have having classes in the Malawian language, Chichewa. Madonna and Guy can now manage some basic words and phrases, such as 'mummy', 'daddy', 'hello' and 'my love'. Madonna also learned a lullaby, called 'Gona Mana', which she plays to David. She fervently believes that adopting David is one of the greatest things she has done. Friends said Ritchie was 'totally in love' with David and it was in his role as a father that Madonna most admired him. Yet, over 2008 the word used more and more to describe their relationship was reportedly 'fiery'. Details of the marriage were leaked on the gossip carousel. There was a media madness, a hysteria. By October of 2008 it was all over. After the divorce was announced she would have to read in newspapers that her husband had allegedly said she 'looked like a granny' onstage compared with her younger backing dancers, and that she could not act, and was 'past it' after she turned 50. It must have wounded.

As in most separations the trivial became important and the important trivial. The pain of it all raised the tension on both sides. And as there was no prenuptial there was the little matter of money —what was to happen to their combined more than £300 million in assets?

When reports appeared that Guy Ritchie was being very British, very stiff upper lip and refusing to take a penny from the marriage, his former wife ordered her aides to take the extremely unusual step of making public details of their financial agreements. Liz Rosenberg for Madonna said Ritchie would get between £50 and £65 million in cash and property, and added, 'I'd assume it's one of the biggest divorce settlements.'

In the deal she announced, Madonna would keep the New York penthouse valued at £3 million, the Beverly Hills home bought for £10 million, the ten-bedroom Georgian town house in Marylebone, London, valued at £8.25 million, and the £7 million next door mews property. Ritchie would get a cash payment of £2.4 million, Ashcombe House in Wiltshire, valued at £14 million in 2008, provisions to buy a property in London equivalent to the former marital home worth £15.25 million, provision for property in New York worth £3 million, a five-storey Georgian town house in Regent's Park, London, valued at £4 million, the Punchbowl pub, valued at £3 million, and artwork and other gifts worth £5 million. He also got maintenance as the father of two boys for up to 15 years worth around £7.5 million. Madonna had made the money matters public as she was angry that Guy appeared to be walking off with nothing.

Her attempt to control the financial side of the break-up backfired. Guy Ritchie was furious for he was getting a lot less. There was a day of furious phone calls between their aides and finally Madonna agreed to put out another statement. It said the first figures were 'misleading and inaccurate'. He was to receive less than £45 million in total, including the property.

Together they would care for the children. But Madonna won the geographical arrangements. Although Guy

Ritchie wanted his sons brought up in England, their legal teams agreed that the children would not be separated and would live with their mother in America. Both boys would divide their time between New York and London. Madonna was concerned about security for her children and wanted money spent on Guy Ritchie's homes to increase it after threats from Muslim extremists in January, 2009. She was said to be 'very concerned' after the threats were posted on some Islamic websites. It seemed that the marriage made in Heaven had turned somewhat hellish. But the brittle feelings calmed with time and with the need to care for the children.

On 27 December 2008, Madonna went to dinner with her close friend Gwyneth Paltrow and her husband Chris Martin. Understandably, she seemed careworn, her skin stretched tight and veins bulging in her forehead. It had been a long day. She and Guy Ritchie had taken their family to the London Kabbalah HQ during the day. He had celebrated Christmas with the boys in Wiltshire while Lourdes was with her mother at the marital home. On Boxing Day he took his sons back to their mother and stayed overnight. A truce had been called.

By January, Madonna was in America training for the FTI Equestrian Festival in Florida. Another chapter in her life was over. She was not going to weep about it: 'You have to get to a point where you care as little about getting smoke blown up your ass as you do when you become a whipping boy for the press because ultimately they both add up to shit. If your joy is derived from what society thinks of you, you're always going to be disappointed. You just to have to keep doing your work, and hope and pray someone is dialling into your frequency.'

A DANGEROUS AGE

Globally, many millions of people are on Madonna's radar and they are waiting for the sparks, the excitement, the controversy and attention-grabbing antics, to detonate once more.

And they will. And probably very soon.